教育部人文社会科学重点研究基地四川大学南亚研究所
教育部国别和区域研究培育基地四川大学南亚研究中心
四川大学南亚与中国西部合作发展研究中心

第一辑

南亚评论

South Asian Review: A Bilingual Publication（Volume I）

曾祥裕 刘嘉伟 ◉ 主 编
程杨冀 邹正鑫 ◉ 副主编

国际文化出版公司
·北京·

图书在版编目（CIP）数据

南亚评论．第一辑 ／ 曾祥裕，刘嘉伟主编．－－ 北京：
国际文化出版公司，2023.6
ISBN 978-7-5125-1487-4

Ⅰ．①南… Ⅱ．①曾… ②刘… Ⅲ．①南亚－研究
Ⅳ．① D735

中国国家版本馆 CIP 数据核字 (2023) 第 002845 号

南亚评论（第一辑）

主　　编	曾祥裕　刘嘉伟
副 主 编	程杨冀　邹正鑫
统筹监制	吴昌荣
责任编辑	马燕冰
品质总监	张震宇
出版发行	国际文化出版公司
经　　销	全国新华书店
印　　刷	北京虎彩文化传播有限公司
开　　本	710 毫米 ×1000 毫米　　16 开
	15 印张　　240 千字
版　　次	2023 年 6 月第 1 版
	2023 年 6 月第 1 次印刷
书　　号	ISBN 978-7-5125-1487-4
定　　价	88.00 元

国际文化出版公司
北京朝阳区东土城路乙 9 号　　　邮编：100013
总编室：（010）64270995　　　传真：（010）64270995
销售热线：（010）64271187
传真：（010）64271187-800
E-mail：icpc@95777.sina.net

编前语

2023 年 6 月，以发表当代南亚问题前沿研究成果、促进中外学术交流为宗旨的《南亚评论》在四川成都诞生。国际问题研究已蔚为显学，各种学术刊物和专著书籍颇为兴旺，在这一背景下创办这份南亚问题的中英双语系列出版物，是出于以下几点考虑。

首先，南亚问题极为重要，中国与南亚国家的关系也极为重要，但专注于南亚现实问题研究的中文刊物数量并不多。中国南亚学界完全专注南亚研究的学术刊物主要有四川大学南亚研究所主办的《南亚研究季刊》（1985 年创刊）和中国社科院亚太与全球战略研究院主办的《南亚研究》（1978 年创刊）。云南省社会科学院和中国（昆明）南亚东南亚研究院主办的《南亚东南亚研究》（1983 年创刊时名为《东南亚》，2009 年改名《东南亚南亚研究》，2018 年改现名）和云南财经大学主办的《印度洋经济体研究》（2014 年创刊）也有一半左右的篇幅刊发有关南亚研究的论文。此外，《当代亚太》《现代国际关系》等刊物也经常刊登有关南亚研究的论文。但是，与美国研究、日本研究、欧洲研究等领域相比，南亚研究仍然相对"冷门"，刊物和专著出版都要少很多。近年来，一些机构开始尝试创办新的出版平台，有关南亚研究成果的刊发阵地可望逐步扩大，我们也希望加入这一大潮，做出自己的贡献。

其次，国内长期缺乏一份有关南亚问题的英文系列出版物，这既不利于中外学术交流，也不利于外界了解中国学界的观点。几十年来，国内已刊发数千篇有关南亚研究的中文论文，到 2022 年 12 月，仅《南亚研究季刊》和《南亚研究》两刊就已累计发文 4205 篇，对诸多问题讨论热烈，创见颇多。然而，由于语言鸿沟的客观存在，中外研究人员的学术对话与交锋非常不够。由于中国研究人员多已具备合格的英语能力，目前的主要问题是，母语非汉语的外国研究人员对中国学界的南亚研究成果与观点所知寥寥。这既是国际南亚学界的一大损失，也造成了中文南亚研究成果在国际学界和舆论场的某种失语。这对双方当然都是不小的损失。

最后，与国内学界颇为兴旺的南亚问题学术出版形成对照的是，国内学界对书评似乎仍然不够重视，很少出版对学术新著的严肃评论与商榷。这既不利于学术交流与争鸣，也不利于学术成果的推广与传播。

有鉴于此，我们决定创办每年定期出版的《南亚评论》双语出版物，向中外研究人员广泛征集中英文稿件，暂定每辑发表 4～6 篇中文正稿和 2～3 篇中文书评，以及相应的英文稿，篇幅约为中文 5～8 万字外加英文 4 万词，总量相当于中文 12～13 万字。受条件所限，《南亚评论》暂定每半年出版一辑，如果以后条件具备，我们会进一步调整出版周期，加大发文量。第一辑译稿由程扬冀进行了全文审读，曾祥裕、刘嘉伟和邹正鑫进行了部分审读。希望这一尝试有助于推介更多的优秀研究成果，也有助于中外南亚学界的对话交流。希望《南亚评论》能够成为南亚研究的生力军，在中外学者和读者的支持与厚爱之下茁壮成长，有朝一日，成为参天大树。

《南亚评论》编委会

2023 年 6 月

目 录

中印海上交流专题

南亚政经 / 外交 / 安全

南亚书评

Table of Contents

Special Topic: Sino-Indian Maritime Exchanges

Book Review

中印海上交流专题

中印海上交流史简论

曾祥裕、朱宇凡 [①]

摘要：本文从史前时代的中印海上交流、佛教的海上传播、中古时代的中印海上贸易、中印在对方的社群与文物遗存四个方面简述中印海上文化交流的基本情况。中印两国特别是中国西南与孟加拉湾地区早在史前就存在初步的海上交流，这对两国的文明演进产生了一定的催化作用。海上通道在佛教对华传播的早期和中期都发挥了重要作用，成为中古时代中印交流的重要载体。中印在中古时代还通过海上通道形成了频繁的商贸交流，为两国的繁荣局面提供了助力。在这种频繁的文化、物质与人员交流的影响下，两国的滨海地区一度活跃着来自对方的居民社群，留下了可观的文化遗存。中印海上交流的历史也为两国在 21 世纪的今天重新扩大海上交往、共建海上命运共同体奠定了历史基础，给人们以多方面的启迪。

关键词：中印文化交流；海洋文明；海上丝绸之路；香料之路

中印两国比邻而居，中印交流源远流长、影响深远，是文明互鉴的典范。多年来，对中印交流的研究主要集中于陆上交流，或关注经由西域的陆上丝绸之路，或侧重经过世界屋脊青藏高原的蕃尼古道，对中印之间经由海洋的交往则较少关注。实际上，中印两大文明均具有深厚的海洋传统，两国的海上交流延续时间长、社会影响大，与陆上交通形成有效互补，值得充分关注。本文将从史前时代的中印海上交流、佛教的海上传播、中古时代的中印海上贸易、中印在对方的社群与文物遗存四个方面简述中印海上文化交流的基本情况。

① 曾祥裕，教育部人文社科重点研究基地四川大学南亚研究所副研究员，主要从事南亚安全与外交、海洋问题、中国外交等方面研究。朱宇凡，中央社会主义学院文化教研部副教授，研究方向为周边关系与海洋安全、中国海外利益等。

一、海上通道与中印交流的开端

追溯中印交往史，人们往往将其追溯到《史记》的最早记载，即张骞通西域并在大夏（Bactria）市场遇当地商人贩售辗转而来的筇竹杖和蜀布[①]，时间在公元前 2 世纪初。此外，印度的《政事论》已提及丝绸及丝衣产于中国（Kauśeyaṃcīnapaṭ tāśca cīnabhūmijāḥ）[②]，一般认为其成书于公元前 4 世纪末。1986 年夏，位于中国西南的四川广汉三星堆遗址出土了一批重要考古遗存，其中的海贝包括一种环纹货贝（monetria annulus 或 ring cowrie，见图 1），大小约为虎斑贝的三分之一，中间有齿形沟槽，既不产于近海地区，更不产于江河湖泊，只产于印度洋深海水域。地处内陆的三星堆出现如此之多的齿贝，只能是从印度洋北部地区（主要孟加拉湾和阿拉伯海之间的地区）直接引入。[③] 而且，三星堆出土的海贝并非由云南各处间接转递而来，应是

---

① 《史记·大宛列传》载，骞曰："臣在大夏时，见邛竹杖、蜀布。问曰：'安得此？'大夏国人曰：'吾贾人往市之身毒。身毒在大夏东南可数千里。其俗土著，大与大夏同，而卑湿暑热云。其人民乘象以战。其国临大水焉。'以骞度之，大夏去汉万二千里，居汉西南。今身毒国又居大夏东南数千里，有蜀物，此其去蜀不远矣。"《史记·西南夷列传》载，及元狩元年，博望侯张骞使大夏来，言居大夏时见蜀布、邛竹杖，使问所从来，曰"从东南身毒国，可数千里，得蜀贾人市"。或闻邛西可二千里有身毒国。骞因盛言大夏在汉西南，慕中国，患匈奴隔其道，诚通蜀，身毒国道便近，有利无害。于是天子乃令王然于、柏始昌、吕越人等，使闲出西夷西，指求身毒国。

② 季羡林：《中印文化交流史》，《季羡林全集》（第十三卷），北京：外语教学与研究出版社，2010 年，第 375 页。原文参见 R. Shamasastry (translated), *Kautilya's Arthasastra*, Bottom of the Hill Publishing, 2010, p. 83. R. P. Kangle (translated), *The Kauṭilīya Arthaśāstra (Vol. 2)*, Motilal Banarsidass Publishers, 8ᵗʰ Reprint: Delhi, 2014 (Second Edition, Bombay University, 1969), p. 105. 朱成明："《利论》译疏"，北京大学博士学位论文，2016 年，第 102 页。一些研究认为此处的 cīnabhūmi 不是中国，可能是今巴控克什米尔的巴尔蒂斯坦等地，但很多研究认为此处应为中国。支持此处为中国的学者又分两派，一派认为这说明《政事论》成书较晚，而另一派认为这恰恰说明中印交往要大大早于现有的文献记载。

③ 段渝："中国西南早期对外交通——先秦两汉的南方丝绸之路"，《历史研究》2009 年第 1 期，第 15 页。薛克翘：《中印文化交流史》，北京：中国大百科全书出版社，2017 年，第 13—14 页。

古蜀人与孟加拉湾地区开展直接经济文化交流的结果。[1] 这是考古学方法所揭示的中国与南亚交流的最早记录，时间大致相当于公元前 11 世纪，比文献记载早近 1000 年。当然，这一交往采取了海陆结合的方式，并不是从印度洋航行到太平洋再登陆，而是从印度洋沿岸直接登陆，然后从陆路进入中国内地。

另外，也有研究认为，张骞在大夏看到的筇竹杖和蜀布并不是从中国西南走陆路贩运到印度，而是循蜀—夜郎—南越—南海而至印度。[2] 这条线路陆地部分约相当于后世的牂牁道，海上部分则大致相当于海上丝绸之路。如果此说无误，则是对中印交通的最早文献记载，涉及的也是两国的海上交通而非陆地交通。

二、佛教的海上传播

一般认为佛教早期从印度向中国传播主要是走陆路，即从西北印度到中亚，再到西域，再到中国内地北方，然后再向东、向南传播。但是，学界关于佛教海上传播路线的讨论从未停止过，梁启超较早提出此说，季羡林认为中国的佛教"可能是先从海道来的，也可能是从陆路来的"。[3] 他作出这一判断的重要依据之一是佛教的核心概念 Buddha 在早期中国有"佛"和"浮屠"两种译法，前者应来自某种西域语言如吐火罗语，而后者应直接来自梵语，但在中国最早流行的恰恰是"浮屠"一语。[4]

近年来的考古发现揭示了佛教对华传播早期海上路径的一种可能性。在中国江苏沿海的孔望山摩崖石刻年代早至东汉末期的桓帝灵帝时代（2 世纪后期），其中部分石刻头有高肉髻，右手呈施无畏印状，两手放在胸前者结

---

① 据段渝，从云南至四川的蜀身毒道上出土海贝的年代最早为春秋时期，而三星堆的年代早在商代中晚期，差不多要早上千年，云南并无这 1000 年间的海贝出土。见段渝："中国西南早期对外交通——先秦两汉的南方丝绸之路"，《历史研究》，2009 年第 1 期，第 17 页。

② 吕昭义："对西汉时中印交通的一点看法"，《南亚研究》，1984 年第 2 期，第 64、67 页。

③ 季羡林："浮屠与佛"，《季羡林全集》（第十五卷），北京：外语教学与研究出版社，2010 年，第 11 页。原稿撰于 1947 年 10 月 9 日。

④ 同上。

枷趺坐，全身有凹形的身光等，被视为佛像（见图2、图3、图4）。据推定，这应该是中国佛教史上最早的佛像雕刻[①]，时间大大早于西向的丝绸之路沿线各石窟造像。一般来说，本土造像应明显晚于宗教教义的传播，故佛教传播到青州、徐州地区时间应该更早。这样一来，佛教传播到中国最东部沿海地区的时间就早于由西向东的陆上传播，其来源只能是海上通道。现存文献也流露出佛教海上传播的重要迹象，比如东汉明帝时的楚王刘英颂浮屠言，而楚王的封地位于江苏等沿海地区，其都城彭城即今日的江苏省徐州市，该地区很容易受到从海上溯长江而上的影响。值得注意的是，楚王所信的佛教使用的是更接近印度本土表述的"浮屠"而不是从西域辗转而来的"佛"，这也表明其所信的佛教直接来自印度，而其途径显然只能是来自海上。[②]

如果说关于佛教早期对华传播的海上通道还有争议的话，此后的中印通过海上通道实现的佛教交流（南海佛教之路）就无可置疑了。一批佛教僧侣循着西汉已开通的海上丝绸之路，陆续往来于中印之间，从魏晋南北朝一直延续到宋元。东晋法显从陆路赴印度，回国则先沿恒河而行抵达今加尔各答附近，义熙七年（411年）秋乘船自狮子国（今斯里兰卡）启程，两天后遇风暴，修补船体破损后继续前行90日才抵达耶婆提（今苏门答腊岛东部）。次年春，法显再次搭船出发，途中再遇暴风并最终在今山东海岸登陆。[③]

值得注意的是，当时往来于中印者中有许多人取海路：僧侣从中国动身时往往沿传统的陆路西行，但归国则常取海路。如西凉僧人智俨曾赴克什米尔，后与当地僧人觉贤一起启航回国（智俨二人赴天竺直接取海路）。幽州李勇沿陆路赴印度求学，后"于南天竺泛海达广州"。南北朝入华的外国僧侣也有很多是泛海而来，如中天竺僧人求那跋陀罗"随舶泛海"并于元嘉十一年（435年）抵达广州。克什米尔王子求那拔摩先赴狮子国并乘船到达爪哇岛，后乘船来华。西天竺僧拘那陀罗（真谛）于梁中大同元年（546年）

---

① 俞伟超、信立祥："孔望山摩崖造像的年代考察中文期刊文章"，《文物》，1981年第7期，第8—15页。

② 吴廷璆、郑彭年："佛教海上传入中国之研究"，《历史研究》，1995年第2期，第30—31页。《后汉书·光武十王列传》载：楚王英……少时好游侠，交通宾客，晚节更喜黄老，学为浮屠斋戒祭祀……诏报曰："楚王诵黄老之微言，尚浮屠之仁祠，洁斋三月，与神为誓，何嫌何疑，当有悔吝？其还赎，以助伊蒲塞桑门之盛馔。"

③ 刘迎胜：《丝绸之路》，南京：江苏人民出版社，2014年9月第1版，第356页。

取海道经扶南（今柬埔寨附近）至南海郡（今广州）。《南齐书·东南夷列传》载天竺道人那迦仙从广州乘扶南海舶归国。[①]上述种种记载都说明，两汉以后，在中国与南亚的交通中海路日渐重要。

中印海上佛教文化交流的大发展还要等到更晚的唐代。咸亨二年（671年），义净在玄奘出发之后第44年从广州循海路赴印求法，所著《高僧传》记述了玄奘归国后46年间61位赴印求法僧的事迹，其中走海路者37人。据其记载，前7人往返均经陆路，其后开始有选择海路者，至第21人开始几乎全部走海路，表明赴印海路日渐兴旺，甚至呈现出取代陆路首要地位的趋势。[②]有分析称义净本人往返走的都是海路，所以对走海路的旅行者更为熟悉，其记载无意间夸大了海路的影响力。义净书中还记载了24名走陆路者，且义净在印游学12年左右，游历东印度、北印度各地，长期在那烂陀寺学习，有充分的时空条件和人员交往机会来熟悉循各种渠道往返印度者。因此，揣测义净因为个人经历而有意无意地偏向海上通道，说服力并不充分。将义净的记述与此前僧侣往返中印的交通方式相比较可发现，中印海上交通的便利程度从汉代到南北朝再到唐代一直在逐步提升。相应地，在中印间旅行的首选方式也从早期的以陆路为主，转变为南北朝的陆上来海上回，到唐代中期变为来回皆通过海路。

三、中古时代的中印海上贸易

现存文献表明，早在西汉（公元前2世纪至公元前后），中印就建立了直接的海上交流。这条通道延续千余年，被称为"南海道"。成书于东汉初年（1世纪末）的《汉书·地理志》描述了从今广东航海通往东南亚、南亚，

---

① 刘迎胜：《丝绸之路》，南京：江苏人民出版社，2014年9月第1版，第357、383页。
② 孟亮："唐代初期中印文化交流图景"，《重庆交通大学学报（社会科学版）》，2019年第1期，第46页。

辗转抵达南亚"已不程国"和"黄支国"的海上丝绸之路，^①其中的黄支通常被认为相当于今印度东南部泰米纳杜邦的康契普腊姆（Kanchipurram），其南约 100 公里的阿里卡梅度（Arikamedu）遗址濒临孟加拉湾，是一处重要港口遗址，^②"黄支"在《汉书》中出现过 4 次。据描述，黄支国地域辽阔，人口众多，其民俗与当时的海南岛差不多，返航时从黄支国行约 10 个月可抵达日南（今越南北部）。虽然相隔万里，但汉与黄支仍频频互动，自汉武帝时代便多次遣使与中国交往，《汉书·平帝传》载"元始二年（2 年）春，黄支国献犀牛"，《汉书·王莽传》又提及"黄支国自三万里贡生犀"。^③犀牛对中国而言是罕见之物，而王莽本人也热衷于营造"祥瑞"并为其称帝制造舆论，所以正史中专门记述了黄支献犀牛，日常之物的交流虽然不见诸记载，却是不难想象的。

此后的南北朝时代，中国陷入南北分裂达 200 多年，南朝国土局促，与通过西域抵达南亚的陆上丝绸之路基本绝缘，但南朝与古印度之间的海上通路仍然畅通，保证了双方交流不致中断。南朝齐永明六年（488 年）成书的《宋书·蛮夷列传》保存了南朝宋元嘉五年（428 年）天竺迦毗黎国^④遣使奉表并赠送金刚指环、摩勒金环诸宝物、赤白鹦鹉各一一事。更重要的是，其致宋文帝的外交文书曰"愿二国信使往来不绝，此反使还，愿赐一使"。^⑤

---

① 《汉书·地理志》载："自日南障塞、徐闻、合浦船行可五月，有都元国，又船行可四月，有邑卢没国；又船行可二十余日，有谌离国；步行可十余日，有夫甘都卢国。自夫甘都卢国船行可二月余，有黄支国，民俗略与珠崖相类。其州广大，户口多，多异物，自武帝以来皆献见。有译长，属黄门，与应募者俱入海市明珠、璧流离、奇石异物，赍黄金，杂缯而往。所至国皆禀食为耦，蛮夷贾船，转送致之。亦利交易，剽杀人。又苦逢风波溺死，不者数年来还。大珠至围二寸以下。平帝元始中，王莽辅政，欲耀威德，厚遗黄支王，令遣使献生犀牛。自黄支船行可八月，到皮宗；船行可二月，到日南、象林界云。黄支之南，有已程不国，汉之译使自此还矣。"

② 熊昭明："汉代海上丝绸之路航线的考古学观察"，《社会科学家》，2017 第 11 期，第 38 页。

③ 刘迎胜：《丝绸之路》，南京：江苏人民出版社，2014 年 9 月第 1 版，第 345 页。

④ 一些研究认为此即迦毗罗卫国，但据国书原文，其地"名迦毗河，东际于海……首罗天护，令国安隐"，显然靠海。薛克翘认为迦毗黎应该指南印度大河高韦里河（Kaveri），其地信奉印度教湿婆派，即所谓"首罗天"，其说可参考。见薛克翘：《中印文化交流史》，北京：中国大百科全书出版社，2017 年，第 39 页。

⑤ 《宋书》（卷九十七）。同样是在元嘉五年，师子国遣使来访，"托四道人遣二白衣送牙台像以为信誓"，元嘉十二年（435 年）再次遣使来访。

现在无法确定宋文帝是否曾遣使随来使前往天竺，如派遣使者，则必然是走海路。另外，现在也无法确认双方此后是否曾频繁交换使者（如有使者也必然循海路），但史书中直到泰始二年（466 年）才再次出现迦毗黎国遣使贡献的记载。[①]

中印海上贸易在唐宋得到大发展，中国出口的瓷器和印度出口的香料都是重要的大宗贸易品，由此可见海上"瓷器之路"或"香料之路"均非虚言。据《唐大和上东征传》，早在公元 750 年的天宝九年，广州城外的"江中有婆罗门、波斯、昆仑等船，并载香药珍宝，积载如山"。[②]1974 年，福建沿海的泉州湾发掘出一艘宋代远洋海船（沉没时间不晚于公元 1274 年，见图、图 6），舱中发现一批珍贵文物，其中未脱水的香料药物重约 2350 千克，应该是来自东南亚或南亚（见图 7、图 8、图 9、图 10）。[③]这是中古香料贸易的罕见存世见证。印度西南海岸的科钦是对华贸易特别是香料贸易的枢纽之一，到明清仍经营着繁盛的对华贸易。当地一名犹太富商经营对华贸易发家致富，专门从中国订制了一批中国风的蓝色瓷砖，用于铺设犹太会堂地板，至今仍保存完好（见图 11、图 12）。[④]喀拉拉的故临（Kollam 或 Quilon）是马拉巴尔海岸一处重要港口，与宋代中国贸易交往密切，据南宋末成书的《诸蕃志》，"故邻国自南毗舟行，顺风五日可到……土俗大率与南毗无异……大食人多寓其国中"。[⑤]近年在此地开展的考古发掘出土瓷器残片 500 多件，铜钱（含残件）1300 多枚，[⑥]瓷器残片包含产自浙江、江西、广东、福建等省的瓷器，年代在 10—14 世纪，铜钱年代在 8—14 世纪。另外，喀拉拉的帕特南遗址也出土大批瓷器残片，主要是 15—19 世纪产自江西和福建的产

---

① 《宋书》（卷五十七）。

② 真人元开著、梁明院校注：《唐大和上东征传校注》，扬州：广陵书社，2010 年 11 月，第 71 页。

③ 笔者 2016 年 6 月 19 日在泉州海上交通史博物馆沉船馆现场考察得知。

④ 笔者 2014 年 3 月 19 日在科钦现场考察得知。

⑤ 赵汝适著、杨博文校释：《诸蕃志校释》（中外交通史籍丛刊），北京：中华书局，2004 年 4 月，第 68 页。

⑥ 冀洛源："二〇一四年印度喀拉拉邦两处出土中国文物遗址的调查与收获"，《紫禁城》，2017 年第 5 期，第 70 页。

品。^① 这些都是中印贸易之繁盛的见证。

在东部的科罗曼德尔海岸同样发现了大批宋元中国瓷器的残片。前述阿里卡梅度（Arikamedu）遗址从 20 世纪 30 年代开始考古发掘，发现有 9—10 世纪的越窑碟子残片，11—12 世纪的越窑瓷、龙泉窑青瓷残片和磁州窑的陶片，以及南宋龙泉窑出产的精美的青瓷碗、龙泉窑深碗残片和小罐残部、青白瓷碟残片，同时出土的还有北宋末年徽宗宣和年间（1119—1125 年）的"宣和通宝"。这说明，在 9—13 世纪的数百年间，中国瓷器曾源源不断地运往这里。附近的可里麦都（Korimedu）遗址散落有中国宋元时代的瓷片，其中有 12—13 世纪南宋时代浙江或福建一带生产的珠光青瓷碗残片、淡色青白釉罐残部，还有 14 世纪以后闽粤一带生产的青花瓷片。^②

从历史变迁的宏观角度来观察可以发现，海上丝绸之路在唐以后的兴旺同中国东南地区经济地位的急剧提升，在时间上是相互重叠的，二者之间存在密切关系。薛克翘指出，南海道为中印交流发挥了非常独特的作用：一是有利于中国东部沿海与印度交流，二是一直保持畅通（陆路则时断时续），三是免去了陆路交流层层设关、处处收税对商贸活动的干扰。^③ 应该说，上述看法都是相当有道理的。

四、中印在对方的社群与文物遗存

中印均具有深厚的航海传统，在漫长的航海活动中，陆续有一些居民泛海而来，在对方的国土长期居住，形成了一定规模的社区，也遗留了一批历史遗存。印度西海岸的马拉巴尔似乎是中国舟舶西行的极西界，如南宋末的赵汝适《诸蕃记》称南毗国（一般认为在马拉巴尔沿岸）"在西南之极……其国最远，番舶罕到"；^④ 又称有"时罗巴、智力干父子，其种类

---

① 冀洛源："二〇一四年印度喀拉拉邦两处出土中国文物遗址的调查与收获"，《紫禁城》，2017 年第 5 期，第 68 页。

② 薛克翘：《中印文化交流史》，北京：中国大百科全书出版社，2017 年，第 211—212 页。

③ 同上，第 25—26 页。

④ 赵汝适著、杨博文校释：《诸蕃志校释》（中外交通史籍丛刊），北京：中华书局，2004 年 4 月，第 66—67 页。

也，今居泉之城南"。[①] 此处的"泉"指现泉州，是中国东南当时的重要港口，而时罗巴、智力干父子当系长居泉州的印度人中的重要人物，赵汝适才会专门记载其姓名，其语气表明赵汝适认为时人对此父子二人相当熟悉，无须更多介绍。20 世纪以来，在福建泉州陆续发现一批具有浓烈印度文化色彩的文化遗存，包括印度教石刻 300 多方，以及一块断裂的泰米尔文石碑，分别收藏在泉州海外交通史博物馆、厦门大学人类博物馆、泉州开元寺（见图 13）、天后宫等。[②] 著名古刹开元寺大雄宝殿后侧的石柱被识别为包含人狮（Naramsinha）和牧童黑天（Krishna as Gopala）等的印度教建材（见图14、图 15、图 16），[③] 最典型的毗湿奴像（高 115 厘米，1934 年出土于泉州南校场，见图 17）和若干神庙建筑残件收藏在海外交通史博物馆，另外还有很多"林伽"图像。这些遗存共同反映了中古时期一批印度居民常年在华生活的若干侧面，表明元代泉州的印度教信仰规模不小，影响较大，有不止一座印度教寺庙和祭坛，[④] 说明元代及以前已有一批印度人逐渐在泉州定居，出现了较大规模的印度教徒社区；[⑤] 印度教毗湿奴和湿婆派均在泉州存在过；印度教与民间信仰产生了某种程度的融合。[⑥] 很多研究认为，泉州的印度教遗存表现出较鲜明的南印风格，[⑦] 这与马拉巴尔海岸的时罗巴父子在泉州定居的情况也可相互印证。泉州的印度教寺庙并不孤立。实际上，泉州之南的广州早在唐代就有 3 座印度教寺庙，据《唐大和上东征传》，天宝九年（750 年）的广州"有婆罗门寺三所，并梵僧居住"，又说有"师子国……往来居住，种类极多"，[⑧] 这里提到的梵僧和师子国居民应该均来自印度和斯

---

① 赵汝适著,杨博文校释:《诸蕃志校释》(中外交通史籍丛刊),北京:中华书局,2004 年 4 月,第 67—68 页。

② 相关研究可参考 David Yu（余得恩）撰、王丽明译:"泉州印度教石刻艺术的比较研究",《海交史研究》,2007 年第 1 期。

③ 邱永辉:《印度教概论》,北京:社会科学文献出版社,2012 年,第 363—364 页。

④ 王丽明:"泉州印度教石刻研究回顾与思考",《海交史研究》,2016 年第 1 期,第 123 页。

⑤ 同上,第 134—136 页。

⑥ 邱永辉:《印度教概论》,北京:社会科学文献出版社,2012 年,第 364 页。

⑦ 王丽明:"泉州印度教石刻研究回顾与思考",《海交史研究》,2016 年第 1 期,第 131—132、134—135 页。

⑧ 真人元开著、梁明院校注:《唐大和上东征传校注》,扬州:广陵书社,2010 年 11 月,第 71 页。

里兰卡等南亚地区。

与此类似的是，在印度国土上也曾经居住着一定规模的中国人。唐代义净记载，在那烂陀寺（Nalanda）以东40余驿有鹿园寺，距此不远有"支那寺"，相传当室利笈多大王时（3世纪晚期）有"支那"即广州僧人20余人至此，至唐代还有3个村子的人属于鹿园寺。[①]据说，这些广州僧人是"从蜀川牂牁道而出"，可能是从四川经牂牁郡（覆盖云贵等地）至印度。[②]另据《史记·西南夷列传》，从中国西南的牂牁江可乘船直达广州，历史上习称的"牂牁道"其实是东南向通往广州的水道而不是西南向的陆路。因此，上述僧侣其实更可能是从四川循水路至贵州，再走水路至广州，最后乘船从南海航海赴印。[③]

宋元时代的中国人在印度东南海岸也形成了一个社区，建造中式宝塔一座。据元代亲自造访印度的汪大渊所撰《岛夷志略》，南印度有"土塔"，"居八丹之平原，木石围绕，有土砖甃塔，高数丈。汉字书云：咸淳三年（1267年）八月毕工。传闻中国之人其年白文（一作旅）彼，为书于石以刻之，至今不磨灭焉"。[④]此处的"八丹"应是泰米尔语"Pattinam"或"Patam"的音译，意为"城墙围起来的城镇"，[⑤]一般认为即那加帕塔姆（Nagapatam），今称那加帕蒂纳姆（Nagapattinam）。这说明至迟到南宋末已有较大规模的中国人常驻印度东南海岸。这一遗址在当地保存了近600年，后来的西方人

---

① 刘迎胜：《丝绸之路》，南京：江苏人民出版社，2014年9月，第355页。"去此寺不远，有一故寺，但有砖基，厥号支那寺。古老相传云，是昔室利笈多大王为支那国僧所造。于时有唐僧二十许人，从蜀川牂牁道而出，向摩诃菩提礼拜。王见敬重，遂施此地，以充停息，给大村封二十四所。于后唐僧亡没，村乃割属余人。现有三村入属鹿园寺矣。准量支那寺，至今可五百余年矣。"见义净著，王邦维校注：《大唐西域求法高僧传校注》（中外交通史籍丛刊），北京：中华书局，1988年9月，第102页。

② 王路平："唐代贵州佛教述论"，《贵州社会科学》，1998年第2期，第49页。

③ 吴焯："西南丝绸之路研究的认识误区"，《历史研究》，1999年第1期，第43—44页。一些研究将"牂牁道"理解为陆路可能是因为广州僧人既然西行抵达四川，则继续西行也是合理的；如果先西行抵达四川，再向东折返广州，最后乘船走海路赴印度，路径过于曲折，于情理有所不合。但是，如果将上述"支那国僧"（广州僧人）理解为"从广州（出发）而来的"僧人，就顺理成章了。

④ 汪大渊著，苏继庼校释《岛夷志略校释》（中外交通史籍丛刊），北京：中华书局，1981年5月，第285—287页。据苏继庼，同书还有"土珠""土布""土粉"之谓，故"土塔"之土应类似于"土产"之土，而非"泥土"之土，相当于"中国"或"中原风土"之意。因此，"土塔"即"中国塔"之意，并非"泥土之塔"。

⑤ 刘迎胜：《丝绸之路》，南京：江苏人民出版社，2014年9月第1版，第433页。

也有记载。16 世纪，葡萄牙人巴尔比（Gasparo Balbi）记述其在那加帕塔姆看到"支那七塔"，是中国古代航海者所建。[1]1615 年，一位名叫巴拉达斯（Manuel Barradas）的葡萄牙耶稣会士记载，当地人"认为（该塔）是由（华人）当印度商业领主时所造：砖结构，尽管多个世纪既无主又失修，却依然巍峨，状况完好"。18 世纪的荷兰东印度公司雇员瓦伦丁（Franqois Valentijn）将其称为 Pagood China（中国塔）。1846 年，英国人埃利奥特（Walter Elliot）对此塔作详细描写并绘图（见图 18），称其高约 30 米，是一座三层四方塔，砖构，紧密贴合，无水泥，第一层和第二层作飞檐造型，每侧中开一门或窗。[2] 盖伊（John Guy）认为"此种风格的塔，最直接的原型是中国宋元时期的佛塔"。[3]此塔应即亨利·玉尔注《马可·波罗游记》时提到的南印度那加帕塔姆西北约 1 英里处的砖塔，俗称"中国塔"。[4] 该塔至 1866 年尚存（见图 19），[5]1867 年 8 月后不久被拆毁，今已不存。建立此塔的目的今已不可考，但印度文化部在"季风计划"的概念文件中指出其在 17—19 世纪一直是航船使用的主要地标，[6]此说可参考，因为前述葡萄牙人巴尔比（Gasparo Balbi）也是在环绕锡兰岛的时候从海上遥望到此塔的，这也与前述巴拉达斯（Manuel Barradas）所载该塔系华人担任当地商业领主所造相符。

到更晚的元明时代，中印海上交往的重心似乎逐步从印度东南部的科罗曼德尔海岸转移到西南部的马拉巴尔海岸，元朝的广东招讨司达鲁花赤杨庭璧四次出访印度都以马拉巴尔为目的地，[7]明朝郑和远航船队多次抵达柯枝

---

[1] 季羡林：《中印文化交流史》，收入《季羡林全集》（第十三卷），外语教学与研究出版社，2010 年，第 471 页。

[2] Walter Elliot, "The Edifice Formerly Known as the Chinese of Jaina Pagoda at Negapatam," *Indian Antiquary*, Vol. 7(1878), p. 64.

[3] 沈丹森："中印海上互动：宋至明初中国海上力量在印度洋沿岸的崛起"，《复旦学报（社会科学版）》，2014 年第 2 期，第 16 页。

[4] 汪大渊著，苏继庼校释《岛夷志略校释》（中外交通史籍丛刊），北京：中华书局，1981 年 5 月，第 286 页。

[5] 图 18 和图 19 均由中国国家图书馆孙丽副研究馆员和刘冰雪副研究馆员协助查找提供，特此致谢。

[6] Ministry of Culture, Government of India, Concept Note: Mausam/ Mawsim: Maritime Routes And Cultural Landscapes, p. 5.

[7] 《元史·列传第九十七》（卷二百一十）。

（Kochi）、古里（Khozikode）等地。《明史·列传第二百十四》称："柯枝，
或言即古盘盘国，宋、梁、隋、唐皆入贡。"永乐九年（1411年），柯枝
可亦里遣使朝贡，后来又要求赐封国王并封其国中之山。郑和第五次出洋在
永乐十五年（1417年）冬，同时也受明成祖之命前往柯枝赐封，并撰碑文铭刻。
碑文曰："乃封可亦里为国王，赐以印章，俾抚治其民，并封其国中之山为
镇国之山，勒碑其上，垂示无穷。"[1]具体碑文参见《明实录》和《明史》。[2]
此碑迄今尚未发现。尽管如此，科钦（即前文的柯枝）民间却长期沿用一种"中
国渔网"（Cheena vala 或 Chinese fishing net，见图20、图21、图22），
一般认为其与13—14世纪的对华贸易有密切关系。《明史》也记述了马拉
巴尔海岸另一航海重镇古里，称其为西洋大国，西滨大海，南距柯枝国……
柯枝舟行三日可至，自锡兰山十日可至。郑和船队非常重视古里，多次将其
作为下西洋的重要据点，马欢《瀛涯胜览》载郑和在古里立碑，碑文称"其
国去中国十万余里，民物咸若，熙嗥同风，刻石于兹，永示万世"。遗憾的
是，此碑也未能发现，为后人留下了诸多遐想。

结论

通过对近代以前中印海上交流史的简要梳理，本文得出如下结论。首先，
中印海上交往源远流长、形式多样。两国的海上交流始于史前，公元之前已
有确定的航线并得到文献记载，此后长期与陆上交流并驾齐驱，中古后期甚
至呈超越陆上交流之势。两国海上交流形式多样，覆盖了经济、社会、文化
等诸多领域，兼具人员交流、物质交流和思想交流的特性，堪称人类文明交
往的一大壮举。其次，中印海上交流的影响深远、意义重大。这一交流在精
神领域促进了中印两大文明的沟通，助推了佛教在亚洲东部特别是沿海地区
的传播与发展；在经济领域增进了整个亚洲东部跨越西太平洋和东印度洋的
物质交流，促进了农作物交流，两国主要港口因海外贸易而一片繁荣，从而
为中国东南沿海经济超越北方，以及印度南部若干政权的长期繁荣，奠定了
强大的物质基础。有研究认为中印经济在中古世界长期领先，甚至一度占据

---

① 刘迎胜：《丝绸之路》，南京：江苏人民出版社，2014年9月第1版，第501页。
② 《明史·列传第二百十四》。

世界国内生产总值（GDP）总额的近一半，而中印海上贸易在其中发挥了重大作用。由此可见，中印海上交流在双边、地区（亚洲东部）和世界经济格局上，均发挥了非常重要的作用。最后，复兴海上文明、建设和谐海洋，应成为中印两国的共同使命。中印两国均具有深厚的海洋传统，但近代以来，两国均在不同程度上丢失了这一古老传统，并先后沦为半殖民地和殖民地。两国丢失海洋权利并导致主权沦亡的历史教训是深刻的，而有效利用海洋禀赋并造福国民的传统也极为深厚。在 21 世纪的今天，中印两国均致力于复兴自身的海洋传统，建设海权大国，而建设服务各国人民共同利益、有效应对共同挑战的和谐海洋，应成为中印两国乃至世界各国的共同主张。我们深信，有着海上友好交往传统的中印两国，将在这一领域携手合作，做出应有的贡献。

附图

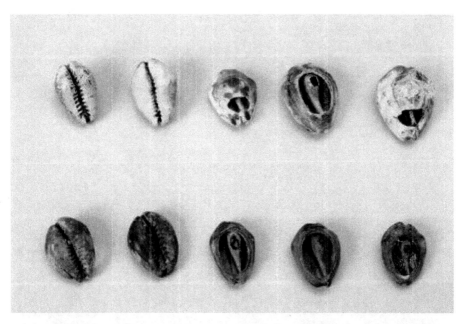

图 1　三星堆出土海贝（距今 3000 多年，长 1.5 厘米左右，大致分黑、白两色，略呈卵圆形，图据三星堆博物馆网站）

图2 孔望山佛教摩崖造像（江苏省连云港市，图据网络）

图3 孔望山佛教摩崖造像（江苏省连云港市，图据网络）

图 4 孔望山佛教摩崖造像（江苏省连云港市，图据网络）

图 5 泉州湾后渚港宋代沉船 1974 年发掘现场（图据泉州海外交通史博物馆沉船馆展板）

图6 泉州湾宋代沉船修复陈列（泉州海外交通史博物馆沉船馆，作者自摄，2016年6月19日）

图7 泉州湾宋代沉船上的香料等货物（图据泉州海外交通史博物馆沉船馆展板）

图 8 泉州湾宋代沉船上的香料等货物（图据泉州海外交通史博物馆沉船馆展板）

图 9 泉州湾宋代沉船上的香料（泉州海外交通史博物馆沉船馆，作者自摄，2016 年 6 月 19 日）

图 10 泉州湾宋代沉船上的香料（泉州海外交通史博物馆沉船馆，作者自摄，2016 年 6 月 19 日）

图 11 科钦的犹太会堂（作者自摄，2014 年 3 月 19 日）

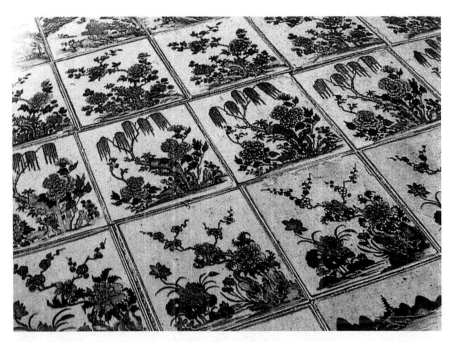

图 12 科钦犹太会堂的中式地板（会堂内部不允许拍摄，图据网络）

图 13 泉州开元寺大雄宝殿（作者自摄，2016 年 6 月 19 日）

图 14　泉州开元寺大雄宝殿背侧的印度教风格石柱（作者自摄，2016 年 6 月 19 日）

图 15 泉州开元寺大雄宝殿背侧的印度教风格石柱（作者自摄，2016 年 6 月 19 日）

图 16 泉州开元寺大雄宝殿背侧的印度教风格石柱（作者自摄，2016 年 6 月 19 日）

图 17　泉州出土毗湿奴像（泉州海外交通史博物馆藏，作者自摄，2016 年 6 月 19 日）

THE TOWER AS IT EXISTED IN 1846.

图18 1846 年的那加帕塔姆"中国塔"［图据 Indian Antiquary Vol. 7（1878）卷末图录，Walter Elliot 委托英属印度马德拉斯管区公共工程部，不知名绘图员绘制］

图 19　1866 年的那加帕塔姆"中国塔"［图据 Indian Antiquary Vol. 7（1878）卷末图录，照片由 Middleton Rayne 拍摄］

图 20 科钦的"中国渔网"（作者自摄，2014 年 3 月 19 日）

图 21 郑和布施碑（斯里兰卡科伦坡国立博物馆藏，作者自摄，2020 年 1 月 17 日）

图 22　郑和布施碑现代拓本（原件藏斯里兰卡科伦坡国立博物馆，现代拓本展示于南京宝船厂遗址公园碑廊，图据网络）

蓝色经济在中国的现状及未来发展

刘嘉伟 [①]

摘要： 在中国语境下，"蓝色经济"不仅与海洋经济密不可分，其内涵也是海洋经济与可持续发展和循环发展的有机融合。本文分别从海洋经济发展、海洋生态环境保护与循环经济发展两个层面介绍中国蓝色经济的现状、面临挑战及发展前景。作为中国现代经济体系的重要组成部分，海洋经济在过去数十年取得了长足发展。中国政府在大幅增加对海洋经济投入的同时，也科学地制定了海洋经济发展的总原则和战略目标。但是，由于客观环境及人们对海洋经济认知的局限性，当前中国海洋经济在迅速发展的同时也暴露出诸多问题。此外，中国的海洋生态环境保护及循环经济发展也历经环境保护—海洋生态环境保护—海洋可持续发展—循环经济认知演变。作为海洋大国，中国将根据自身经济发展程度、经济发展规律科学推动蓝色经济发展，为人类社会经济进步贡献自身力量。

关键词： 蓝色经济；海洋生态环境；可持续发展；循环经济；中国

比利时经济学家、企业家冈特·鲍利（Gunter Pauli）被普遍认为是"蓝色经济"概念、"蓝色经济"模式的创始人。2012年2月，随着鲍利的著作《蓝色经济》（*The Blue Economy*）中文版在中国首次出版发行，"蓝色经济"这一新兴概念被首次引入中国，并在中国学术界、商界乃至政府内部引起了广泛关注与巨大反响。对于冈特·鲍利而言，蓝色经济是生态系统与经济体系的有机融合，强调了地球资源与环境的保护以及可持续发展。中国虽然接受了蓝色经济这一重要概念，但由于国情及认知上的差异，中国对于蓝色经济概念有着自己特有的理解和定义。冈特·鲍利倡导的蓝色经济更接近于中国国内讨论的广义蓝色经济，而狭义蓝色经济则更多地聚焦于海洋经济领域本身。本文尝试从中国国内对蓝色经济概念的认知入手，介绍蓝色经济在中

① 刘嘉伟，副研究员，四川大学南亚与中国西部合作发展研究中心执行主任，主要研究领域为中印经济、印度政治、能源政策和公共外交等。

国的现状及发展状况。

一、什么是蓝色经济

如前文所述，蓝色经济是一个相对较新的概念。当前在中国，不论是政府还是学术界尚未给其赋予一个权威统一的定义或解释。国内通常认为蓝色经济有广义与狭义之分。上海辞书出版社出版的《管理学大辞典》将广义蓝色经济定义为循环经济，即以资源节约和循环利用为特征，与环境保持和谐的经济发展模式，把经济活动组织成一个"资源—产品—再生资源"的反馈式流程，强调低开采、高利用、低排放。冈特·鲍利在接受媒体采访时，也认可了其蓝色经济理论与循环经济理论的相似性。狭义蓝色经济特指海洋经济，包括为开发海洋资源和依赖海洋空间而进行的生产活动，以及直接或间接为开发海洋资源及空间开展的相关服务性产业活动。上述活动根据 2003年 5 月中国国务院发布的《全国海洋经济发展规划纲要》，可以综合定义为开发利用海洋的各类海洋产业及相关经济活动的总和。[①]

中国国内分别从广义和狭义两个层面分别定义蓝色经济，主要源于以下原因。一是蓝色经济的理论体系尚不够明确，其内涵与外延有许多需进一步厘清的部分。蓝色经济是一个跨学科的综合领域，其内容涉及经济学、社会学、政治学以及自然科学，甚为复杂；冈特·鲍利在提出蓝色经济概念时立足于其经济运营实务，更偏向微观经济领域，对理论体系而言尚有较大欠缺。二是蓝色经济模式是更高级的经济发展与管理模式，是中国经济发展进入更高阶段的改革方向，但在短时间内完全改变中国经济发展模式几无可能，需按由部分到全面、由初级到高级的方式逐步发展。三是蓝色经济概念的引入正值中国海洋经济迅速发展时期，政府及学术界自然偏向于将蓝色经济与海洋经济概念紧密结合、共同分析。

中国是海洋大国，海洋经济发展潜力巨大。进入新千年，随着综合国力的进一步提升，中国经济开启了全方位、综合发展模式，对海洋经济的重视也上升到历史新高点。2003 年，中国政府首次制定《全国海洋经济发

---

① 中华人民共和国中央人民政府：《2003 年中国全国海洋经济发展规划纲要》，http://www.gov.cn/gongbao/content/2003/content_62156.htm，2003 年 5 月 9 日。

展规划纲要》，确定了 2001—2010 年这十年的中国海洋经济发展战略及目标，此事件被认为是中国海洋经济高速增长的开端；2012 年，中国共产党第十八次全国代表大会明确提出"建设海洋强国"的战略目标和重大任务，标志着中国区域发展从陆域经济延伸到海洋经济并进入具体实施阶段。在海洋经济发展受到高度重视的背景下，引入中国的蓝色经济概念自然被学界和政府视为海洋经济概念的补充、发展以及演进。中国海洋问题研究的最高学府——中国海洋大学认为蓝色经济是在海洋科技、海洋经济与海洋文化发展到一定阶段而出现的社会经济现象，它以海洋经济为主题，以海带陆、以陆促海、海陆结合、海陆统筹为特色的区域经济。[①]值得一提的是，2011 年 1 月，国务院批准在山东建立蓝色经济区。这里的蓝色经济区，即特指以海洋经济为支柱产业，涵盖社会经济、自然生态、科技文化的地理区域，从定义上更接近海洋经济。

从上文的陈述可见，当前中国对蓝色经济概念的理解认知同冈特·鲍利最初始的定义存在差别，同其他西方发达国家亦有所不同。蓝色是海洋的代名词，与海洋有关的概念通常使用蓝色来描述。因此，在中国语境下，蓝色经济不仅在中文字面上与海洋经济密不可分，其内涵也是海洋经济与可持续发展和循环发展的有机融合。2016 年 3 月，中国国务院公布了《中华人民共和国国民经济和社会发展第十三个五年规划纲要》，其中第四十一章的标题即"拓展蓝色经济空间"，明确指出中国在"十三五"期间将"坚持陆海统筹，发展海洋经济，科学开发海洋资源，保护海洋生态环境，维护海洋权益，建设海洋强国"。[②]从这一决定中国 2016—2020 年发展方向的最重要规划可以清晰地看到，海洋经济与科学开发海洋资源、保护海洋生态环境是中国政府当前认可的蓝色经济内涵中最主要的两个组成部分。本文据此分别从海洋经济发展、海洋生态环境保护与循环经济发展两个层面介绍中国蓝色经济现状、面临挑战及发展前景。

---

① 中国海洋大学官方网站，http://www.ouc.edu.cn/lsjj/list.htm。
② 中华人民共和国中央人民政府:《中华人民共和国国民经济和社会发展第十三个五年规划纲要》，http://www.gov.cn/xinwen/2016-03/17/content_5054992.htm，2016 年 3 月 17 日。

二、中国海洋经济现状及发展状况

自古以来，中国都是海洋资源大国。从自然资源禀赋看，中国海洋经济发展潜力尤为巨大。

（一）中国海洋经济现状 [①]

中国自然资源部海洋战略规划与经济司统计，2018 年中国全国海洋生产总值达 83415 亿元人民币，年增长率为 6.7%；2018 年中国国内生产总值为 90.03 万亿元人民币，年增长率为 6.6%，海洋生产总值占国内生产总值的比重为 9.3%，两者增速基本持平。全国海洋生产总值中，第一产业生产总值约为 3640 亿元人民币，第二产业生产总值约为 30858 亿元人民币，第三产业生产总值约为 48916 亿元人民币，第三产业在全国海洋经济中占比超过半数，产值占海洋生产总值的 58.6%；全国涉海就业人员总数已达 3684 万人。

自然资源部海洋战略规划与经济司统计规定，海洋经济生产总值是指按市场价格计算的沿海地区常住单位在一定时期内海洋经济活动的最终成果，是海洋产业和海洋相关产业之和。2018 年中国海洋相关产业生产总值为 30449 亿元人民币，海洋产业生产总值为 52965 亿元人民币。从产值上看，滨海旅游业、海洋交通运输业和海洋渔业仍是中国海洋经济的支柱产业，2018 年产值分别为 16078 亿元人民币、6522 亿元人民币和 4801 亿元人民币。

2018 年中国海洋生产总值

	总量（亿元人民币）	增速（%）
海洋生产总值	83415	6.7
一、海洋产业	52965	6.2
（一）主要海洋产业	33609	4.0

[①] 本章数据皆引用中国自然资源部海洋战略规划与经济司 2019 年 4 月发布的《2018 年中国海洋经济统计公报》，http://gi.mnr.gov.cn/201904/P0201904113381 41849830.doc，2019 年 4 月 11 日。

	总量（亿元人民币）	增速（%）
滨海旅游业	16078	8.3
海洋交通运输业	6522	5.5
海洋渔业	4801	−0.2
海洋工程建筑业	1905	−3.8
海洋油气业	1477	3.3
海洋化工业	1119	3.1
海洋船舶工业	997	−9.8
海洋生物医药业	413	9.6
海洋电力业	172	12.8
海洋矿业	71	0.5
海洋盐业	39	−16.6
海水利用业	17	7.9
（二）海洋科研教育管理服务业	19356	10.2
二、海洋相关产业	30449	—

注：表格引用《2018 年中国海洋经济统计公报》，因公报对部分具体数据采用了四舍五入的统计方法，导致总计与分项合计不能一致。

从上表可见，海洋生物医药业、海洋电力业、海水利用业等新兴产业增速领先，海洋盐业、海洋船舶工业、海洋工程建筑业等传统产业尽管产值占比高，但皆呈负增长之势，中国海洋经济结构更新正逐步进行。

（二）中国发展海洋经济的各阶段

对海洋经济的重视与关注首先源自西方国家，20 世纪 60 年代，西方国家为保持经济高速增长、解决传统自然资源逐渐枯竭难题，将眼光转向了资源丰富的海洋，并将海洋经济上升为国民经济的重要组成部分。为给发展海洋经济提供必要理论支持，20 世纪 60 年代末 70 年代初，美国学者率先提出了海洋经济学的概念，而 70 年代则成为海洋经济学完善以及快速发展的黄金时期。彼时中国尚处在改革开放初始阶段，对海洋的开发与利用仍属于较初级阶段，海洋经济发展缺乏系统性、呈碎片化发展状态。20 世纪最后20 年，改革开放政策的顺利实施将中国带入经济飞速发展的科学轨道，随着综合国力的不断增强，中国对海洋经济的重视也随之提升。总体来说，中国海洋经济发展可大致分为三阶段。

1. 初步发展阶段（1949—2000 年）。1949 年中华人民共和国成立以来，中国政府一直将海洋资源的开发与利用纳入整体经济发展规划之中，但由于整体经济实力不足，缺乏先进的理论与科学技术，对海洋的开发利用一直处于初级阶段，长期局限于渔业、矿业、交通运输等传统领域，对海洋经济发展更是缺乏整体规划。改革开放以来，随着国民经济的迅速发展以及先进理论与技术的引进，中国对海洋的重视程度迅速增加。1998 年，国务院新闻办公室发布了《中国海洋事业的发展》白皮书，在联合国海洋年对外介绍了中国海洋事业的发展情况，并对外公开宣示了中国对海洋的重视。本阶段中国政府尽管重视海洋，对海洋经济仍缺乏科学的认识和系统规划，中国海洋经济发展尚处初始阶段、增长速度有限。

2. 高速发展阶段（2001—2010 年）。在本阶段的十年期间，海洋经济在中国得到了前所未有的发展：一是海洋经济地位上升，被正式确定为国家规划。2003 年 5 月，中国国务院发布了《全国海洋经济发展规划纲要》，明确提出发展海洋经济对于促进沿海地区经济合理布局和产业结构调整，保持国民经济持续健康快速发展具有重要意义。发展规划纲在确定发展海洋经济原则的基础上，首次提出中国海洋经济发展的总目标："海洋经济在国民经济中所占比重进一步提高，海洋经济结构和产业布局得到优化，海洋科学技术贡献率显著加大，海洋支柱产业、新兴产业快速发展，海洋产业国际竞争能力进一步加强，海洋生态环境质量明显改善。形成各具特色的海洋经济区域，海洋经济成为国民经济新的增长点，逐步把我国建设成为海洋强国。"[1]二是海洋经济总量增长迅速。《全国海洋经济发展规划纲要》规定了全国海洋经济增长具体目标是："到 2005 年，海洋产业增加值占国内生产总值的 4% 左右；2010 年达到 5% 以上，逐步使海洋产业成为国民经济的支柱产

---

① 中华人民共和国中央人民政府：《2003 年中国全国海洋经济发展规划纲要》，http://www.gov.cn/gongbao/content/2003/content_62156.htm，2003 年 5 月 9 日。

业。"实际上，在 2001—2010 年十年期间，中国海洋经济发展已经远超发展规划纲要原定目标。全国海洋生产总值从 2001 年的 9519 亿元人民币增加到 2010 年的 38439 亿元人民币，年均增长率超过 13%，而 2001—2010 年中国国内生产总值年均增速为 10.7%，海洋经济增长走到了国民经济增长的前面；2010 年，海洋生产总值占国内生产总值比重为 9.7%。三是海洋产业趋向合理，海洋经济进入有序发展阶段。到 2010 年，中国的海洋经济已经形成了较为完整的产业体系，第一产业占比明显下降，初步形成了"第三产业—第二产业—第一产业"的科学结构，中国海洋经济初步实现了高速、稳定增长。

3. 科学发展阶段（2011—2020 年）。在这个阶段，中国政府、学术界对海洋经济的认识有了更为显著的发展，可持续发展、循环发展的理念被逐步引入：一是发展海洋经济从国家规划进一步上升为重大国家战略。2012 年，中国共产党第十八次全国代表大会报告提出了中国要提高海洋资源开发能力，发展海洋经济，保护海洋生态环境，坚决维护国家海洋权益，建设海洋强国；[①] 同年 9 月，中国国务院印发了《全国海洋经济发展"十二五"规划》，在综合分析了中国海洋经济发展趋势的基础上，确定了"十二五"期间全国海洋经济发展的主要目标。2016 年 3 月，中国国务院印发了《中华人民共和国国民经济和社会发展第十三个五年规划纲要》，提出了蓝色经济空间概念，并确定了"十三五"期间海洋经济发展战略。2017 年，中国共产党第十九次全国代表大会报告中在"建设现代化经济体系"这一部分中提出了加快建设海洋强国，将海洋经济正式纳入中国现代化经济体系中，进一步明确了海洋经济的重要地位。二是海洋产业结构更趋完善，海洋经济发展更加科学。在这一阶段，中国海洋经济的发展不再一味追求速度，海洋生产总值的增速逐渐下降、趋向平稳，政府、企业在海洋生态环境保护中的投入大幅提升，海洋产业技术创新迅速发展，生态保护、可持续发展、循环经济在海洋经济发展中的权重逐步提升，海洋产业结构不断发生良性变化，高科技产业、可持续发展产业增速明显，在海洋经济中的地位亦逐步上升。

---

① 胡锦涛:《坚定不移沿着中国特色社会主义道路前进为建成小康社会而奋斗——在中国共产党第十八次全国代表大会上的报告》,北京:人民出版社,2013 年版,第 17 页。

（三）中国海洋经济发展面临的主要问题

过去数十年，海洋经济作为中国现代经济体系的重要组成部分，取得了长足发展；中国政府在大幅增加对海洋经济投入的同时，也科学地制定了海洋经济发展的总原则和战略目标。但是，由于客观环境及人们对海洋经济认知的局限性，当前中国海洋经济在迅速发展的同时也暴露出以下四个主要问题。

1. 海洋经济对整体国民经济发展的支持尚不够。中国政府对海洋经济未来发展规划了宏大蓝图，并希望海洋经济能成为中国现代化经济体系的重要组成部分、中国国民经济的重要支柱。但目前中国海洋经济对国民经济发展的支持仍旧不足，2018年中国海洋生产总值占当年国内生产总值的9.3%，远低于发达国家15%~20%的占比，距离实现我国战略目标尚有较大距离。

2. 传统产业仍占据海洋产业主流。尽管海洋生物医药业、海洋电力业、海水利用等新兴产业增长迅速，但其发展时间尚短，相较于传统产业占比较低。当前中国海洋经济发展仍需依靠滨海旅游业、海洋交通运输业和海洋渔业等传统产业。这在客观上为中国未来海洋经济结构调整和产业升级留下了不小的负担。

3. 海洋生态环境压力较大。尽管中国政府很早就将海洋生态环境保护置于与海洋经济发展相同的地位，出台了一系列保护海洋生态环境的政策。但由于技术水平、经营理念等方面的问题，当前中国海洋经济发展方式仍较为粗放，一些地区在落实中央海洋生态环境保护政策不到位，继续坚持唯经济增长论；此外，过去数十年对海洋掠夺性开发的负面影响短期内难以消除，中国面对的海洋环境尤其是近海环境保护压力巨大。

4. 对海洋经济发展的认识仍不够全面。当前中国国内对海洋经济的重视程度已大幅提升，各级政府、公私企业亦将发展海洋经济列为未来重点，加大了资金、物质资源上的投入。但各方在发展海洋经济时仍过多考虑沿岸、近海，对远海、深海、大洋的规划、设计远远不够，而上述领域必将是全球未来海洋经济发展的重点区域。认识不够全面恐造成理念落后，进而影响中国海洋经济发展跻身世界先进国家行列。

三、中国的海洋生态环境保护及循环经济的发展状况

（一）中国海洋生态环境及循环经济的发展历史

总体来说，中国对于海洋生态环境保护及循环经济的认识演进大致可以按以下顺序区分：环境保护—海洋生态环境保护—海洋可持续发展—循环经济。中华人民共和国成立以来便将环境保护列为政府关注的要点之一，但由于经济发展落后、相关体制不健全、群众认知有限等客观问题，中国的环境保护（含海洋生态环境保护）长期缺乏系统性和科学性，一直到 1989 年，第七届全国人民代表大会常务委员会第十一次会议才通过第一部《中华人民共和国环境保护法》。在这部环境保护法中，海洋被列为环境的重要组成部分，并在随后的数年里，海洋生态环境保护逐渐演变为一个完整、独立的概念，体现在中国政策制定和执行进程之中。1996 年，中国国家海洋局出版了《中国海洋 21 世纪议程》，在进一步完善了海洋生态环境保护概念，并第一次正式将其提升至海洋可持续发展层面，提出了中国海洋事业可持续发展的战略。1998 年，国务院新闻办公室发布了《中国海洋事业的发展》白皮书，白皮书涵盖"海洋可持续发展战略""合理开发利用海洋资源""保护和保全海洋环境""发展海洋科学技术和教育""实施海洋综合管理""海洋事务的国际合作"[1]6 章，更加系统地阐述了中国对海洋生态环境保护和可持续发展的立场、态度及具体举措。

近年来，随着海洋经济在中国的迅速发展，海洋生态环境保护和可持续发展理念被纳入海洋经济科学框架之内，得到更大的重视。2000 年，《中华人民共和国海洋环境保护法》正式颁布实施，海洋生态环境保护首次获得独立司法保障。2003 年《全国海洋经济发展规划纲要》在发展海洋经济的指导原则中明确指出"坚持经济发展与资源、环境保护并举，保障海洋经济的可持续发展。加强海洋生态环境保护与建设，海洋经济发展规模和速度要与资源和环境承载能力相适应，走产业现代化与生态环境相协调的可持续发

---

[1] 国务院新闻办公室网站，《中国海洋事业的发展》，http://www.scio.gov.cn/zfbps/ndhf/1998/Document/307963/307963.htm，2000 年 9 月 10 日。

展之路"，①并在海洋经济发展目标中加入了海洋生态环境与资源保护目标。同年，中华人民共和国生态环境部开始发布年度《中国近岸海域环境质量公报》；值得一提的是，2018年，公报被正式更名为《中国海洋生态环境状况公报》。此后，海洋生态环境保护与可持续发展频繁出现在中国所有涉及海洋的重要政策规划中。

2012年，蓝色经济理念被引入中国；同年，循环经济首次出现了中国政府涉海洋政策文件之中。中国国务院2012年9月发布的《全国海洋经济发展"十二五"规划》首次提到了循环经济发展。该规划在基本原则中提出"统筹考虑海洋生态环境保护与陆源污染防治，大力发展海洋循环经济，加强海洋资源节约集约利用，推进海洋产业节能减排与清洁生产，强化海洋生态环境保护和防灾减灾，不断增强海洋经济可持续发展能力"，②在第八章"推进海洋经济绿色发展"中更进一步阐述了如何大力发展循环经济，包括"鼓励涉海企业加大海洋资源循环利用技术研发和应用等方面的投入，引导园区及企业开展海洋领域循环经济示范。重点围绕海水养殖业、海水利用业、海洋盐业和盐化工等领域，探索构筑沿海地区循环产业体系。积极开展有关循环经济的信息咨询和技术推广，支持涉海企业参与循环经济领域的国际交流与合作，引进国外先进的循环经济技术和模式"。③在规划期至2020年的《全国海洋经济发展"十三五"规划》中，循环经济再次被提及。

在上述阶段我们可以看到，一方面，循环经济概念已经被引入中国经济发展战略之中，并开始逐步演进发展；另一方面，基于中国基本国情和认知习惯，本阶段的循环经济仍置于海洋领域，成为中国海洋经济的重要组成。

（二）中国海洋生态环境保护及循环经济发展现状及未来发展

自《海洋环境保护法》实施以来，过去十余年中国在海洋生态环境保护事业中投入了大量人力、物力，并引入了世界最先进的技术与科学理念，取得了令人振奋的成绩。根据《2018年中国海洋生态环境状况公报》，2018

---

① 中华人民共和国中央人民政府：《2003年中国全国海洋经济发展规划纲要》，http://www.gov.cn/gongbao/content/2003/content_62156.htm，2003年5月9日。

② 国务院：《全国海洋经济发展"十二五"规划》，http://www.gov.cn/xxgk/pub/govpublic/mrlm/201301/t20130117_65866.html，2012年9月16日。

③ 同上。

年我国海洋生态环境状况整体稳中向好，海水环境质量总体有所改善，符合一类海水水质标准的海域面积占管辖海域面积的 96.3%，近海海域优良水质点位比例 74.6%，典型海洋生态系统健康状况和海洋保护区保护对象基本保持稳定，海洋倾倒区、海洋油气区环境质量基本符合海洋功能区域环境保护要求，海洋渔业水域环境质量总体良好。[①]

在当前中国，海洋生态环境保护整体职责由生态环境部承担，具体职责则由各地方政府及地方生态环境部门承担。为切实做好相关保护工作，生态环境部除部署指导完成相关任务外，还组建了"中央生态环境保护督查小组"直接前往一线督查、推动相关环保工作顺利进行。为赋予生态环境部门在保护海洋生态环境时拥有必要的权力，全国人大常委会不定期成立执法检查组，赴地方监督检查《中华人民共和国海洋环境保护法》贯彻执行情况。而在更高层面，中央政府成立了全国海洋经济发展部际联席会议，统筹海洋经济发展以及海洋生态环境保护与循环经济发展。

当前及未来中国保护海洋生态环境及发展循环经济的基本原则是"绿色发展、生态优先"，也就是坚持开发与保护并重，加强海洋资源集约节约利用，强化海洋环境污染源头控制，切实保护海洋生态环境。[②]节约利用海洋资源，推动海洋产业低碳发展将是未来发展的主要趋势，主要举措如下。

（1）推进海洋传统产业优化升级。推进海洋渔业、海洋油气业、海洋船舶工业、海洋交通运输业、海洋盐业与化工业的转型升级，引入更为绿色、安全的生产技术，严格控制开放强度，加强受产业影响的相关环境的保护与修复。

（2）促进海洋新兴产业迅速发展。加大对海洋药物和生物制品业、海水利用业、海洋可再生能源业的投入力度，重视资源的节约和再生，将新兴产业与循环经济发展模式有机地结合起来。

（3）强化海洋生态的保护与修复。实施强制保护和严格管控，建立海洋生态保护红线制度，实施海洋督察制度，开展常态化海洋督察；同时在重要区域开展生态修复和生物多样性保护工作。此外，中国政府正加强海洋气

---

① 中华人民共和国生态环境部，《2018 年中国海洋生态环境状况公报》，http://hys.mee.gov.cn/dtxx/201905/P020190529532197736567.pdf，2019 年 5 月。

② 国家发展改革委、国家海洋局，《全国海洋经济发展"十三五"规划》，http://images.mofcom.gov.cn/www/201709/20170907170048332.pdf，2017 年 5 月。

候变化研究，提高海洋灾害监测、风险评估和防灾减灾能力，加强海上救灾战略预置，提升海上突发环境事故应急能力。

综上所述，蓝色经济是未来经济必然进入的更为科学的发展模式，但何时推动蓝色经济发展、如何推动蓝色经济发展与一国的基本国情密切相关。中国将根据自身经济发展程度、经济发展规律科学推动蓝色经济发展，为人类社会经济进步贡献自身力量。

气候变化对中印海洋安全的影响

邹正鑫 [①]

摘要：中国和印度同为海洋大国，气候变化及其引发的次生问题对中印海洋安全与发展构成重大挑战。本文认为在海洋经济安全方面，气候变化引发的海洋水文要素的变化，以及由此产生的一系列次生灾害严重制约沿海地区经济社会发展，对海上交通线安全，海洋渔业、海洋资源开发等构成新挑战。在海洋主权安全方面，受海平面上升、海洋气象水文条件的改变以及极端天气的综合影响，两国大陆架之外部分岛礁面临被淹没或收缩的处境，也影响到了沿海和岛礁军事布防，对海上军事行动提出更高要求。在海洋公共安全方面，气候变化引发的大规模移民、海上防灾减灾和污染防治等对海洋公共安全提出新挑战。在海洋地缘安全方面，气候变化引发的海洋地理环境变化也将加剧大国博弈，导致中印海上竞合关系更加复杂。作为发展中大国，在从海洋大国迈向海洋强国的过程中，中印必须处理好海洋安全与发展的关系，采取联合行动，有效应对气候变化背景下日益恶化的海洋环境。

关键词：气候变化；中印海洋安全；气候移民；海上通道

气候变化是当今人类社会面临的重要环境问题，在对自然生态系统、人类生存环境和社会经济发展产生影响的同时，也对海洋安全构成严重挑战。中印同为海洋大国，气候变化引发的次生问题制约着两国海权发展。因而，分析和研究气候变化的海洋响应及其对中印两国海洋安全与发展的影响具有重要的现实意义和战略意义。当前，学术界在这一方面的研究尚不充分，也未就气候变化与海洋安全之间的关系进行全面探讨。鉴于此，本文立足于地理上更靠近中印的太平洋和印度洋广阔水域，探讨海洋领域的气候变化及其对中印海洋经济安全、海洋主权安全、海洋公共安全和海洋地缘安全等方面的影响，从而提出应对之策。

---

① 邹正鑫,印度德里大学政治学博士研究生,四川大学南亚与中国西部合作发展研究中心主任助理,主要研究印度洋安全问题、印度政治及中印关系。

海洋与大气层是相互关联的整体系统，两者不断进行着热量和气体的交换。1971—2010 年，海洋吸收了由空气、海水、陆地和融冰存储的所有多余热量的 93%，因此，气候变化对海洋的影响也更为深远。联合国 2017 年发布的第一次全球海洋综合评估技术摘要显示，与气候变化相关的海洋变化主要表现在：海水温度上升、海平面上升、海洋酸化、海水盐度多变、海洋分层程度加强、海洋环流变化、风暴和其他极端天气事件频繁、海水溶解氧水平降低等多方面。[①]

从经济利益到国家安全，乃至大国地位的追求方面来讲，海洋对中印两国都有着重要的现实意义。两国也都认识到气候变化对海洋生态系统的危害，以及对各自追求海权的消极影响。两国积极参与到全球气候变化的多边讨论中。2015 年，中国和印度发表关于气候变化的联合声明，指出气候变化及其负面影响是全人类的共同关切和 21 世纪最大的全球挑战之一，需要在《联合国气候变化框架公约》及其《京都议定书》等可持续发展框架下通过国际合作解决，表示中印双方将携手并与其他缔约方一道，共同推动多边谈判进程于 2015 年在公约下达成全面、平衡、公平和有效的协议，以确保公约的全面、有效和持续实施。[②]两国在政府层面和全球及区域的多边策层面开展了卓有成效的合作，是应对气候变化的积极参与者和贡献者。随着两国海权的发展，气候变化在海洋领域的不利影响将对两国海洋安全持续构成挑战。

一、气候变化对中印海洋经济安全的影响

海洋以其广阔性、便利性和资源富集性成为国家经济发展的重要基础。中印两国都为滨海大国，非常重视沿海地带和远海"蓝色经济"的发展。然而，气候变化引发的海洋气候水文要素的变化，以及由此产生的一系列次生灾害严重制约沿海地区经济社会发展，对海上交通线安全，海洋渔业、海洋

---

① 联合国：《第一次全球海洋综合评估技术摘要——气候变化和大气层的有关变化对海洋的影响》,2017 年, https://www.uncclearn.org/sites/default/files/inventory/1705753-c-impacts-of-climate-change_print-body.pdf, 第 3—6 页。

② 中央政府门户网站：《中华人民共和国政府和印度共和国政府关于气候变化的联合声明》, http://www.gov.cn/xinwen/2015-05/15/content_2 862749.htm?gs_ws=tsina_635675440362130507,2015 年 5 月 15 日。

资源开发等构成新挑战。

（一）制约沿海地区经济发展

全球气候变化背景下，多种灾害共同作用，使沿海地区受到极为复杂的影响：海平面上升导致潮位升高，风暴潮致灾程度增强，海水入侵面积和范围加大，洪涝灾害加剧；潮位和波高增大，减弱沿岸防护堤坝的能力，海岸和低地侵蚀加重；海平面上升和淡水资源短缺使得滨海淡水受到污染，农田盐碱化，河口区咸潮入侵，增加排污难度，破坏生态平衡。[①] 中印海岸线漫长且经济发达城市大多处于沿海地带，受到气候变化的影响也将更为直接。

印度海岸线长约 7500 公里，沿海分布着 12 个主要港口和 200 多个非主要港口，港口是印度对外经济发展的重要依托，但印度各港口配套基础设施建设较为落后，易受到气候变化引发的次生灾害的影响，如海平面上升将改变海岸附近陆基泥沙的动态变化，导致港池、航道水深不够而影响港口的吞吐能力；泥沙的运动也可能导致航道淤塞、原有航线废弃等，加大运输的成本和风险。印度"海洋花环"[②] 项目中的沿海社区发展包括渔业以及鱼产品加工和增值产品开发，沿海农业、手工业和小企业，海洋旅游休闲设施等，以上种种的发展都依赖海洋环境。而海平面上升压缩沿海社区人民的生存空间，酸化和咸化海水倒灌使海滨和内河淡水污染，农田盐碱化严重，农业产量锐减。海水的酸化、盐度增加以及海洋分层和环流等导致渔业资源短缺，鱼产品的安全无法得到保障。海洋极端天气也导致海洋旅游业和海洋设施发展缓慢。

中国沿海地区经济发达、人口密集、生态环境脆弱，是气候变化影响的敏感区域。《2019 年中国气候变化海洋蓝皮书》显示，1980—2018 年，中国沿海海表温度平均每 10 年升高 0.23℃；沿海海平面平均每年上升 3.3 毫米；沿海极值高水位平均每年上升 4.5 毫米；沿海气温平均每 10 年上升 0.37℃，[③]

---

① 黎鑫、张韧、李倩等："气候变化对国家海洋战略影响评估"，《国防科技》，2012 年第 3 期，第 53 页。

② Ministry of Shipping, Government of India, "Concept Note on Sagar Mala Project: Working Paper," October 28, 2014.

③ 中国海洋发展研究中心：《自然资源部发布〈2019 年中国气候变化海洋蓝皮书〉》，http://aoc.ouc.edu.cn/2019/1001/c9828a270601/pagem.psp，2019 年 10 月 1 日。

而且以上变化呈逐年递增态势，近几年增加值创历史新高。中国沿海区分布着五大城市群，是中国经济发展和对外贸易的重要引擎，气候变化对城市群的功能发挥以及居民的生命财产安全构成严重威胁。天津、上海、广州等城市由于受到海平面上升和风暴潮、台风、暴雨的综合影响，面临洪水和低地被淹没的巨大风险；海平面上升导致潮位升高，枯水期长江、珠江、黄河等面临海水倒灌和水质污染的危险；风暴潮、台风以及海平面上升的综合作用将导致海岸和河口三角洲侵蚀严重；海平面上升也将使港口和河道废弃，降低运输能力。

（二）挑战海上能源通道安全

海上能源通道主要指海上运输航线、海峡水道以及接驳货物的港口。气候变化引起的环境变化威胁着货运船舶的航行和关键枢纽水道安全，进一步加剧了两国传统能源通道的运输风险。两国的地缘位置和经济崛起决定了海洋运输在对外贸易中的核心地位。太平洋和印度洋是重要的国际运输线路，其东西两侧的马六甲海峡和霍尔木兹海峡更是沟通各大洋的"关键枢纽"。然而海平面上升改变了海峡水道的宽度、深度和明暗礁分布等地貌环境，海洋气象水文要素的变化引起风暴、台风等极端天气多发，海水温度和盐度变化导致的海洋分层程度增强和海洋环流机制紊乱，这些都给船舶航行带来不安全因素。

海上通道面临的另一个严重安全威胁是海盗。印度洋是重要的海路运输通道和战略通道，承载着全球 90% 的货物贸易和 60% 的石油运输，中国出口到中东、非洲、欧洲的货物一半以上，石油进口 80% 需途经印度洋。[①] 而印度处于印度洋的中心位置，该区域不仅涉及其海上运输安全，更关乎其海洋主权安全。但印度洋东西两端的具有战略意义的马六甲海峡和亚丁湾，是海盗活动高危区域。海盗通过武装抢劫过往商船，获取经济利益。海盗的产生是综合作用的结果，其中气候变化是主要原因之一。全球变暖和降水减少导致部分地区粮食和水资源供应不足，热带气旋、洪水等自然灾害侵蚀，以及近海渔业资源枯竭和海洋污染等综合因素致使沿岸居民陷入赤贫，许多渔

---

① 许可："印度洋的海盗威胁与中国的印度洋战略"，《南亚研究》，2011 年第 1 期，第 2—9 页。

民为解决生计问题而铤而走险。生存环境的进一步恶化有可能导致更为严重的海盗和海上恐怖主义活动，给海上运输安全带来巨大挑战。

（三）威胁海洋渔业安全和海洋资源开发安全

海洋渔业资源是海洋经济的重要组成部分。对中印两国来说，庞大的人口基数决定了对海产品的严重依赖，海产关乎两国人民的食物供应与安全问题。然而，气候变化引发的全球洋流、水域含盐度、酸度的改变等严重威胁着海洋渔业资源安全。海水气温升高和全球洋流的无规律调整引起鱼类大规模迁徙或灭绝，相关渔场面临资源枯竭，影响国内水产经济发展和国民的营养均衡，增大食物供应的压力。同时也会造成渔场拥挤，大量渔民面临巨大的失业和经济压力。水体含盐度和酸度的改变，以及海洋污染等直接导致鱼类污染，进而产生食品安全问题，以及由此产生一系列附加的经济成本。此外，海洋渔业资源枯竭也会造成捕鱼商业公司资金链的断裂和倒闭，加剧相关海洋国家的资源纠纷。目前来看，经济、资源与海洋生态系统之间的矛盾日益突出，这是全世界所面临的共同挑战，也是海洋大国中印迫切需要解决的重要问题。

海洋资源开发是一个过程，包括资源勘探、资源开采、资源处理以及运输等一系列环节。中印两国均重视海洋科考和油气开采，在各自海域都布置有大量海上钻井平台，为国家经济发展提供必要动能。然而在全球气候变化背景下，海上勘探、开采和运输等必然面临巨大风险。比如，海平面上升直接威胁到海上钻井平台及施工人员的安全；海水盐度、酸度以及洋流等气象水文变化对海上科考提出更高要求，需要重新评估海洋资源的可开采性或开发难度；再如，海上风暴、台风等极端恶劣天气增多考验海上钻井平台的稳定性，对其提出更高的技术要求，也会影响海上作业的正常开展。以上种种势必会加大对海洋资源考察和开发的技术难度，提高经济成本。中印两国在印度洋科考方面有较为成功的合作经历，但伴随着气候变化的不利影响的日益突出，可能会制约两国海洋经济领域合作的广度和深度，对两国的海洋经济发展造成不利影响。

二、气候变化对中印海洋主权安全的影响

气候变化以及由此产生的一系列负面效应对海洋国家的主权安全构成挑战。在海平面上升、海洋气象水文条件的改变以及极端天气的综合影响下，中印两国大陆架之外岛礁面临被淹没或收缩的处境，这使部分海域和岛礁主权争端风险加大。气候变化也恶化了海洋生态系统，影响沿海和岛礁军事布防，对海上军事行动提出更高要求。

（一）海平面上升将使岛礁淹没，部分海域和岛礁主权争端风险加大

海平面的持续上升，将导致大陆海岸线收缩，部分岛屿被淹没或者变为岛礁。中印两国的领海、毗连区、专属经济区等也将发生重大变化。具体表现在：两国海拔极低的岛屿将会被海水淹没，而对于本身拥有领海、毗连区、专属经济区和大陆架的岛屿来说，一旦岛屿被完全淹没则意味着将失去一大片管辖的海域；海拔较低的岛屿或海岸高地，将会部分地被淹没，并且更容易遭受极端海平面事件的侵袭，使这些岛屿的人口、资源以及设施遭受极大破坏，失去了生存条件，同样将失去专属经济区和大陆架。[①]

中国拥有的岛屿达6700多个，岛屿在经济建设、国防建设，甚至在政治、外交中的作用都举足轻重，而且事关中国的海域疆界。海平面继续上升可能淹没南海岛屿，部分岛屿永久消失水下，部分岛屿面积逐渐变小等。这不仅影响到中国的海洋主权，也会加大中国与所谓"主权声索国"之间的矛盾纠纷。如中国和越南之间围绕岛屿主权和经济利益的争端由来已久，部分岛屿变小或消失势必会加大两国海洋分歧，使目前的海洋局势更加复杂。

另一个例子是印度与孟加拉国新穆尔岛（New Moore）（孟加拉国称南达尔帕蒂岛）的主权争端。新穆尔岛位于孟加拉湾，约10.5平方公里，小岛周围蕴藏着储量巨大的油气资源，印孟两国围绕岛屿主权问题争夺了近30年。然而随着全球变暖海平面上升的影响，小岛在2010年遭海水淹没而消失。据报道，印度外交部发言人已明确表示："小岛消失不影响两国之间

的争端解决，我们仍要对小岛所在的海域进行主权控制。事实上，由于两国间仍有诸多小岛存在领土争端，所以印度不会因为新穆尔岛的消失就放弃对它的主权。"两国都宣称对该岛拥有主权，并就该岛所拥有的经济专属区（丰富的油气资源）产生争议。①

（二）海平面上升和极端天气增加将影响沿海和岛礁军事布防

气候变化引发的海平面上升和极端天气增加也将影响沿海和岛礁军事布防。突出的例子是 2014 年 10 月，印度东部海军司令部所在地维沙卡帕特南（Vishakhapatnam）遭遇 4 级飓风"赫德赫德"（Hudhud）袭击，导致整个城市受损严重，海军基地的机场和其他军事设施严重受损。②中印两国沿海港口众多，港口因其优越的地理位置和水文条件成为贸易物流的集散地，同时也是海军驻扎的理想地，是舰船建造、停泊和维修的主要基地。然而，海平面上升将和极端天气导致海岸线发展改变而失去理想的驻泊基地。海岸线向大陆移动，改变了水深和水底泥沙形态，海水流向和盐度、酸度等的变化对军舰驻泊提出新挑战，而不得不调整军事战略部署，包括人员、军事设施的重新部署或转移，气象水文条件的变化也要求舰艇作战参数等相应调整等。

海平面上升和极端天气增加也会对岛礁的军事布防造成威胁，尤其是当这些岛屿作为重要防御基地时，将会直接影响军事设施和驻扎环境，使官兵被迫转移，改变了海战场部署格局，削弱了海上防御纵深，从而间接影响到海洋主权的稳固。③岛礁是重要的战略基地，这一点从美国在海外的军事基地可见一斑。例如，美国在关岛的海军基地，海外飞地可以构成军事行动的"桥头堡"和"前哨"，利用地理优势在海外行动中先发制人，实现对邻近区域的战略优势。位于印度洋东部，介于孟加拉湾与缅甸海之间、十度海峡之北的安达曼群岛，扼守马六甲海峡与印度洋的咽喉，对印度的战略意义重大。

① "Island claimed by India and Bangladesh sinks below waves," *The Guardian*, March 24, 2010, https://www.theguardian.com/world/cif-green/2010/mar/24/india-bangladesh-sea-levels.

② "Vizag first Indian city directly hit by cyclone Hudhud," *The Times of India*, October 18, 2014, https://timesofindia.indiatimes.com/city/visakhapatnam/Vizag-first-Indian-city-directly-hit-by-cyclone-Hudhud/articleshow/44864271.cms.

③ 黎鑫、张韧、李倩等："气候变化对国家海洋战略影响评估"，《国防科技》，2012年第 3 期，第 54 页。

印度退役海军准将阿尼尔·贾伊·辛格（Anil Jai Singh）指出，每年有12万艘船只来往于印度洋，其中有近7万艘船只是通过马六甲海峡进入；他认为印度"必须真正监视中国的活动，需要在安达曼群岛配备足够的装备"。[1] 然而，在全球气候变化的背景下，这些岛屿的环境变化必然导致国家海洋战略的调整，岛礁军事布防成本的增加。

（三）气候变化对海上军事行动提出更高要求

如今，全球的地缘战略重心进一步向西太平洋和印度洋地区转移，围绕海洋的军事行动构成国际政治的主战场。然而，气候变化及其不利效应对海上军事行动提出更高的要求。有专家指出，全球冰雪融化有可能造成海水密度的变化，从而降低北纬地区海水的密度，而较暖和的低纬度地区蒸发量大而海水密度提高，海水盐度变化可能会导致潜艇浮力和水下武器的性能发生变化。[2] 随着海水密度的变化，它可能会改变水下声学特性，对声呐性能产生不利影响。最近的一项研究得出的结论是，到21世纪中叶，未来的化石燃料二氧化碳排放可能导致酸化增加，低频吸声率显著下降。[3] 此外，海水作业也可能受到不断改变的温跃层的影响，温跃层可能导致热水和冷水流的流动模式发生重大转变。例如，印度洋流可能会受海洋季风变化的影响。

未来的极端天气事件也可能会阻碍海军海面作战部署。恶劣的天气会对舰艇军事人员的身心健康造成影响。例如，在较温暖的气候条件下，航空母舰甲板上的表面温度可能会达到高温，从而给甲板机组人员的正常工作带来很大压力。高温也会对维持高频率操作的舰艇产生负面影响。各种极端恶劣天气也对船员和水手的水下训练构成挑战。最后，气候变化可能会对舰载作战系统，尤其是一些高精准武器的性能参数产生不利影响。以上种种由气候变化导致的对军事人员、舰艇等产生的不利影响都对海上军事行动提出了更

---

[1] 观察者网："监视中国动向，印度海军启用第三座安达曼群岛航空基地"，https://www.guancha.cn/military-affairs/2019_01_24_488080.shtml，2019年1月24日。

[2] National Development Council, "National Security Implications of Climate Change for U.S. Naval Forces," Washington DC: National Academies Press, 2011, pp. 107–108.

[3] Hester, Keith C., Edward T. Peltzer, William J. Kirkwood and Peter G. Brewer, "Unanticipated Consequences of Ocean Acidification: A Noisier Ocean at Lower pH," *Geophysical Research Letters*, Vol. 35, 2008.

高要求。随着印度印度洋战略的进一步深入实施，以及中国在印度洋战略存在的进一步加强，两国在处理双方安全关系的同时，更要深入考虑气候变化等因素对两国海上安全的影响。

三、气候变化对中印海洋公共安全的影响

公共安全是海洋安全的重要组成部分。气候变化以及由此引发的大规模移民对中印国家安全构成挑战，也严重影响着海洋公共安全。此外，海上防灾减灾和海洋污染治理等也是维护海洋公共安全的应有之义。

（一）气候移民

气候变化会引发印度洋地区大规模的人口迁移。研究表明，非洲和南亚沿海国家的荒漠化可能引发环境恶化，移民和冲突的恶性循环。2019 年 4 月，联合国难民署（UNHCR）公布的数据显示，自 2010 年以来，因气候变化相关灾害而流离失所的人数已上升至 2150 万人。另据澳大利亚智库经济与和平研究所（IEP）预测，到 2050 年，至少有 12 亿人可能因此类气候相关事件而流离失所。[1] 在印度洋区域，最脆弱的国家可能位于南亚。气候移民挑战着虚弱国家的政府治理能力。如果印度洋和太平洋上的岛屿国家人民为躲避不断恶化的环境、极端恶劣天气或政治动荡与军事冲突等移民，作为滨海大陆国家的中印无疑是最佳选择。因而，移民很可能会严重增加沿海社区的冲突风险。同时也可能促使国家更积极地动用海上力量来防止难民涌入，进行更多的预防性部署来应对可能发生的冲突。凡此种种都会增加海上和沿海地区的公共安全压力。

研究表明，印度洋变暖的速度较其他热带海洋更快，正在形成一个"温水池"，正在改变西南季风的强度，未来天气异常和极端事件会更频繁。[2] 可以预想，海平面上升和极端天气增加势必会使岛上居民面临疾病和饥荒，

---

① Tetsuji Ida, "Climate refugees—the world's forgotten victims," Economic Forum, June 18, 2021, https://www.weforum.org/agenda/2021/06/climate-refugees-the-world-s-for-gotten-victims/.

② Roxy, M.K., Ritika Kapoor, Terray Pascal and Masson Sabastien, "The Curious Case of Indian Ocean Warming," *Journal of Climate,* 27(22), pp. 8501–8509.

海水的酸化和污染侵蚀农田和淡水系统，导致生存环境崩溃。图瓦卢、马尔代夫、塞舌尔、瑙鲁和萨摩亚独立国等一些海岛国家已经因为近年来全球海平面的不断上升而逐渐丧失土地，其居民面临无家可归的风险。在 20 世纪的最后 10 年，海平面上升已经使太平洋岛国图瓦卢失去了 1% 的领土，2000 年 2 月的特大大潮几乎吞没了整个图瓦卢。每逢大潮期间，图瓦卢都会有 30% 左右的国土被海水淹没。2001 年，图瓦卢对外宣布本国所有的努力均告失败，该国将于 50 年后在世界版图上消失，全国 1.1 万国民将不得不放弃家园，陆续迁往与其签订协议的新西兰。[①] 作为区域大国的中印对地区安全治理负有责任，气候移民及其产生的公共安全问题考验着崛起的负责任大国的国际责任。

（二）海上防灾减灾

印度洋和太平洋地区的经济崛起正在导致海上活动的增加，从海上资源开发到货物和人员的运输，包括海运和空运。这有利于全球的物流畅通，也增加了由于海上（包括航空）事故造成的人身安全风险。2014 年发生的马来西亚客机 MH-370 和韩国"世越"号（Sewol）渡轮灾难就是鲜明的例子，表明海上防灾减灾不仅关乎海上人员和设施安全，也对地区海洋公共安全构成威胁。在未来，随着海上气候日益恶劣、海平面上升以及地区安全局势的演变，防灾减灾维护海洋公共安全也将变得更为迫切。

在全球气候变化背景下，海上防灾减灾工作形势严峻。据估计，到 2050 年，暴露于热带气旋风险之下的城市人口将从 3.1 亿人增加至 6.8 亿人。到 2070 年，暴露于海平面上升和洪水危险之下的城市资产可达 35 万亿美元，10 倍于目前的水平。地震、海啸、飓风和洪水带来的经济损失严重影响了基础设施、能源、农业、环境、水资源、健康和教育等关键部门。[②] 对中印来说，两国拥有漫长的海岸线且沿海聚集众多的经济发达城市和大量人口，沿海社区也是两国未来发展的重要支撑。受气候变化引发的海平面上升和海

---

① 王慧、李廷廷："气候变化背景下海洋安全的新挑战"，《浙江海洋学院学报（人文科学版）》，2014 年第 3 期，第 4 页。

② 联合国新闻："国际减灾日：秘书长特别代表格拉瑟强调自然灾害同气候变化与实现可持续发展目标之间关系密切"，https://news.un.org/zh/audio/2017/10/1001341，2017 年 10 月 12 日。

水气象水文因素，以及日益频繁的极端天气的影响，两国沿海及海上防灾设施建设、水资源保护、海洋生态体系建设等都面临挑战。中印两国在海上防灾减灾方面有着较为成功的合作经历。通过双边访问、召开会议、联合研究和军事演习等形式，两国加强在海洋防灾减灾、海洋科研、海洋环保、极地科考等方面的合作。[①] 无论是海上相关协议、科研考察还是海军演习，围绕的主题主要都是海上防灾减灾。这表明，两国在认识到海洋对各自的战略重要性的同时，也认识到海上问题远非一国之力可以解决，合作是解决问题最有效的途径。

气候变化的全球影响性和海洋的无国界性决定了国际合作是解决问题的可取途径。中印两国在海洋上虽有竞争，但受共同威胁因素的驱使，两国在海上尤其是印度洋上有众多合作空间和潜力。中印自 2008 年起就一直在协调其政策与海军行动，包括借助"打击索马里海盗联络小组"（CGPCS）相互协调，共同在亚丁湾－索马里执行护航任务。两国军方高层多次就联合打击海盗举行对话，拟定合作方案和实施细则。近年来，两国也多次在双边多边场合中协调相互立场，谋求联合反海盗护航、海上防灾减灾和海上救援等联合行动。[②] 在气候变化背景下，两国在海洋领域的合作途径也将越来越广。反海盗平台虽为维护海洋公共安全进行的有益探索，但在合作中建立的信息共享和合作行动等平台也为海上防灾减灾提供了便利，两国海军更是海上防灾减灾的主力军。同时也要看到，气候变化及其引发的一系列次生问题阻碍了海上防灾减灾的顺利开展，进而加剧了海上本就脆弱的安全环境。

四、气候变化对中印海洋地缘安全的影响

海洋地缘安全是大国海权追求的重要目标。北极新航道的开辟将调整世界经济运行结构，同时也将对亚太等低地国家造成严重影响。中印两国现阶段的海上互动表现为一种复杂的竞合关系，随着海洋地理环境的变迁，两国海上关系也将发生变化。

---

① 国家海洋局："陈连增副局长率团访问印度"，http://www.soa.gov.cn/xw/hyyw_90/201504/t20150423_37103.html，2015 年 4 月 23 日。

② 新华网："国际护航研讨会 2 月 23 日在南京举行"，http://news.xinhuanet.com/mil/2012-02/23/c_111560746.htm，2012 年 2 月 23 日。

（一）北极航道

历史上，通过北冰洋有两条途径可以连通起太平洋和大西洋。一条是著名的"西北航道"，它穿越了加拿大西部的大片岛屿；另一条就是"北海航道"，它是沿着亚洲北部海岸线伸展。由于全球气候变暖，北极冰层加速融化，估计不出 10 年，"西北航道"在夏季至少有一个月可通航；再过 15 年，"西北航道"每年将会有几个月的时间可以通航；最快到 2080 年整条航道可完全贯通。[①]北冰洋一旦全面通航，便可成为北美洲、北欧地区和东北亚国家之间最快捷的通道，也将极大缩短现有的航程。在这种情况之下，谁控制了北冰洋，谁就控制了世界经济新走廊的主动权。

中印虽远离北极航道，但北极航道的开通具有改变世界地缘政治的深远意义，对中印两国海洋安全也有一定影响。印度积极参与到北极事务中，加强对北极的科学研究、谋求成为北极理事会观察员国、加强与北极国家的能源合作、积极进行北极外交等。《中国的北极政策》白皮书指出作为负责任的大国，中国愿本着"尊重、合作、共赢、可持续"的基本原则，与有关各方一道，抓住北极发展的历史性机遇，积极应对北极变化带来的挑战，共同认识北极、保护北极、利用北极和参与治理北极，积极推动共建"一带一路"倡议涉北极合作，积极推动构建人类命运共同体，为北极的和平稳定和可持续发展做出贡献。这一定程度上将导致中印海洋安全战略的调整，未来的竞争可能不仅局限于从西太平洋到印度洋的广阔地区，还会延伸到关乎能源、经济发展的北极地区，可能使两国的海上安全关系更加复杂。

（二）中印海洋互动

中印均重视海权概念和海洋能力的发展，两国不断增强的海上势力存在交集，两国的崛起对区域乃至全球海洋空间均有巨大影响，在印度洋区域则更多地表现为一种竞争态势。在气候变化的背景下，不排除两国在更广范围、更深层次上竞争的可能性，对两国的地缘安全构成挑战。气候变化加剧了海

---

① 王慧、李廷廷，"气候变化背景下海洋安全的新挑战"，《浙江海洋学院学报（人文科学版）》，2014 年 6 月，第 2 页。

洋环境的脆弱性，使原有的双边合作难以深化，原有的合作基础不再存在。例如，两国在维护海上交通线安全方面，如果气候变化导致国际航线调整而远离两国本土或靠近其他大洋国家，中印两国可以发挥的作用就会受限，即降低两国参与的深度和广度。

但也应认识到，气候变化可能是两国海上安全合作新的渠道。目前来看，两国多是从现实主义国际政治立场出发，把国家安全置于首要地位，视对方为竞争对手，但随着海洋环境日益恶化，崛起的两大国势必会探索可能的合作途径应对气候问题。突出的例子是两国在北极地区的竞争与合作。气候变化对北极战略通道的影响更为严重，众多国家在这一地区的战略博弈也更为激烈。同为海洋大国的中印，自然也将目光投向这一区域，这是两国海洋战略发展的必然，与国际政治环境发展密切相关。中印在北极地区的海上通道战略并不清晰，都处于起步阶段。中国的海洋通道战略主要是以海洋科学研究为主，兼有其他方式。相较而言，印度对北极地区海上战略通道的利益诉求更为明显，采取的战略手段更为直接。但同时两国都表示出合作的意愿并作出积极努力。因而，从地缘安全角度来看，气候变化具有正、反两方面的效应，中印应从大局出发，维护公平正义的海洋秩序和自己合法的海洋区域，共同应对气候变化背景下日益严峻的海洋安全环境。

结论

气候变化与海洋安全是人类面临的两大安全与发展挑战，两者之间的相互影响更是恶化了人类生存条件。在海洋经济方面，气候变化制约沿海地区经济发展，威胁海上交通线安全，限制海洋资源开发；在海洋主权方面，海平面上升及海洋气象水文条件的改变增加了岛屿主权的争端风险，影响沿海和岛礁军事布防，同时也对海上军事行动提出了更高要求；在海洋公共安全方面，气候变化引发气候移民、海上灾害、海洋污染等诸多公共安全问题；在海洋地缘安全方面，气候变化可能使全球地缘政治中心发生转移，也必将引发大国的海上博弈和海上安全问题。

日渐紧迫的气候挑战要求各国采取积极措施，共同行动起来。中印作为两大发展中大国，在从海洋大国迈向海洋强国的过程中，必须处理好海洋安全与发展的关系，采取联合行动，有效应对气候变化背景下日益恶化的海洋生态环境。具体来看，两国应在政府立法、教育科研、产业合作和国际交流等方面开展相关实践，主动应对气候挑战。首先，政府应通过立法，制定海洋发展规划和行动计划，并确保政策落地实施；其次，加强对海洋水文气象等的科学研究和教育，建立海水检测分析数据平台，为政策制定提供参考；再次，加强海洋相关产业合作，鼓励引导民间参与，共同维护海上生态环境安全；最后，探索国际合作治理新模式，优化海洋合作体制机制。应对气候变化和海洋安全威胁，中印两国应发挥引领作用，维护自身海洋安全和发展利益，塑造绿色、和谐、可持续发展的海洋生态安全环境。

南亚政经 / 外交 / 安全

2014年以来印控克什米尔内部武装冲突新态势：
现状、原因与影响

曾维维 [①]

内容提要： 2014年莫迪政府上台后，印控查谟和克什米尔内部的武装冲突呈现出新的特点，其原因主要是经济停滞、特殊地位废除、社交媒体普及和安全部队不规范执法等。新特点包括涌现出如抵挡阵线等新兴本土武装组织，袭击目标更侧重于安全部队，无人机用于武装活动，社交媒体被用于宣传动员克什米尔青年并增强了招募能力等。印控克什米尔武装冲突的新态势促使印度政府加大对武装组织的打击力度，在克什米尔问题上对巴态度更为强硬。这又使得克什米尔问题进一步复杂化，印巴关系陷入僵局，和平解决克什米尔争端变得更为困难。印控克什米尔武装的外溢加大南亚地区安全隐患，对南亚区域合作提出挑战。

关键词： 克什米尔问题；武装组织；抵抗阵线；印巴关系

20世纪80年代伊始，受伊朗革命和阿富汗战争的影响，印控克什米尔山谷萌生出伊斯兰武装组织和运动，对当地的经济发展和社会安全都产生了重大影响。这些武装团体以安全部队、重要人物和平民为目标，采取自杀式袭击等手段，在当地发动了数以千计的武装袭击，旨在谋求印控克什米尔独立。在这一过程中，印巴两国围绕克什米尔问题相互指责，巴基斯坦认为印度在克什米尔侵犯人权，而印度认为巴基斯坦给予武装活动资金和技术上的支持，印巴两国的边境武装冲突时常发生。这种局面对当地经济发展和政治稳定都造成了严重影响，降低了两国政治互信，严重冲击印巴关系，使得南亚局势更为动荡和复杂。

---

① 曾维维，教育部人文社科重点研究基地四川大学南亚研究所硕士研究生，主要关注印度西北地区的分裂主义与民族主义研究。

一、印控克什米尔内部武装冲突的新变化

随着带有浓厚印度教民族主义色彩的莫迪政府的上台，印控克什米尔内部的武装冲突出现了一系列新态势，不仅涌现了新兴的本土武装组织，其袭击对象更侧重为安全部队，无人机技术也逐步运用到武装活动中，武装组织的招募能力稳步提升。

（一）袭击对象与袭击手段改变

近 30 年来，目标各异的武装组织在印控克什米尔地区活动频繁，不断发动袭击事件，造成大量的平民、警察和安全部队人员伤亡，截至 2021 年底已有 45280 人丧生。[①] 从袭击的时间分布来看，袭击事件在 20 世纪 90 年代达到峰值，21 世纪初逐渐下降，2014 年莫迪上台后又相对前几年呈螺旋上升趋势。从袭击致死对象来看，2008 年前平民死亡率一直高于安全部队的死亡率（见图 1），而 2014—2021 年间，武装分子的死伤人数已跃居首位，安全部队次之，平民最低（见图 2）。前期平民死亡率高与武装分子的无差别袭击有一定关系。"虔诚军"长期对印度目标无差别袭击，通常采取投掷手榴弹、引爆汽车炸弹、自杀式袭击等手段，在人流量密集的交通枢纽、公共场所对重量级人物、军警和平民发动袭击。[②] 而近年来，武装组织的主要袭击对象变为安全部队、警察等执法人员（见表 1）。

---

① "Datasheet - Jammu & Kashmir," South Asia Terrorism Portal, https://www.satp.org/datasheet-terrorist-attack/fatalities/india-jammukashmir, 2022 年 2 月 26 日。

② 李康安：《虔诚军的起源和发展》，硕士学位论文，北京大学国际政治专业，2011 年，第 18 页。

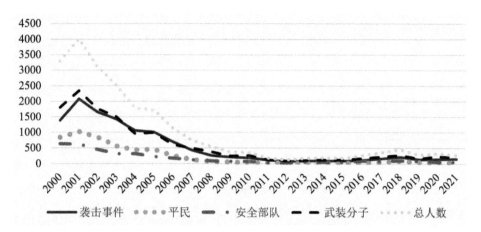

图1 2000—2021年印控克什米尔武装袭击情况

数据来源：South Asia Terrorism Portal. [1]

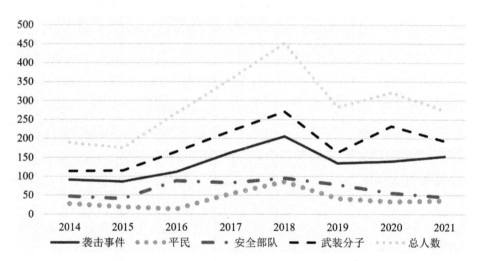

图2 2014—2021年印控克什米尔武装袭击情况

数据来源：South Asia Terrorism Portal. [2]

[1] "Datasheet - Jammu & Kashmir, Yearly Fatalities," South Asia Terrorism Portal, https://www.satp.org/datasheet-terrorist-attack/arrest/india-jammukashmir, 2022年2月26日。

[2] Ibid.

表 1 2014—2021 年克什米尔袭击事件（部分）

时间	地点	死伤人数	武装组织	详情
2014 年 12 月 5 日	乌里（Uri）	21 人死亡	虔诚军（Lashkar-e-Taiba）	虔诚军武装组织袭击乌里一军营，枪战共造成 21 人死亡，包括 11 名安全部队人员，2 名平民和 8 名武装分子
2015 年 12 月 7 日	阿纳恩特纳格（Anantnag）	6 人受伤		武装分子袭击中央后备警察部队，造成 6 名士兵受伤
2015 年 12 月 24 日	阿纳恩特纳格（Anantnag）	2 人受伤	圣战者党（Hizbul Mujahideen）	2 名警察在游行值班中遭武装人员袭击受伤
2016 年 6 月 25 日	普尔瓦马（Pulwama）	10 人死亡，20 人受伤	虔诚军（Lashkar-e-Taiba）	武装分子在普尔瓦马的帕姆波雷镇（Pampore）袭击安全部队，造成 8 名中央后备警察死亡，超 20 人受伤，2 名武装成员亦丧生
2016 年 9 月 18 日	乌里（Uri）	22 人死亡	穆罕默德军（Jaish-e-Mohammed）	武装分子对乌里军营发动大规模手榴弹袭击，造成 18 名士兵死亡，4 名武装分子在枪战中丧生。此次袭击被认为是 20 年来对克什米尔安全部队最致命的袭击
2016 年 10 月 19 日	查谟（Jammu）	5 人死亡		武装分子袭击讷格罗达（Nagrota）一军营，3 名印军人员和 2 名武装人员死亡
2017 年 2 月 12 日	库尔加姆（Kulgam）	7 人死亡，3 人受伤		武装分子与安全部队爆发冲突，4 名武装分子、2 名士兵和 1 名男子死亡，3 名士兵受伤。
2017 年 2 月 14 日	班迪波拉（Bandipora）	4 人死亡，7 人受伤		安全部队与武装分子发生冲突导致 3 名士兵和 1 名武装分子死亡，6 名安全人员和 1 名平民受伤
2017 年 2 月 23 日	斯胡皮延（Shopian）	3 人死亡，6 人受伤	圣战者党（Hizbul Mujahideen）	武装分子在凌晨伏击一支车队，造成 3 名士兵死亡，包含 1 名平民在内的 6 人受伤

时间	地点	死伤人数	武装组织	详情
2017 年 4 月 27 日	库普瓦拉 (Kupwara)	5 人死亡		武装分子袭击潘兹加姆（Panzgam）地区的一个军营，3 名士兵身亡，2 名武装分子被击毙
2017 年 8 月 26 日	普尔瓦马 (Pulwama)	11 人死亡		武装分子对警察大楼发动自杀式袭击从而引发与安全部队的枪战，8 名安全人员和 3 名武装人员死亡
2017 年 10 月 4 日	斯利那加 (Srinagar)	5 人死亡	穆罕默德军（Jaish-e-Mohammed）	4 名武装分子冲进斯利那加机场附近的边境安全部队 (BSF) 营地枪杀 1 名警察并全部身亡
2017 年 11 月 2 日	阿南特纳格 (Anantnag)	5 人受伤		武装分子向中央后备警察部队车辆开火，导致 5 名警察受伤
2017 年 12 月 31 日	普尔瓦马 (Pulwama)	7 人死亡	穆罕默德军（Jaish-e-Mohammed）	武装人员袭击准军事基地，造成 5 名士兵死亡，2 名武装人员丧生
2018 年 1 月 1 日	普尔瓦马 (Pulwama)	8 人死亡，3 人受伤	穆罕默德军（Jaish-e-Mohammed）	3 名武装分子闯入位于莱塔波拉村庄的（Lethapora)中央后备警察营地(包括准军事部队第 185 营的集团训练中心、弹药库）被打死，另有 5 名警察身亡，3 人受伤
2018 年 2 月 10 日	查谟 (Jammu)	10 人死亡，11 人受伤	穆罕默德军（Jaish-e-Mohammed）	武装分子偷袭查谟和克什米尔轻步兵第 36 旅营地，造成 5 名士兵和 1 名平民死亡，4 名武装成员在搜查中被打死
2019 年 2 月 1 日	普尔瓦马 (Pulwama)	46 人死亡，29 人受伤	穆罕默德军（Jaish-e-Mohammed）	武装人员阿迪尔·达尔（Adil Dar）驾驶装载有 300 斤炸药的汽车撞向安全部队车队，造成 46 名警察身亡，这是 1989 年后针对国家安保人员的伤亡最惨重袭击
2020 年 4 月 7 日	阿纳恩特纳格 (Anantnag)	1 人死亡	抵抗阵线（The Resistance Front）	1 名中央后备警察被杀

续表

时 间	地 点	死伤人数	武装组织	详 情
2020 年 4 月 8 日	巴拉穆拉（Baramula）	3 人死亡，2 人受伤	抵抗阵线（The Resistance Front）	巴拉穆拉区索波尔地区的一次武装袭击造成 3 人死亡，2 人受伤
2020 年 5 月 3 日	库普瓦拉（Kupwara）	7 人死亡		武装分子与安全部队交火，5 名士兵死亡（其中包括一上校、少校和当地副督察）和 2 名武装成员死亡
2021 年 2 月 19 日	布德甘区（Budgam）	4 人死亡，1 人受伤	虔诚军（Lashkar-e-Taiba）	一次武装冲突中，3 名武装分子和 1 名警察身亡，1 名警察受伤
2021 年 10 月 10—11 日	蓬奇（Poonch）	5 人死亡		武装分子朝执行任务的印度军队和查谟和克什米尔警察开火，造成 5 名士兵死亡
2021 年 12 月 13 日	斯利那加（Srinagar）	3 人死亡，11 人受伤		3 名武装分子袭击一辆警察营地附近的公共汽车
2021 年 12 月 31 日	斯利那加（Srinagar）	3 人死亡，4 人受伤	穆罕默德军（Jaish-e-Mohammed）	位于斯利那加的潘萨霍克（Panthachowk）发生枪战，3 名穆罕默德军成员死亡，4 名警察受伤
2022 年 1 月 13 日	库尔加姆（Kulgam）	2 人死亡，5 人受伤	穆罕默德军（Jaish-e-Mohammed）	武装分子袭击安全部队阵地，造成 1 名警察和 1 名武装分子丧生
2022 年 3 月 6 日	斯利那加（Srinagar）	1 人死亡，24 人受伤		武装分子对安全部队进行了手榴弹袭击，造成 1 位平民死亡，包含 1 名警察在内的 24 人受伤
2022 年 3 月 12 日	斯胡皮延（Shopian）	1 人死亡	抵抗阵线（The Resistance Front）	1 名休假的警察在家遭枪杀
2022 年 5 月 7 日	斯利那加（Srinagar）	1 人死亡	抵抗阵线（The Resistance Front）	1 名抵抗阵线成员开枪打死 1 名警察
2022 年 8 月 11 日	拉朱里（Rajouri）	5 人死亡，2 人受伤		2 名持枪和手榴弹的武装分子在独立日前夕袭击达尔哈尔地区并在袭击中死亡，袭击还造成了 3 名士兵的死亡和 2 名士兵受伤

信息来源：各大新闻网站资料整理而成

武装组织近年来以印方安全部队和中央后备警察等为主要袭击目标，采取"独狼"策略或少数袭击者突袭军事基地、军车和警察局等要地，其行动更具目的性和组织性，在袭击对象上更有策划和区分。

近年来，武装组织不仅在袭击目标上有所转变，在袭击手段上也有所革新。除传统的炸弹袭击外，无人机技术也开始用于在印控克什米尔开展武装袭击。据印度官方数据，印度安全人员在 2019 年发现了 167 架来自巴基斯坦的无人机，[①] 在查谟和克什米尔多地均有无人机活动。[②] 印方安全部队认为是巴方的武装分子借助无人机将武器、弹药、毒品和资金输送到控制线的另一侧，[③] 采取如伏击、肇事逃逸、遥控炸弹等游击战术来攻击印方军事基地，[④] 2021 年 6 月的查谟空军基地遇袭就是典型例子，查谟和克什米尔警察局局长迪尔巴格·辛格（Dilbag Singh）称虔诚军涉嫌在查谟机场的空军基地利用无人机投掷爆炸物，造成 2 名人员受伤。[⑤]

目前的无人机装置仍较为简易，杀伤力有限。无人机重量轻，荷载有限，可降落高度有限，这就意味着无人机袭击可能不够精确。[⑥] 尽管如此，无人机用于武装袭击的确给印方安全部队带来了新的困扰，迫使印方在查谟多地

---

① 王卓一："无人机频繁'光顾'印军基地，印在克什米尔遭遇安全新挑战"，澎湃新闻，https://m.thepaper.cn/newsDetail_forward_13357451，2022 年 2 月 2 日。

② "Suspected drone activity reported from three places in Jammu and Kashmir's Samba," *Times of India*, August 2, 2021, https://timesofindia.indiatimes.com/india/suspected-drone-activity-reported-from-three-places-in-jammu-and-kashmirs-samba/articleshow/84963484.cms，2022 年 2 月 2 日。

③ Irfan Amin Malik, "Content Creators, Vloggers in J&K Are Suffering After the 'Temporary' Ban on Drones," The Wire, August 13, 2021, https://thewire.in/government/content-creators-vloggers-in-jk-are-suffering-after-the-temporary-ban-on-drones, 2022 年 2 月 5 日。

④ "India says two drones intercepted over Kashmir army base," Aljazeera, June 28, 2021, https://www.aljazeera.com/news/2021/6/28/india-says-two-drones-intercepted-over-kashmir-army-base，2022 年 2 月 5 日。

⑤ "LeT suspected to be behind IAF station attack, drones may have come from across border: DGP," *India Today*, June 29, 2021, https://www.indiatoday.in/india/story/let-suspected-to-be-behind-iaf-station-attack-drones-may-have-come-from-across-border-dgp-1820889-2021-06-29，2022 年 2 月 5 日。

⑥ Deeptiman Tiwary, "Blast at IAF base in Jammu: Two drones dropped 2 kg 'high grade' IEDs from 100 m height, flew back," *The Indian Express*, June 28, 2021, https://indianexpress.com/article/india/blast-at-iaf-base-in-jammu-2-drones-dropped-2-kg-high-grade-ieds-from-100-m-height-flew-back-7378721/，2022 年 2 月 5 日。

部署反无人机系统，斯利那加县政府已禁止销售、拥有、储存、使用或运输无人机。[①] 边境安全部队的总部副检察长称，无人机用于走私毒品和武器将会是一种"巨大挑战"。[②] 随着无人机技术的发展和改良，无人机未来可能承载威力更大的爆炸装置，对印度安全人员的威胁也会进一步升级。

（二）招募人数增加

随着互联网技术的普及，激进思想得以迅速在网上传播，印控克什米尔武装团体的招募能力也显著提升，特别是在 2014 年莫迪政府执政以来，武装团体的人员招募呈螺旋上升的趋势。

印方安全部队近年来大力打击武装分子，在 2016 年、2017 年和 2018 年分别击毙 140 名、210 名、191 名武装分子，但招募人数并未下降，且在 2018 年达到峰值（见图 3）。安全部队于 2020 年对恐怖组织发起全面攻势，两月间共击毙 52 名武装分子，但当地青年加入武装组织的人数不减反增，本地招募从 4 月 7 日的 6 人跃升至 6 月 8 日的 43 人。[③]

① "Express News Service, IED-laden drone shot down near LOC in Jammu and Kashmir," *The Indian Express*, July 23, 2021，https://indianexpress.com/article/india/ied-drone-shot-down-loc-kashmir-7418069/，2022 年 2 月 6 日。

② Shakir Mir, "Armed Attacks, Drones: Why Is Jammu Seeing a Rise in Militant Activity?" The Quint, August 25, 2022, https://www.thequint.com/news/india/armed-attacks-drones-why-is-jammu-seeing-a-rise-in-militant-activity#read-more，2022 年 9 月 24 日。

③ Abhishek Bhalla, "Kashmir: Big spike in local terror recruitment amid lockdown even as forces killed top commanders," *India Today*, June 8, 2020，https://www.indiatoday.in/india/story/kashmir-big-spike-in-local-terror-recruitment-amid-covid-19-lockdown-even-as-army-nabbed-top-commanders-1686871-2020-06-08，2022 年 2 月 6 日。

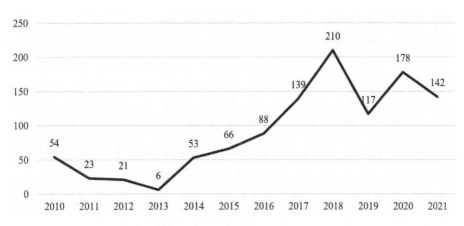

图 3 2010—2020 年恐怖分子招募人数

数据来源：*The Economic Times*,[1]The Print.[2]

武装组织的招募地选择和成员构成也发生新变化。21 世纪初，虔诚军等武装组织主要从巴基斯坦旁遮普省和印控克什米尔靠近控制线的地区招募成员，但其招募重点在 2015 年左右转移到南克什米尔，普尔瓦马（Pulwama）、斯胡皮延（Shopian）、阿南特纳格（Anantnag）和库尔加姆（Kulgam）成为热门招募地。[3]与此同时，印控克什米尔武装组织的外国人比例也在不断下降，从 2016 年的 77% 下降到 2017 年的 60%、2018 年的 45%、2019 年的 19% 和 2020 年的 15%。[4]换言之，这些武装组织的本土人员比例在不断

① "Local recruitment in militant groups rises alarmingly in Kashmir," *The Economic Times*, June 3, 2018, https://economictimes.indiatimes.com/news/defence/local-recruitment-in-militant-groups-rises-alarmingly-in-kashmir/articleshow/64436108.cms，2022 年 3 月 6 日。

② Snehesh Alex Philip, "Kashmir terrorist numbers & local recruitment dip, but 'dormant' Pakistan intruders resurface," The Print, February 28, 2022, https://theprint.in/defence/kashmir-terrorist-numbers-local-recruitment-dip-but-dormant-pakistan-intruders-resurface/850792/，2022 年 3 月 6 日。

③ Khalid Shah, Parjanya Bhatt, Shubhangi Pandey, "Kashmir Conflict Tracker," Observer Research Foundation, October 22, 2018, https://www.orfonline.org/kashmir-conflict-tracker-45120/，2022 年 3 月 7 日。

④ Rohith Sai Narayan Stambamkadi, "Crowdsourcing violence: Decoding online propaganda of new militant groups in Kashmir," Observer Research Foundation, January 19, 2022, https://www.orfonline.org/expert-speak/crowdsourcing-violence/，2022 年 3 月 7 日。

攀升，目前活跃在印控克什米尔地区的武装成员已多为本土青年。

（三）出现新的武装组织

活跃在印控克什米尔的武装组织众多，斗争目标各异。以宗教思想为动员工具的组织具有鲜明的反印特征，倾向于将克什米尔与查谟分离并同巴基斯坦合并；具有克什米尔民族主义倾向的组织则试图建立独立的克什米尔国家，[①] 这一类以查谟和克什米尔解放阵线（Jammu Kashmir Liberation Front, JKLF）为典型代表。不过，查谟和克什米尔解放阵线已在 21 世纪初淡出人们视野，印控克什米尔目前仍较活跃的武装组织是带伊斯兰色彩的虔诚军、穆罕默德军和真主圣战党。虔诚军和穆罕默德军的总部均设在巴基斯坦境内，[②] 其成员往往越界渗入印控克什米尔地区发动袭击。

2019 年后，印度对克什米尔实控线的管控更为严格，沿控制线的武装渗透活动也呈现下降趋势，从 2019 年的 130 起下降到 2020 年的 36 起和 2021 年的 31 起。[③] 武装组织的人员来源也从跨境渗透转变为本土培养，抵抗阵线（The Resistance Front , TRF）、人民反法西斯阵线（People's Anti-Fascist Front, PAFF）、联合解放阵线（United Liberation Front, ULF) 等新武装组织逐步兴起，特别是抵抗阵线因声称对多个袭击事件负责而名声大噪，频繁出现于主流媒体的报道中。在 2019 年 10 月 12 日于斯利那加发生的手榴弹袭击事件、[④]2020 年 4 月 5 日的库普瓦拉（Kupwara）袭击事

---

① 刘向阳："克什米尔地区恐怖主义问题综述"，载《国际资料信息》，2010 年第 4 期，第 1 页。

② Asad Hashim, "Profile: What is Jaish-e-Muhammad?" Aljazeera, May 1, 2019, https://www.aljazeera.com/news/2019/5/1/profile-what-is-jaish-e-muhammad, 2021 年 12 月 24 日。

③ Peerzada Ashiq, "Over 100 terrorists waiting across border, says BSF," *The Hindu*, January 24, 2022, https://www.thehindu.com/news/national/other-states/over-100-terrorists-waiting-across-border-says-bsf/article38320313.ece, 2022 年 1 月 4 日。

④ "'Faceless Force', 'Invisible Outfit': What is TRF and Its Sinister Plan for Kashmir," News 18, December 20, 2021, https://www.news18.com/news/opinion/faceless-force-invisible-outfit-what-is-trf-and-its-sinister-plan-for-kashmir-4574888.html, 2022 年 1 月 4 日。

件、[①]2021 年 6 月 22 日针对警督达尔的枪杀事件、[②]2021 年 8 月 9 日阿南特纳格（Anantnag）县的印人党夫妇枪杀事件中均出现其身影。[③]

这些新武装组织的宣传活动有强烈的非宗教特征，多采用世俗化名字，口号上强调"抵抗"而不是具有宗教色彩的"圣战"。比如，解放阵线的宣传口号是"抵抗直到胜利"；[④]联合解放阵线使用"抵抗存在"作为其口号，将印方安全部队称为"占领军"，将政府称为"占领政权"，激进组织的成员自称"自由战士"，占领、抵抗和自由斗争的标语高频出现。虽然抵抗阵线等武装组织在宣传口号上有意突出其世俗属性，但实际袭击行动仍带有某种宗教色彩。如在 2020 年 10 月 7 日的袭击事件中，肇事者将人质按是否穆斯林进行分类，开枪射杀了一名印度教徒和一名锡克教徒。[⑤]

除此之外，新的武装组织还呈现出本土化和与外部武装组织界限模糊的双重特点。不同于虔诚军等外部武装组织，抵抗阵线诞生于印控克什米尔的特殊地位被废除后，其目的是抵制印度统治，成员多系克什米尔本土青年，袭击对象则包括外地人、反恐官员以及帮助"外来者"的本地人，具有明显

---

① "'Pak Has Launched New Terror Outfits with Local Names but Let, JeM Cadres to Fool the World'," News 18, May 21, 2020, https://www.news18.com/news/india/pak-has-launched-new-terror-outfits-with-local-names-but-let-jem-cadres-to-fool-the-world-2630861. html, 2022 年 1 月 4 日。

② "Police Officer Shot Dead by Terrorists Outside Srinagar Mosque; Terror Group TRF Claims Responsibility," News 18, June 22, 2021, https://www.news18.com/news/india/jammu-and-kashmir-cop-killed-in-terrorist-attack-outside-mosque-in-srinagar-3879461.html, 2022 年 1 月 6 日。

③ "BJP Leader, Wife Shot Dead in Anantnag; TRF Claims Responsibility for Attack," News 18, August 9, 2021, https://www.news18.com/news/india/bjp-leader-wife-from-kul-gam-shot-dead-in-anantnag-dgp-says-let-behind-killing-4063871.html, 2022 年 1 月 6 日。

④ Manu Pubby, "The Resistance Front: New name of terror groups in Kashmir," *The Economic Times*, April 29, 2020, https://economictimes.indiatimes.com/news/defence/the-resistance-front-new-name-of-terror-groups-in-kashmir/articleshow/75440416.cms?from=mdr, 2022 年 1 月 7 日。

⑤ "After prominent Kashmiri Pandit chemist, 2 teachers killed in Srinagar," *Tribune India*, October 8, 2021, https://www.tribuneindia.com/news/j-k/after-prominent-kashmiri-pandit-chemist-2-teachers-killed-in-srinagar-321410, 2022 年 9 月 25 日。

的本土化特征。^①不过，印方仍然强调抵抗阵线是虔诚军的本土化影子组织，认为其核心人员其实是虔诚军和穆罕默德军的领导人。^②印方一些安全人士强调，抵抗阵线等本土化世俗武装组织的出现，是巴基斯坦为了逃避国际压力并确保各组织协同合作而进行人力、武器和训练整合的结果。^③世界危机组织的观察人士也认为："抵抗阵线和其他'圣战'武装组织存在合作，抵抗阵线只是另一个名字。"^④印方媒体报道还强调，抵抗阵线在印控克什米尔的活动得到了虔诚军和穆罕默德军的全力支持。^⑤一些报道称穆罕默德军成员承认虔诚军和抵抗阵线在行动上在进行合作，^⑥甚至引用抵抗阵线成员被捕后的供词来凸显其与虔诚军的密切联系。^⑦种种迹象表明，抵抗阵线与虔诚军等外部组织确有密切合作和成员交叉的情况，二者的界限具有一定的模糊性。

---

① Manoj Gupta, "In New Kashmir 'Strategy Note', Terror Group TRF Threatens Non-Locals and Locals Who Help Them: Sources," News 18, October 18, 2021, https://www.news18.com/news/india/in-new-kashmir-strategy-note-terror-group-trf-threatens-non-locals-and-locals-who-help-them-sources-4334279.html, 2022 年 1 月 10 日。

② Shishir Gupta, "Pak launches terror's new face in Kashmir, Imran Khan follows up on Twitter," *Hindustan times*, May 8, 2020, https://www.hindustantimes.com/india-news/pak-launches-terror-s-new-face-in-kashmir-imran-khan-follows-up-on-twitter/story-vDmvByzke-owrW8OKruhS3M.html, 2022 年 1 月 10 日。

③ Khalid Shah, "Pakistan using COVID-19 as a cover for cross border militancy," Observer Research Foundation, April 29, 2020, https://www.orfonline.org/expert-speak/paki-stan-using-covid19-cover-crossborder-militancy-65377/?amp, 2022 年 2 月 2 日。

④ International Crisis Group, "Raising the Stakes in Jammu and Kashmir," *Asia Report*, No.310, August 5, 2020, pp.16–17.

⑤ "'Pak Has Launched New Terror Outfits with Local Names but Let, JeM Cadres to Fool the World'," News 18, May 21, 2020, https://www.news18.com/news/india/pak-has-launched-new-terror-outfits-with-local-names-but-let-jem-cadres-to-fool-the-world-2630861.html, 2022 年 2 月 2 日。

⑥ Kamaljit Kaur Sandhu, "J&K: 5 terrorists, including top JeM commander Zahid Wani, killed in dual encounters," *India Today*, January 30, 2022, https://www.indiatoday.in/india/story/jammu-kashmir-let-terrorists-jem-commander-zahid-wani-dual-encounters-pulwa-ma-budgam-1906313-2022-01-30, 2022 年 2 月 2 日。

⑦ Ashraf Wani, "J&K: Three militant associates arrested in Ganderbal, arms and ammunition recovered," *India Today*, January 29, 2022, 2022 年 2 月 2 日。

二、印控克什米尔内部武装冲突出现新态势的原因

经济停滞、政策调整和社交媒体普及是近年来印控克什米尔武装冲突出现新态势的重要原因。

（一）经济持续低迷

近年来，由于印控克什米尔遭受封控、新冠疫情肆虐、武装袭击频发等原因，印控克什米尔经济增长缓慢，旅游业受到严重影响。印控克什米尔人均收入排名在印度国内长期靠后，2019–2020 财年的人均收入在全印仅排第 25 位，较前一年下降 2 名。[①] 旅游业对印控克什米尔经济的贡献仅次于园艺和农业，但 2019 年开始加码的各种管控措施和随后的新冠疫情暴发导致游客数量大减。2018 年访问克什米尔山谷的游客数量为 830758 人，到 2019 年下降到 565532 名，但 2020 年 1—11 月间仅接待游客 25922 名，[②] 可以说是断崖式下降。这给印控克什米尔经济发展带来了极为严重的负面影响。[③]

经济停滞导致当地失业率大幅提升。自 2019 年 8 月到 2020 年 2 月，整个印控克什米尔有超过 20% 的人口处于失业状态，到 7 月份的平均失业率为仍为 17.9%，是印度平均失业率（9.5%）的近 2 倍。[④] 在这种背景下，加入武装组织所获得的高报酬对失业青年就产生了吸引力。据印度情报机构计算，每位克什米尔武装成员平均每年可获得 30 万卢比的报酬，外国成员最高可获得 50 万卢比。他们只要加入武装组织即可获得一笔预付款，若本

---

① "Indian states by GDP per capita," *Statistics times*, https://statisticstimes.com/economy/india/indian-states-gdp-per-capita.php, 2021 年 10 月 9 日。

② Abha Lakshmi Singh, Saleha Jamal, "Impact assessment of lockdown amid COVID-19 pandemic on tourism industry of Kashmir Valley, India," *Research in Globalization*, Vol.3, December 2021, p.8.

③ Chaitanya Mallapur, "India's Covid-19 lockdown may cause 38 million job losses in the travel and tourism industry," Scroll.in, April 14, 2020, https://scroll.in/article/959045/indias-covid-19-lockdown-may-cause-38-mil lion-job-losses-in-the-travel-and-tourism-industry, 2021 年 10 月 9 日。

④ Niha Dagia, "Perpetual Silence: Kashmir's Economy Slumps Under Lockdown," *The Diplomat*, August 14, 2020, https://thediplomat.com/2020/08/perpetual-silence-kashmirs-economy-slumps-under-lockdown/, 2021 年 10 月 16 日。

人在行动中死亡，家人还会获得武装组织一定的经济照抚。[①]这也解释了印控克什米尔武装团体在印方安全部队的打击下招募人数仍上升的原因。

印控克什米尔武装分子数量的上升与当地经济的发展迟缓密不可分，所招募的武装成员多为低收入青年，学者通过对1989—2008年间被杀的虔诚军成员传记进行研究发现，虔诚军成员平均年龄为17岁，[②]观察者基金会2018年的研究与之印证，武装分子的主要年龄段集中在15～25岁。[③]并且武装分子通常来自中下阶层的低收入人群，排名前五的职业是工厂工人、农民、裁缝、电工和劳工。"尽管虔诚军面向全体社会进行招募，但大多数招募的武装分子为最底层人群。"[④]由此可见，经济低迷下的低收入青年更容易被吸纳到武装组织中。

（二）修宪的负面影响

2019年8月5日，印度政府宣布废除《印度宪法》第370条，取消赋予印控克什米尔的特殊地位。印度政府认为修宪对防止恐怖主义、维护印度统一、促进经济发展和确保克什米尔民主治理均有重要意义。印度内政部长阿米特·沙阿（Amit Shah）表示："只要有第370条，恐怖主义就不能消灭。第370条的存在是民主没有渗透到查谟和克什米尔的原因。"[⑤]莫迪总理也表示，宪法第370条应该对印控克什米尔的"分裂主义、恐怖主义、裙带关系和普遍的腐败"负责，认为将印控克什米尔完全融入印度将促进经济发展

---

① Dr. Sanjay Kumar, *Indo-Pak Tension Solution for Conflict or Cooperation*, New Delhi: G.B. Books, 2016, p.167.

② Don Rassler, C. Christine Fair, Anirban Ghosh, Arif Jamal, Nadia Shoeb, "The Fighters of Lashkar-e-Taiba: Recruitment, Training, Deployment and Death," *Combating Terrorism Center at West Point*, April 2013, p.18.

③ Khalid Shah, Parjanya Bhatt, Shubhangi Pandey, "Kashmir Conflict Tracker," Observer Research Foundation, October 22, 2018, https://www.orfonline.org/kashmir-conflict-tracker-45120/, 2021年11月5日。

④ Abou Zahab, "I shall be waiting for you at the door of paradise," in Aparna Rao eds., *The Practice of War: Production, Reproduction and Communication of Armed Violence*, New York: Berghahn Books, 2008, p.136.

⑤ Rakesh Mohan Chaturvedi, "Article 370: cause of corruption and terrorism: Amit Shah," *The Economic Times*, August 6, 2019, https://economictimes.indiatimes.com/news/politics-and-nation/article-370-cause-of-corruption-and-terrorism-amit-shah/articleshow/70546744.cms, 2022年2月3日。

并恢复当地青年对印度的信心。[①]

印度政府对这一举措予以高度评价，但此举却严重挫伤了印控克什米尔民众的情绪，在该地引发了广泛愤怒，当地居民普遍对印度政府感到失望，[②]一些山谷的居民甚至认为印度政府已将他们视为"二等公民"。[③]更何况，印方在高度重视反恐的同时，对地方政府的腐败和治理不善等问题却不够重视，民众对此颇为失望，投票率持续走低，暴力和反抗事件卷土重来。[④]2019年印控克什米尔的对示威者投石事件激增到1999起，其中1193起发生在8月5日修宪后。[⑤]另有研究认为，修宪举动加剧了分离主义者和克什米尔民众的不满，甚至催生了抵抗阵线等新的本土武装组织，[⑥]也加剧了武装分子的招募活动。

（三）社交媒体对激进言论的传播

互联网的广泛普及为武装组织的宣传动员和培训联络提供了载体。到

①　"In first speech on Article 370, PM Modi talks development in J&K," *India To-day*, August 8, 2019, https://www.indiatoday.in/india/story/pm-narendra-modi-speech-arti-cle-370-highlights-development-agenda-jammu-kashmir-ladakh-1578882-2019-08-08，2022年3月7日。

②　Concerned Citizens Group, "India: Sixth and Seventh Reports of the Concerned Cit-izens' Group on Kashmir Sep 17-18, 2019 and Nov 22-26, 2019," South Asia Citizens Web, December 2019, http://www.sacw.net/article14242.html，2022年2月3日。

③　Ayjaz Wani, "Life in Kashmir after Article 370," *Observer Research Foundation Special Report*, No. 99, January 28, 2020, p.7.

④　Freedom House, "Indian Kashmir," www.freedomhouse.org/country/indian-kash-mir/freedom-world/2020，2022年1月4日。Hakeem Irfan, "Parties Fear 'Cadre Alienation' after Low Turnout in Valley," *The Economic Times*, April 27, 2019, https://economictimes.in-diatimes.com/news/elections/lok-sabha/india/parties-fear-cadre-alienation-after-low-turnout-in-valley/articleshow/69067557.cms，2022年2月3日。

⑤　"1,999 stone-pelting incidents in 2019 in J-K, 1,193 post abrogation of Article 370," *The Economic Times*, January 7, 2020, https://economictimes.indiatimes.com/news/politics-and-nation/1999-stone-pelting-incidents-in-2019-in-j-k-1193-post-abrogation-of-article-370/articleshow/73129411.cms?utm_source=contentofinterest&utm_medium=text&utm_cam-paign=cppst，2022年2月3日。

⑥　Happymon Jacob, "Toward a Kashmir Endgame? How India and Pakistan Could Negotiate a Lasting Solution," United States Institute of Peace, No. 474, August 2020, p.13.

2015年底，印控克什米尔地区社交媒体的使用人数达到70%，[①]印控克什米尔一些武装组织公开在网上发表激进言论，在社交媒体上更新武装行动信息，以此来扩大支持阵营，鼓动当地人拿起武器。[②]每次与安全部队交锋后，武装组织的管理人员就会借网络媒体发声，称颂死去的武装分子是"烈士"。有别于传统对武装分子形象的隐藏，社交媒体动员更倾向塑造个人"英雄"形象，真主圣战党首领布尔汉·瓦尼（Burhan Wani）以身着战服、手持步枪的形象成为武装分子的"明星人物"，[③]其照片和视频在印控克什米尔地区广为流传，吸引许多对政府不满的青年投身其阵营中。互联网不仅为武装组织提供了新的动员方式，也提升了其招募率。克什米尔警方2015年的一项研究表明，武装组织有过半数的人员是受互联网激进言论的刺激而加入的。[④]更严重的是，武装组织不仅利用WhatsApp和Telegram等平台动员群众，也利用互联网向新成员介绍武器、爆炸装置和攻击计划。[⑤]

印度当局一度借助切断固定电话、手机和互联网等通信服务来遏制武装组织的招募和行动，但收效甚微。即使印度政府限制了高速互联网通信，信息仍通过较低流量的图像和短信文本传播，许多武装组织转向虚拟专用网络（VPN）以绕过政府管控，在瓦尼被杀一周内的近12.6万条社交媒体评论

---

① Justin Rowlatt, "How smartphones are shaping Kashmir's insurgency," BBC, July 12, 2016, http://www.bbc.com/news/world-asia-india-36771838, 2022年1月3日。

② Ayushman Kaul, "The Resistance Front: new terrorist group in Jammu and Kashmir amplifies attacks on social media," Medium, July 16, 2020, https://medium.com/dfrlab/the-resistance-front-new-terrorist-group-in-jammu-and-kashmir-amplifies-attacks-on-social-media-d71fd7362275, 2022年3月5日。

③ Vinay Kaura, "Countering insurgency in Kashmir: The cyber dimension," Observer Research Foundation, January 10, 2017, https://www.orfonline.org/research/countering-insurgency-kashmir-cyber-dimension/#_ednref52, 2022年1月17日。

④ Rohith Sai Narayan Stambamkadi, "Crowdsourcing violence: Decoding online propaganda of new militant groups in Kashmir," Observer Research Foundation, January 19, 2022, https://www.orfonline.org/expert-speak/crowdsourcing-violence/, 2022年4月2日。

⑤ Aditya Gowdara Shivamurthy, "The Aftermath of Article 370: A Review of Technological Developments in Kashmir," Observer Research Foundation, May 16, 2021, https://www.orfonline.org/expert-speak/the-aftermath-of-article-370/, 2022年1月17日。

中，有 45% 来自未知位置。[①]从激进组织的 Telegram 频道可看出，其当前的内容产出、消息传递和叙事构建比过去要更加集中。[②]为规避暴露风险，武装组织开始减少发布人数，其宣传材料由匿名管理员发布，很少通过个人渠道来发布内容。此外，不少武装组织还转向更新、更小、更晦涩的平台，如 nandbox、TamTam 等，[③]以此逃避监管与打击。

（四）安全部队执法乱象的影响

近年来，印度进一步加大对印控克什米尔武装团体的打击力度，相继实施"冷静"（Operation Calm Down）行动和"全力以赴"（Operation All Out）行动，但在具体过程也存在不少简单粗暴乃至侵犯居民正当权益的现象，严重加剧了当地穆斯林群众对印军和当局的不满，加深了当地居民对政府的不信任和反感，[④]导致地方政府的治理能力和威信进一步下降，最终也极大地损害了印度政府的形象。[⑤]

特别严重的是，军警在执行《武装部队特别授权法》的过程中存在诸多不足，安全人员经常使用《公共安全法》来逮捕或拘留无辜的青少年甚至未成年人，拘留时间从几小时到几年不等。如果高等法院否决安全部队开具的拘留令，安全部队在被拘者获释前又经常提出新的指控，以确保能继续将其拘留——这被称为"旋转门"逮捕。一个调查小组指出，在 2019 年 8 月 5 日之后的几周内，数百名青少年在夜间突袭中被警察或准军事人员从家中带

---

① Himanshi Dhawan, "Pakistan may be waging proxy war in cyberspace too," *The Times of India*, July 19, 2016, https://timesofindia.indiatimes.com/india/Pakistan-may-be-waging-proxy-war-in-cyberspace-too/articleshow/53273657.cms, 2022 年 4 月 1 日。

② Rohith Sai Narayan Stambamkadi, "Crowdsourcing violence: Decoding online propaganda of new militant groups in Kashmir," Observer Research Foundation, January 19, 2022, https://www.orfonline.org/expert-speak/crowdsourcing-violence/, 2022 年 4 月 1 日。

③ Kabir Taneja, Khalid Shah, "The Social Media Anatomy of New Radical Groups in Kashmir," Global Network on Extremism & Technology, February 24, 2021, https://gnet-research.org/2021/02/24/the-social-media-anatomy-of-new-radical-groups-in-kashmir/, 2022 年 2 月 17 日。

④ 王译鹤：《印度西北部恐怖主义研究》，云南师范大学 2018 年硕士学位论文，第 56 页。

⑤ 邓红英："论印度在印控克什米尔的治理政策及其问题"，《南亚研究》，2015 年第 3 期，第 3 页。

走，受到"非法拘留"。[①]印方一名高级警官承认，警方过去曾"无缘无故"地抓捕年轻男子，并承认警方处理对武装分子持同情态度的年轻人的方法可能会对他们造成创伤。[②]总体来说，印方安全部队的不规范执法损害了当地民众应有的自由生活，限制了当地政府的能力，激发了穆斯林民众更强的不满情绪，招致国际社会的指责，也损害了印军的形象和地位。[③]

而军警的过激行为客观上促使不少印控克什米尔年轻人加入武装组织。国际危机小组的报告显示，2018 年的武装镇压活动造成包括平民在内的 500多人死亡，加剧了当地对武装活动的支持。[④]一些研究认为，安全部队对包括和平抗议者甚至旁观者在内的印控克什米尔青年不分青红皂白地使用武力，导致越来越多的青年参与暴力示威或加入武装组织中。[⑤]例如，赛义德（Syed Tajamul Imran）在目睹其弟弟被非法拘留后选择加入武装组织，[⑥]布尔汉·瓦尼（Burhan Wani）自述是在遭安全部队殴打后才选择加入武装组织，运用社交媒体并成为一些青年的"偶像"并鼓动更多的年轻人加入了武装组织。[⑦]

---

① Jean Drèze, Kavita Krishnan, Maimoona Mollah, Vimal Bhai, "Kashmir caged: A fact-finding report," India Culture Forum, August 14, 2019, https://indianculturalforum.in/2019/08/14/kashmir-caged-a-fact-finding-report/, 2021 年 12 月 4 日。

② Fahad Shah, "India's Militant Pipeline," *Foreign Policy*, December 18, 2019, https://foreignpolicy.com/2019/12/18/jailed-stone-throwing-join-terrorist-militant-group-kashmir-radicalization/, 2021 年 12 月 4 日。

③ Attar Rabbani: "Jammu & Kashmir and the Armed Forces Special Powers Act," *South Asian Survey*, Vol. 8, No. 2, March 5, 2014, pp.270–274.

④ Laurel Miller: "Deadly Kashmir Suicide Bombing Ratchets up India-Pakistan Tensions," Crisis Group, February 22, 2019, https://www.crisisgroup.org/asia/south-asia/kashmir/deadly-kashmir-suicide-bombing-ratchets-india-pakistan-tensions, 2022 年 1 月 3 日。

⑤ Khalid Shah, "Ideological Shift, Public Support and Social Media: The 'New' in Kashmir's 'New Militancy'," *Observer Research Foundation Occasional Paper*, No.231, January 10, 2020, p.27.

⑥ Syed Tajamul Imran, "On the securitisation of truth and facts: how I lost my brother," *Inverse Journal*, June 27, 2020, https://www.inversejournal.com/2020/06/27/on-securitisation-of-truth-and-facts-how-i-lost-my-brother-by-syed-tajamul-imran/, 2022 年 1 月 3 日。

⑦ Ramachandra Guha, "Distrust, Discontent and Alienation: Kashmir During the Modi Years," The Wire, April 4, 2019, https://thewire.in/politics/distrust-discontent-and-alienation-kashmir-during-the-modi-years, 2021 年 12 月 19 日。

三、印控克什米尔内部武装冲突新态势的影响

近年来，印控克什米尔的武装组织本土化特征凸显，加入武装组织的印控克什米尔青年较之前明显增多；互联网的鼓动宣传和信息传递使印度政府对武装团体的打击难度明显上升；无人机等新技术的应用也为安全部队的防控和反制措施构成新的挑战，对印度政府内部管控和印巴关系乃至地区安全都造成了巨大影响。

（一）推动印度政府加大对武装组织的打击力度

当地武装招募增加以及互联网和社交媒体的激进思想宣传对印度政府构成了巨大挑战，印度政府实施了"冷静"行动和"全力以赴"行动来打击武装组织。[①] "冷静行动"在 2016 年 7 月布尔汉·瓦尼被枪杀后，政府在 9 月份将整个旅调入南克什米尔，往普尔瓦马、斯胡皮延、阿南特纳格和库尔甘地区额外部署了 4000 多名士兵。"全力以赴"行动于 2017 年发起，旨在用军事手段消除武装组织网络和指挥官。据《今日印度》报道，有多达 258 名武装分子被列为打击目标，被打击的武装成员涵盖了虔诚军、穆罕默德军、真主圣战党和巴德尔等组织。[②] 据报道，截至 2017 年底，该行动就消灭了 210 名武装分子。[③]

为确保对武装组织的打击力度，印度政府整合多个部门的资源，于 2019 年成立恐怖融资监测组（Terror Financing Monitoring Group，TMG），由印

---

① "Kashmir violence: Army begins operation 'Calm Down'," *The Hindu*, September 14, 2016, https://www.thehindu.com/news/national/Kashmir-violence-Army-begins-operation-%E2%80%98Calm-Down%E2%80%99/article55949400.ece，2021 年 12 月 19 日。

② Jitendra Bahadur Singh, "Operation All-Out: Army's master plan to flush out terrorists from Kashmir," *India Today*, June 22, 2017, https://www.indiatoday.in/india/story/kashmir-terrorism-all-out-plan-lashkar-hizbul-jaish-militants-984216-2017-06-22，2021 年 12 月 20 日。

③ Sameer Yasir, "Kashmir in 2017: Operation All-Out was a success, but will force alone win hearts in the Valley?" *First Post*, December 26, 2017, https://www.firstpost.com/india/kashmir-in-2017-operation-all-out-was-a-success-but-will-force-alone-win-hearts-in-the-valley-4275529.html，2022 年 9 月 24 日。

控克什米尔政府、军队、中央武装警察部队（Central Armed Police Forces，CAPFs）和其他安全机构监测当地武装的袭击情况，印度内政部、国防部和印控克什米尔政府持续监测当地的安全局势。除此之外，印方还积极采取加强国际边界部署、修建边界围栏、改进情报和行动协调、为安全部队配备先进武器以及对渗透者采取主动打击等措施来遏制对边境的渗透活动。①

针对社交媒体在印控克什米尔激进化中的作用，印度政府在社交媒体上大力展开反武装叙事，在极端条件下甚至采取了切断互联网通信的措施。为了打击反印宣传，印度在社交媒体上积极塑造武装部队的正面形象，具体措施包括上传武装部队帮助当地人、呼吁武装分子投降、投降者与家人团聚的视频，希望借此削弱当地居民对印军的负面印象。②另一方面，在废除赋予印控克什米尔特殊地位的宪法条款后，印度当局以安全考量为名，封锁了印控克什米尔大部分地区，切断了手机、互联网和固定电话等对外通信渠道。实际上，切断互联网通信已成为印度当局经常采取的应急措施。修宪后，为防止出现大规模的抗议和武装袭击活动，印度政府宣布关闭印控克什米尔的互联网通信，直到 2021 年 2 月 6 日，长达 552 天的互联网限制才被解除。③截至 2022 年 9 月，印度互联网服务关闭次数已达 673 次，其中印控克什米尔断网 406 次（见图 4），武装活动和社群关系紧张是断网的最主要原因。④

---

① "2019-2020 Annual Report," Ministry of Home Affairs of India, p.276.

② Aditya Gowdara Shivamurthy, "Building Indian Narratives and Battling New Militancy in Kashmir," Observer Research Foundation Issue Brief, No. 480, July 26, 2021.

③ "After Almost 550 Days, 4G Mobile Internet to Be Restored in J&K," The Quint, February 6, 2021, https://www.thequint.com/news/india/4g-mobile-internet-being-restored-in-jammu-and-kashmir，2022 年 9 月 25 日。

④ 许振华："印媒：印度 5 年来因恐怖活动和社区紧张关闭互联网逾 350 次"，澎湃新闻，2019 年 12 月 18 日，https://m.thepaper.cn/newsDetail_forward_5277363，2022 年 5 月 1 日。

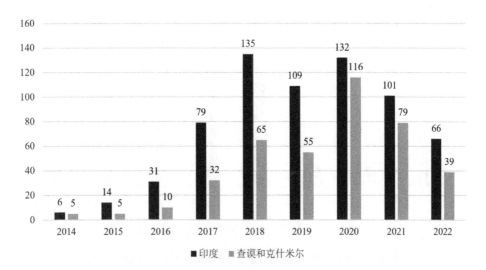

图 4 印度和印控克什米尔通信中断的次数

数据来源：Software Freedom Law Center.[1]

在印方安全部队的强力打击之下，印控克什米尔武装分子的死亡人数近年来明显增多（见图 5）。但军警的强硬行动也激起了一些当地人的不满，且军警打击武装组织的行动总体成效仍然有限，武装分子投降率仍非常低。

---

[1] Software Freedom Law Center, "India's Shutdown Numbers," https://internetshutdowns.in/, 2022 年 9 月 25 日。Software Freedom Law Center, "J&K Shutdown Numbers," https://internetshutdowns.in/static-page/jammu-kashmir/, 2022 年 9 月 25 日。

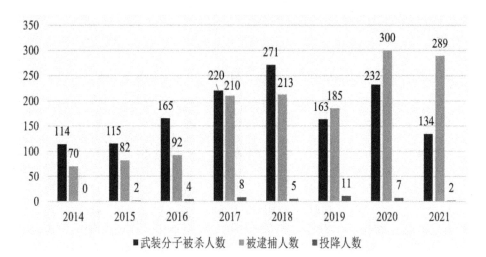

图 5 2014—2021 年武装分子被杀、被捕、投降情况

数据来源：South Asia Terrorism Portal. [1]

（二）促使克什米尔问题复杂化

在打击反政府武装的过程中，印控克什米尔的政治民主也受到了更大的制约，这就削弱了印控克什米尔主流政党的影响力，禁锢了当地媒体发展，限制了当地民众的政治权利和言论自由。自由之家（Freedom House）对印控克什米尔 2021 年自由度的评分仅为 27 分（总分 100），[2] 认为当地的政治多元化、公民的政治参与和自由表达等方面受到了诸多限制。《查谟和克什米尔重组法》颁布后，安全部队拘留了包括克什米尔当地政党和国大党成员在内的数千名党员和活动人士，超 5000 人被捕，这不仅大大降低了印控克什米尔主流政党的竞争力，也削弱了民众参政的能力。[3] 印方在改变印控克什米尔行政地位的同时也打击当地媒体、限制言论自由。2020 年 6 月出

---

① "Datasheet - Jammu & Kashmir," South Asia Terrorism Portal, https://www.satp. org/datasheet-terrorist-attack/arrest/india-jammukashmir, 2022 年 2 月 26 日。

② "Freedom in World, Indian Kashmir," *Freedom House*, 2021, https://freedomhouse. org/country/indian-kashmir/freedom-world/2021, 2022 年 3 月 4 日。

③ 同上。

台的一项媒体政策赋予政府官员审查"假新闻，抄袭、不道德或反国家内容"的权力，并允许对记者和媒体组织采取行动，外界质疑此举会将新闻媒体变成印度政府喉舌。该政策实施后，已有数名记者遭到传讯和指控，当地新闻杂志《克什米尔瓦拉》（The Kashmir Walla）的主编法赫德（Fahad Shah）因报道警察在斯利那加枪战事件中的疑似不当行为而遭到传唤。[①]同年10月，印度国家调查局又以涉嫌为分离主义活动提供资金为名搜查了当地英语日报《大克什米尔》（Greater Kashmir）的办公室。[②]2021年，印度新闻自由指数下降到180个国家中的第142名，[③]有报道称多名记者因工作而遭到警察和安全部队恐吓殴打。[④]除去打击媒体记者外，印度政府还通过禁止媒体广告投放的手段来消耗媒体财力，借此限制言路。据悉，印控克什米尔政府已禁止34家报纸刊登广告，暂停13家出版物的广告业务，警告了17家"涉嫌抄袭"和"内容不良"的新闻出版物。[⑤]印度当局还监控克什米尔大学的研究，师生在审查和自我审查的体制监测下都避免探索敏感话题。在新冠肺炎病毒大流行和断网政策的双重影响下，当地教育受到严重限制，学校被封锁、远程教育受阻。[⑥]对政党和新闻业的打击也形成寒蝉效应，民众的参政热情和对政府的信任程度下降，对印度政府的疏离淡漠感更甚。

军警有罪不罚的现象加深了本地人对反政府武装组织的同情，也促使印

① Irfan Amin Malik, "Why Journalists Are Worried About the New Media Policy in Jammu and Kashmir," The Wire, July 17, 2020, https://thewire.in/media/kashmir-new-media-policy-press-freedom, 2022 年 4 月 8 日。

② "Kashmir daily office, activists' homes raided by Indian agency," Aljazeera, October 18, 2020, https://www.aljazeera.com/news/2020/10/28/indian-agency-raid-multiple-locations-in-kashmir, 2022 年 4 月 8 日。

③ "Data of press freedom ranking 2021," Reporters Without Borders, 2021, https://rsf.org/en/ranking, 2022 年 4 月 10 日。

④ Quratulain Rehbar, "State Intimidation Forces Kashmiri Journalists to Self-Censor," Article 14, Mar 12, 2021, https://www.article-14.com/post/how-state-intimidation-forces-kashmiri-journalists-to-self-censor, 2022 年 4 月 10 日。

⑤ Azaan Javaid, "J&K de-empanels 34 newspapers, suspends ads for 13, issues notice to 17 for 'malpractice'," The Print, January 17, 2011, https://theprint.in/india/jk-de-empanels-34-newspapers-suspends-ads-for-13-issues-notice-to-17-for-malpractice/586914/, 2022 年 4 月 5 日。

⑥ "Freedom in World, Indian Kashmir," Freedom House, 2021, https://freedomhouse.org/country/indian-kashmir/freedom-world/2021, 2022 年 1 月 4 日。

控克什米尔地区出现大规模抗议活动。克什米尔群众通过投掷石块、阻挠安全部队执法、参加武装分子葬礼等形式表达抗议和不满。当安全部队追捕武装分子时，多次出现民众游走街头，以静坐或包围（gherao）的形式阻碍安全部队行动的情况，甚至有人群聚集在安全部队和武装分子的交战地，围成屏障并向安全部队投掷石块，为武装分子争取逃跑时间。[1] 武装分子的葬礼也成为武装组织公开表达诉求的途径，经常有大批哀悼者参加武装分子的公共葬礼游行，借此表达不满，有时更会引发与安全部队的冲突，游行经常升级为街头抗议和冲突。[2]

近年来，印控克什米尔群众的愤懑情绪加深，这进一步提升了武装招募人员的本土比重，群众的抵抗活动和武装袭击交织，也加大了印方安全部队的打击难度，促使克什米尔问题复杂化。

（三）加剧印巴关系僵局

印度长期将印控克什米尔的武装活动视为巴基斯坦的"代理人"袭击，认为新出现的抵抗阵线是虔诚军的影子组织，印控克什米尔武装活动的烈度牵动印巴两国的关系发展。2014年莫迪在宣誓就职前一天与巴基斯坦总理纳瓦兹·谢利夫在新德里进行会谈，双方都表示愿意开启双边关系新时代，[3] 2015年12月，莫迪访问巴基斯坦。[4] 就在外界猜测印巴关系或将出现历史性转折之际，次年的乌里袭击事件令印巴关系突然下跌到多年来的最低点，也使得印度对巴态度更为强硬。

2016年，虔诚军袭击位于乌里镇的印度陆军基地，袭击造成19名士兵

---

[1] David Devadas, *The Generation of Rage in Kashmir*, Oxford: Oxford University Press, July 16, 2018, p.21.

[2] Muzamil Jaleel, "Jammu and Kashmir: Encounters fuel militant hiring, says official report," *The Indian Express*, June 9, 2018, https://indianexpress.com/article/india/jammu-and-kashmir-encounters-fuel-militant-hiring-says-official-report-ramzan-ceasefire-burhan-wani-5196477/, 2022年4月5日。

[3] "Indian PM Modi holds talks with Sharif," Aljazeera, May 27, 2014, https://www.aljazeera.com/news/2014/5/27/indian-pm-modi-holds-talks-with-sharif, 2021年11月21日。

[4] 晗宇："印度总理莫迪圣诞日突访巴基斯坦"，BBC中文，2015年12月25日 https://www.bbc.com/zhongwen/simp/world/2015/12/151225_india_pakistan, 2022年4月5日。

身亡。[1] 印方将此次袭击称为安全部队 20 年来遭受的最致命袭击，[2] 第一时间在印控克什米尔地区实施大规模宵禁并部署大量军警，在乌里袭击事件 11 天后采取先发制人措施，对巴控克什米尔地区的武装组织据点发起报复性的"外科手术式打击"。[3] 印度总理莫迪还强悍地表示："印度永远铭记乌里袭击，将不遗余力地在世界上孤立巴基斯坦。"[4]

2016 年的乌里袭击让印巴关系陷入僵局，2019 年的普尔瓦马袭击更是加深了两国之间的矛盾。2019 年袭击发生后，印方立刻展开巴拉科特空袭，跨越停火线摧毁穆罕默德军的营地，[5] 并取消巴基斯坦最惠国待遇。巴方以降低与印度外交关系级别并中断双边贸易、终止与印度所有文化活动回应，两国关系剑拔弩张。普瓦尔马袭击是 48 年以来双方军机首次飞越停火线，亦是两国拥有核武器后的又一次较大规模正面冲突。[6] 此前，印巴双方在停火线附近经常发生摩擦，但都未超越停火线，在领空问题上都相对谨慎，此次的越境空袭表明双方在印控克什米尔武装冲突问题上矛盾更深，印度对巴态度更为强硬。

两国在近两年虽未爆发大规模的武装冲突，但印控克什米尔的武装袭击问题仍是横亘在印巴之间的难题。2021 年 3 月的"巴基斯坦日"前一天，

---

① "Tents set on fire, troops shot while coming out," *The Hindu*, September 18, 2016, https://www.thehindu.com/news/national/Tents-set-on-fire-troops-shot-while-coming-out/article14986872.ece?homepage=true，2022 年 2 月 3 日。

② "Militants attack Indian army base in Kashmir 'killing 17'," BBC News, September 18, 2016, https://www.bbc.com/news/world-asia-india-37399969，2021 年 11 月 17 日。

③ Umair Jamal, "Pawn to E4," *Pakistan Today*, October 2, 2016.

④ Liz Mathew, "PM Modi speaks to people of Pakistan: Let us go to war against poverty, unemployment… let's see who wins," *The Indian Express*, September 25, 2016, https://indianexpress.com/article/india/india-news-india/pm-narendra-modi-speaks-to-the-people-of-pakistan-lets-go-to-war-against-poverty-unemployment-lets-see-who-wins-3048329/，2022 年 3 月 4 日。

⑤ "IAF jets strike and destroy Jaish camp across LoC, 200 killed: Sources," *Hindustan Times*, February 26, 2019, https://www.hindustantimes.com/india-news/pakistan-army-says-indian-jets-intruded-airspace/story-AuuwxJVTByKuxoJlr0cAQP.html，2022 年 3 月 4 日。

⑥ "India airstrike in Pakistan: IAF crosses LoC first time since 1971 war," *India Today*, February 26, 2019, https://www.indiatoday.in/india/story/india-airstrike-in-pakistan-iaf-crosses-loc-first-time-since-1971-war-1465178-2019-02-26，2022 年 3 月 4 日。

印度总理莫迪向巴基斯坦总理伊姆兰·汗（Imran Khan）发出祝福，称印度人民渴望与巴基斯坦人民建立友好关系。但莫迪也强调，没有"恐怖主义行为"的环境是两国关系改善的必要条件。伊姆兰·汗和陆军参谋长卡马尔·贾韦德·巴杰瓦（Qamar Javed Bajwa）都表示"愿意实现印巴关系缓和"，但均强调"印度必须首先迈出第一步"。[①]2022 年 1 月，伊姆拉·汗公布首个国家安全政策（National Security Policy, NSP），该政策寻求和近邻和睦相处，但也强调"公正和平地解决查谟和克什米尔争端仍然是我们双边关系的核心"。[②]总之，印控克什米尔内部武装冲突频发，双方各不退步，和平解决克什米尔争端仍道阻且长，印巴关系的僵局也迟迟难以得到有效缓解。

（四）加剧南亚局势动荡

抵抗阵线等新兴本土武装组织在印控克什米尔的频繁活跃并不意味着虔诚军、穆罕默德军和圣战者党等外部武装组织的谢幕，外部武装组织和本土武装组织的人员交叉和协同作战现象值得警觉。随着以虔诚军为代表的外部武装组织影响力不断壮大，南亚邻国可能受到武装活动外溢的影响，成为印控克什米尔武装的成员招募地和活动中转站。孟加拉国、尼泊尔和马尔代夫均有虔诚军活动的身影。据在孟加拉国被捕的虔诚军成员招供，他们已在孟活动 15 年，为组织招募成员并规划后勤工作。[③]印度情报局称有近千名虔诚军成员在马尔代夫活动，[④]此说法的具体数据未必可靠，但却点出了马

---

① 许振华："莫迪罕见向巴基斯坦献国庆祝福，印巴之间可否真'和好'"，澎湃新闻，2021 年 3 月 24 日，https://www.thepaper.cn/newsDetail_forward_11863594，2022 年 2 月 3 日。

② Sajjad Hussain, "Pakistan wants improved ties with India but unresolved Jammu & Kashmir dispute stymies relations: says new security policy," The Print, January 14, 2022, https://theprint.in/world/pakistan-wants-improved-ties-with-india-but-unresolved-jammu-kashmir-dispute-stymies-relations-says-new-security-policy/804014/，2022 年 3 月 4 日。

③ David Montero, "Pakistani militants expand abroad, starting in Bangladesh," The Christian Science Monitor, August 5, 2010, https://www.csmonitor.com/World/Asia-South-Central/2010/0805/Pakistani-militants-expand-abroad-starting-in-Bangladesh，2022 年 4 月 2 日。

④ "Protests in Maldives over settling 2 Guantanamo Bay terrorists," Policy Research Group, https://www.poreg.org/protests-in-maldives-over-settling-2-guantanamo-bay-terrorists/，2022 年 4 月 2 日。

尔代夫的安全风险。虔诚军人员在尼泊尔被捕也证实有虔诚军人员在尼泊尔活动。[1] 尼泊尔容易成为印控克什米尔武装组织的中转站，这是因为尼泊尔和印度的开放边界管控松弛，首都机场安检薄弱，对旅客筛查简易，乔装的虔诚军成员有可能从尼泊尔边境潜入印度制造袭击。[2] 虔诚军不仅将邻国作为活动中转站，对邻国境内武装组织的支持也对目标国产生重大影响。虔诚军曾支援孟加拉国的伊斯兰圣战运动（Harkat-ul-Jihad-al Islami Bangladesh, HUJI-B）一批手榴弹，这些手榴弹被 7 次用于袭击或暗杀孟加拉国重要官员。[3] 2016 年达卡餐厅袭击事件的肇事者孟加拉圣战者组织（Jamat-ul Mujahideen Bangladesh, JMB）也受到虔诚军的暗中支持。[4] 活跃在尼泊尔的印度圣战者组织（Indian Mujahideen, IM）据信得到虔诚军和穆罕默德军等组织的资金和技术援助，在尼泊尔和印度多地发动炸弹袭击，造成数百名平民伤亡。[5] 外部武装组织将印度邻国视为招募"圣战者"的沃土和开展反印活动的根据地，武装活动的外溢提高了邻国安全管控和协同治理的门槛，加剧了南亚安全局势的不稳定性。

在"泛伊斯兰主义"激进思想盛行的背景下，印控克什米尔武装组织与其他组织的协同合作对印度乃至南亚的安全局势都将带来巨大冲击。虔诚军、穆罕默德军等活跃在印控克什米尔的武装组织同南亚各激进组织有密切

---

[1]　Outlook Web Desk, "A Global Threat," https://www.outlookindia.com/website/story/a-global-threat/285277, 2022 年 3 月 4 日。

[2]　"Country Reports on Terrorism 2018," United States Department of State Publication, October 2019, p.175, https://www.state.gov/wp-content/uploads/2019/11/Country-Reports-on-Terrorism-2018-FINAL.pdf, 2022 年 9 月 25 日。

[3]　Animesh Roul, "Terror and Politics: Lashkar-e-Taiba, HuJI and Assassinations in Bangladesh," Society for the Study of Peace and Conflict, https://www.sspconline.org/LashkareTaibaHuJIandAssassinationsinBangladesh, 2022 年 2 月 26 日。

[4]　Gloria Methri, "Bangladesh Minister Claims 'Pakistan's ISI Strengthening Terror Roots in Dhaka'," Republic World, November 24, 2021, https://www.republicworld.com/world-news/rest-of-the-world-news/bangladesh-minister-claims-pakistans-isi-strengthening-terror-roots-in-dhaka.html, 2022 年 3 月 7 日。

[5]　FP Staff, "Nepal emerges biggest hub for Indian Mujahideen, Says US report; porous border makes India vulnerable to terror attacks," *First Post*, November 7, 2019, https://www.firstpost.com/india/nepal-emerges-biggest-hub-for-indian-mujahideen-says-us-report-porous-border-makes-india-vulnerable-to-terror-attacks-7616161.html, 2022 年 1 月 7 日。

联系，在融资、培训、招募和行动等领域都有密切合作。[①]"基地"组织曾向虔诚军提供资金援助，虔诚军在拉合尔的总部即由本·拉登赠与，[②] 伊斯兰圣战者运动（Harkat-ul-Mujahideen, HuM）成员曾在阿富汗接受"基地"组织的培训，[③] "伊斯兰国"南亚分支（Islamic State in Khorasan Province, ISKP）近几年致力于在印控克什米尔招募成员，其成员包含前虔诚军人员。[④] 印控克什米尔的外部武装组织曾与在南亚活跃的多个武装组织联合行动，如前阿富汗外交部长穆罕默德·哈尼夫·阿特马尔（Mohammad Haneef Atma）曾指责虔诚军与阿富汗塔利班、巴基斯坦塔利班、"基地"组织、乌兹别克斯坦伊斯兰运动等并肩作战。[⑤] 目前阿富汗国内局势尚未稳定，存在权力真空地带，虔诚军等印控克什米尔武装组织有可能借此在阿扩大影响。据报道，虔诚军等组织在 2021 年阿富汗塔利班夺权之前就开始将基地逐步迁移到阿富汗境内，在 2021 年 6 月间，已有超万名"圣战战士"进入阿富汗。[⑥] 塔利班发言人苏海尔·沙欣（Suhail Shaheen）2021 年 9 月在答记者问时还

① Ashley J. Tellis, "The Menace That Is Lashkar-e-Taiba," https://carnegieendowment.org/2012/03/13/menace-that-is-lashkar-e-taiba-pub-47512, Carnegie Endowment for International Peace, March 13, 2012, 2022 年 1 月 7 日。

② "Jaish-I-Mohammed," The Unites Nations Security Council, https://www.un.org/securitycouncil/sanctions/1267/aq_sanctions_list/summaries/entity/jaish-i-mohammed, 2022 年 2 月 5 日。

③ Dan Rothem, "Terrorism Project," Center for Defense Information Research Assistant, July 9, 2002, http://web.archive.org/web/20020925061001/http://www.cdi.org/terrorism/harakat.cfm, 2022 年 1 月 16 日。

④ Devesh K. Pandey, "ISKP has been attempting to recruit Indians," The Hindu, August 28, 2021, https://www.thehindu.com/news/national/iskp-has-been-attempting-to-recruit-indians/article36154252.ece，2022 年 1 月 16 日。

⑤ Riya Baibhawi, "Lashkar-e-Taiba, Other Pakistan Based Terror Outfits Aiding Taliban: Afghan Minister," Republic World, August 4, 2021, https://www.republicworld.com/world-news/rest-of-the-world-news/lashkar-e-taiba-other-pakistan-based-terror-outfits-aiding-taliban-afghan-minister.html, 2022 年 4 月 18 日。

⑥ Siddhant Sibbal, "Pak's Lashkar-e-Taiba shifting base into country, Afghan government tells India," DAN India, July 26, 2021, https://zeenews.india.com/india/pakistan-based-lashkar-e-taiba-shifting-base-into-the-country-afghan-govt-tells-india-2379275.html，2022 年 4 月 17 日。

公开表示，塔利班有权为克什米尔或其他国家的穆斯林发声。[①] 阿富汗塔利班执政给印控克什米尔各武装组织以极大的鼓舞，而虔诚军等组织在阿壮大也可能增加印控克什米尔武装冲突的风险，加大印度边境管理的难度。不仅如此，虔诚军等印控克什米尔武装组织与其他武装组织的合作也会增加南亚各国在武装袭击上的安全隐患。

发生在印控克什米尔的重大武装冲突不仅影响印巴关系走向，对南亚区域合作也有不可小觑的影响。2016 年 9 月乌里袭击事件发生后，印度指责巴基斯坦"支持"穆罕默德军策划此次袭击，宣布不参加同年 11 月在伊斯兰堡举行的南盟首脑会议，阿富汗、孟加拉国和不丹等紧随其后，一半成员国缺席导致此次南盟峰会被迫取消。[②] 此后，巴基斯坦外交部长库雷希 (Shah Mahmood Qureshi) 又于 2021 年 1 月 3 日主动向印度发出邀约。[③] 印方予以拒绝，称"自 2016 年峰会取消以来，局势未发生重大变化"。[④] 总之，印控克什米尔武装冲突严重恶化了印巴关系，拖累了南盟区域一体化进程，影响了南亚区域合作。

总的来看，互联网的隐匿性和网络空间监管机制的不完善增加了安全部队的打击难度，"一刀切"式的断网措施也未能有效阻止信息在武装组织间的传递，单纯审查、删除对政府形象不利的信息不足以抑制反政府武装思想的传播。印控克什米尔民主自由受限，以及武装执法中存在的不公正现象，都激起了民众反感，也为印控克什米尔武装的活动提供土壤，提升了其本土

---

① Vineet Khare, "Afghanistan: Taliban says it will 'raise voice for Kashmir Muslims'," *BBC News*, September 3, 2021, https://www.bbc.co.uk/news/world-asia-india-58419719, 2022 年 4 月 17 日。

② Mahua Venkatesh, "Saarc summit collapses after India and three other members pull out," *Hindustan Times*, September 26, 2016, https://www.hindustantimes.com/world-news/saarc-summit-collapses-after-india-and-3-other-members-pull-out/story-kIMWfSqirGLzB-6MEfuS3CN.html，2022 年 3 月 11 日。

③ "If not in person, join virtually: Pakistan invites India for 19th SAARC summit," *India Today*, January 3, 2022, https://timesofindia.indiatimes.com/world/pakistan/if-not-in-person-join-virtually-pakistan-invites-india-for-19th-saarc-summit/articleshow/88670319.cms，2022 年 3 月 28 日。

④ Niranjan Marjani, "Is Regional Integration Still Relevant for India in South Asia?" *The Diplomat*, January 11, 2022, https://thediplomat.com/2022/01/is-regional-integration-still-relevant-for-india-in-south-asia/，2022 年 3 月 28 日。

招募率，促使克什米尔问题更为复杂化。印巴将克什米尔问题的解决视为两国关系缓解的前提，出于对国内政治考量各不让步，印度更是将巴视为外部武装组织的"支持者"，印巴关系短时间难以取得突破进展。印控克什米尔武装的外溢也会提高南亚邻国安全管控的隐患，加剧南亚安全局势动荡，双方就印控克什米尔问题争执不下，影响南亚区域合作的开展。印度政府应利用社交媒体塑造清廉为民、公正不阿、专业尽责的政府警察形象，构建稳健安全的网络情报网，精准有效打击武装组织；采用务实态度促进当地经济发展，提升青年就业率；摒弃历史遗留下的成见与负担，开展双边乃至区域反武装活动合作，积极解决印控克什米尔武装问题。

结 论

莫迪政府二次胜选执政后废除宪法第 370 条，为了加强对印控克什米尔的管控，采取了中断通信、实施大规模宵禁、严厉打击武装组织等措施。但是，修宪举措加深了很多印控克什米尔居民对政治进程的失望，加剧了认同危机。安全部队在打击武装组织的过程中也存在滥用职权的现象，反而加深了当地居民的厌恶，变相促进了武装组织的招募活动。中断通信网络并未阻止信息在武装组织间传递，反而促使其探寻更为隐蔽的社交平台来传递消息，断网也给当地居民造成一定恐慌，不便于民众的正常生活。印方持续将印控克什米尔的一切武装袭击事件与巴基斯坦捆绑的叙事方式也不利于缓和克什米尔局势，加深两国之间的隔阂，影响到两国信任机制的建设。

可以预见，在互联网助推武装动员、经济不景气和身份认同危机相互交织的影响下，印控克什米尔武装组织的本土化招募趋势将更为显著，新兴本土武装组织也会更为活跃。断网和封控等措施虽不无成效，但并不足以根本解决当地的动荡局势。要长期缓和当地局势，印度政府仍需慎重考虑印控克什米尔的独特环境和独特认同，设法缓和山谷人民的疏离和淡漠情绪；巧用媒体舆论塑造警察正面形象；要更为重视内部治理问题，激发经济活力，提升执法人员素质、规范安全部队行为。只有通过一套强硬打击、有效治理和适当安抚相结合的综合性措施，才有望大幅削减当地民众对武装组织的支持度，降低武装组织的招募能力，除此之外，应转变将巴基斯坦与武装冲突捆绑的叙事方式，通过经济合作促进信任机制的建立，为有效解决印控克什米尔武装冲突问题创造条件。

南亚书评

探索"龙象共舞"之道

曾祥裕 [①]

中印人口之和高达 27.46 亿人，相当于世界总人口（75.93 亿人）的 36.16%；两国国土面积之和约 1258 万平方公里，相当于亚洲的 28.22%、欧亚大陆的 22.97% 或世界陆地总面积的 8.44%；国民生产总值之和达到 16.327 万亿美元，相当于世界总额（85.931 万亿美元）的 19.00%。显而易见的是，中印都是世界上最主要的发展中国家，中印关系对两国利益、亚洲的安定乃至世界的和平与发展都有极为重要的意义。

四川大学南亚研究所杨文武研究员主编的《中国与印度共赢性发展互动机制研究》一书从机制入手，探索中印共赢性发展，在理论和实践上均有较大启发性。

以互动机制助推"龙象共舞"

多年来，研究人员对中印合作实现共赢性发展的必要性已有较充分论述，但共赢性发展的潜力始终未能充分发挥，分歧乃至摩擦不时浮出水面，时起时落似乎成为中印关系的一种节律。比如印度在 2020 年以后连续出台措施限制中国对印投资、中印边界西段经历 2017 年夏洞朗对峙之后的最大规模对峙、印度国内出现专门识别移除中国手机应用的应用（称为 Remove China Apps），印方一些机构和乃至个别颇受尊重的智库在新冠疫情期间甚至炮制了某些表演意味浓厚的针对中国的言论和举措。在中印建交 70 周年的 2020 年，出现这些现象无疑非常令人遗憾，同时也促使人们反思中印共赢性合作的步子迈不快的原因为何，出路何在。

对于这一问题，《中国与印度共赢性发展互动机制研究》一书从国际制度的角度给出了自己的解答。该书借鉴新自由制度主义国际关系理论的思路，

---

① 曾祥裕，教育部人文社科重点研究基地四川大学南亚研究所副研究员，主要从事南亚安全与外交、海洋问题、中国外交等方面研究。

主张以制度或者说机制来促进中印合作的稳定化、常态化和全面化，提出构建政治、经济、安全和人文交流等四位一体的共赢性互动机制体系，充分发挥政治增信、经济互利、安全共赢、人文互鉴的引领作用，将中印共赢性合作推向更高水平。尽管作者高度重视机制的作用，但也没有简单化地将机制视为万能，而是较为客观地指出，中印互动机制正处于"基于利益泛化形成的低度合作机制"阶段，开始向"基于制度分化形成的中度合作机制"过渡，但尚未形成"基于价值固化形成的深度合作机制"。这一判断应该是比较符合实际的。

补齐政党交往短板，提升政治互动成效

该书从政治、经济、安全和人文交流四个方面，全景式地呈现了中印共赢性发展的互动机制。这些梳理颇为详尽，如第三章的五个简表详细罗列了中印国家元首与政府首脑的交流情况（1949—2018）、中印以成员国身份加入的国际或区域多边组织、1973—2016年中国与印度已建友好省邦/城市（不含港澳台）的情况、中印人大与议会交往情况、中国共产党与印度国大党高层往来情况等，资料性颇强。

但比起各种已有机制，笔者倒是对某些缺位的重要机制尤其感兴趣。比如，该书第三章（王娟娟撰稿）从政府交往、议会外交和政党外交三个层面全面梳理了中印在政治层面的互动机制，其对于议会外交和政党外交的论述颇有新意。特别是作者在比较之后指出，中方与以印度共产党和印度共产党（马克思主义）为代表的"左"翼政党，以国大党（Congress）为代表的传统全国性政党有较多党际交往，但与现执政党印度人民党（BJP）交往偏少，机制化程度低，和地方政党的交往也较为薄弱。这一观察可谓切中肯綮。实际上，就党员人数而言，印度人民党已成为世界第一大党；就执政地位而言，印度人民党不仅于1996年5月13日、1998年3月—2004年5月和2014年5月至今三度执掌中央政权，现在还掌握着印度19个邦及中央直辖区的政权（此外，印方于中印边界争议区东段设立的伪"阿鲁纳恰尔邦"也由其执政），而仅北方邦的人口就高达2.3亿左右，远超绝大多数国家；就社会思潮而论，以印度人民党及其母体国民志愿服务团（RSS）为代表的"印度教民族主义"渐成气候，已成为印度社会和政坛举足轻重的力量。因此，不

管出于何种考虑，进一步开展面向印度人民党的政党外交都很有必要。印度是联邦制国家，中央的执政党未必能执掌地方政权。实际上，在西孟加拉、马哈拉施特拉、特伦甘纳、泰米尔纳度、比哈尔、奥里萨、北方邦等地都有非常强大的地方性政党，或单独执政，或与全国性政党联合执政。与地方性政党开展党际交流，既有助于拓宽中印政党交流的领域，也有利于承接地气，打通合作项目具体落地的相应关节，同样是一项亟待开展的工作。

建设卫生交流机制，提升中印国民福利

《中国与印度共赢性发展互动机制研究》的第六章（杨文武、孙莎岚撰稿）提供了另一个鲜明案例。在全面介绍中印在科技、教育、文化等领域交流机制之余，该章明确指出两国在卫生领域尚未建立有效互动机制。实际上，这一缺位不仅不利于中印的国家间关系，也不利于两国的民生改善和公共安全，实在是两国人民的一大损失。印度在仿制药领域有一定优势，已建立较有竞争力的制药产业。即便由于专利原因中国难以大规模进口印度仿制药，但两国药企仍可交流经验、互通有无。特别是在中国适度鼓励部分仿制药生产、推动仿制药产业国际化的当下，与印度药品行业的交流更有必要。印度一些知名私立医疗机构的医疗水准较高且价格低廉，赴印医疗旅游已成为印度旅游业的特色领域。相比每年超过50万的赴印旅游医疗群体而言，赴印从事医疗旅游的中国人仍然是寥寥无几。在这一领域中印开展合作不仅大有可为，而且直接造福于两国人民和相关产业，社会效益明显。与上述处于领先地位的部分私立医疗机构形成对比的是，印度大批公立医疗机构投资不足、经费短缺、人手甚至医药均有不足，公共卫生政策存在隐患，这些因素已在公共卫生领域积累了不小的风险。通过中印在卫生领域的交流合作，合理借鉴中方和其他国家的一些有效做法，必然有利于提升印度的公共卫生水平。在新冠肺炎疫情肆虐之际，上述缺位的负效应正进一步凸显，而及时补齐这一短板应成为两国决策者的一大任务。

提升微观动力，打通微循环

对中印的共赢性合作，两国高层不能说不重视，各种规划设计不能说少，

仅以该书而论就可阅读到众多的乃至令人眼花缭乱的机制与相应设计。但令人尴尬的是，尽管存在这些数量繁多、种类多样的互动机制，中印交流仍然称不上密切，两国合作仍不够有力。个中原因之一，该书将其称为"微观动力不足"，即在宏观上顶层高度重视，上层积极推动，但在具体落实上公司企业、行业协会、企业家等微观主体严重缺位，导致交往与合作的动力难以释放。针对这一情况，该书提出构建多层次、多主体广泛参与的互动机制体系，重点是鼓励地方政府和企业、民间组织、非政府组织乃至家庭等经济主体的参与，同时加强部分微观机制的操作性，以避免"有机制无进展"的尴尬状态。

这里强调微循环当然不是要削弱大循环的重要性，而是针对薄弱环节的针对性措施。展望未来，中印共赢性发展互动机制体系必须既能"顶天"又要"立地"。唯此，中印共赢性发展才能成为现实。

走近古印度治国安邦之书——《政事论》

高刚　南评 ①

　　《政事论》（也译《利论》）是印度古典现实主义的代表作，其作者憍底利耶是印度历史上有名的政治家和战略家，也是孔雀王朝开国皇帝旃陀罗笈多的重要谋臣和首任宰相。他因强烈的现实主义思想而被后人称作"印度的马基雅维利"。他关于印度的国家治理、对外政策和霸权争夺的一系列思想都集中体现在《政事论》一书中。从现代学科意义来说，《政事论》涉及政治思想、政治制度、法律、经济、外交和军事等众多方面，对研究古印度相关领域的学者有很重要的参考意义，其本身也富有研究价值。近年来，印度学界和战略研究界提出要从传统文献中汲取外交智慧，发掘本土战略思想，以创造出具有印度特色的国际关系理论，关于《政事论》和憍底利耶思想的研究也不断趋热。

　　由四川大学南亚研究所曾祥裕副研究员和北京师范大学—香港浸会大学联合国际学院魏楚雄教授合著的《〈政事论〉国际政治思想研究》一书，是国内首部系统引介和研究《政事论》国际政治思想的学术专著，具有较强的开拓性。对印度战略文化和古典外交思想等领域的研究者而言，本书颇有参考价值。在此仅就笔者的已有研究和阅读体会，简要谈一谈此书的学术价值和不足之处。

一、逐层深入，完成多重学术任务

　　《〈政事论〉国际政治思想研究》采取逐层深入的方法，完成了多项重要工作。一是对《政事论》的基本情况进行详尽阐述，让初学者可以很快对其有一个宏观的把握。作者系统论述了近年来国内外的研究现状，为国内相关领域研究者提供了重要参考资料。尤其具有学术价值的是，作者在第一章

---

　　①　高刚，四川大学南亚研究所助理研究员，主要从事印度外交与安全、印度与斯里兰卡关系、《政事论》与印度古代战略文化等研究。南评，四川大学南亚研究所研究人员。

总结和归纳了"现有研究路径"，为国内学者的进一步研究提供了路径参考和方向指引。二是对"国家七要素论""曼荼罗国际体系""六种外交政策""谍报活动"及"战争和军事思想"等原著中重点涉及国际政治的部分进行了深入剖析。这部分有助于读者在纷繁复杂的材料中进行快速定位，系统地掌握《政事论》的核心国际政治思想。三是在初步引介的基础上，从理论方面向前进一步深入，对《政事论》思想和西方现实主义国际关系理论进行横向比较研究。对于印度传统政治思想不熟悉的国际关系专业学生，可以凭借这一部分对《政事论》的国际政治思想有更加准确的认识。四是对于《政事论》的思想与印度外交实践之间的关系进行了分析和探究，重点阐述了"曼荼罗"思想对印度历史和当代印度外交实践的影响。

特别值得一提的是，《〈政事论〉国际政治思想研究》在研究方法上提倡"整体观"：主张在面对原著中频繁出现各种不同甚至互相矛盾的观点之时，采用整体思维，进行全面考察，而后再审慎地做出较为合理而全面的评价。这一主张并非无的放矢。实际上，《政事论》原著体大思精、内容庞杂，憍底利耶也常列举多方观点逐一批驳后才引出自己的观点。初学者容易陷入原著的"汪洋大海"中，不易抓住憍氏思想的全貌，很容易出现只关注原著部分内容、某些核心术语甚至是生硬解读或偏离原著的情况。在从国际关系角度解读《政事论》的作品之中，这种倾向并不罕见。有鉴于此，"整体性"的研究方法应该说是较有启发意义的。

二、立足现实，思考未来研究方向

此书在结论部分指出了《政事论》研究的难点和将来的研究方向。对于今后的研究方向，作者较为敏锐地指出了几个可能的工作方向：一是国内亟须可靠翔实的《政事论》中译本，为深入研究奠定基础。二是要加强对《政事论》多学科交叉的综合研究。三是要扩大对于印度传统国际政治思想的研究范围，除《政事论》外也要涉及各种印度史诗、法论、往事书及其他政治著作。四是要强化《政事论》思想与印度历史和当今外交实践之间的对照性研究。可以说，这几点对国内《政事论》的深入研究大有裨益。

笔者认为，除了上述几个方面外，另一个可供探索的研究方向是将《政事论》与中国古代同类型著作进行比较研究。其实，古典时期的战略性著作往往具有思想共通性。这里简要地举一个例子，如《政事论》中提出了国家构成的七要素（君主、辅臣、国土与居民、要塞、财富、军队、盟友）。对于这些要素，可以对比中国西汉政论家贾谊在《过秦论》中的相似分析。贾谊对商鞅变法时期秦国国力的发展分析状况如下："秦孝公据崤函之固，拥雍州之地，君臣固守以窥周室，有席卷天下，包举宇内，囊括四海之意，并吞八荒之心。当是时也，商君佐之，内里法度，务耕织，修守战之具，外连横而斗诸侯。于是秦人拱手而取西河之外。"这里涉及关塞、土地、君王、大臣、战略意图、法制、经济、军备、外交等多个因素，与侨底利耶的"国家七要素论"不谋而合。

当然，目前西方和印度学界已经有一些类似探索性研究，但他们多依据的是中国古代著作的英译版本，研究程度往往不够深入。相较而言，国内学者在这方面更加具有语言和文化优势。而且，近十几年来中国国际关系学界已经对中国先秦时期经典论著的国际政治思想进行了系统梳理，也产生了多部高质量的学术论著和大量期刊文章。这些成果为中印古典文献国际政治思想的比较研究提供了重要支撑。更重要的是，中国学界的研究路径也可为《政事论》研究提供了重要参考。例如，国内学者曾提出的中国传统国际政治思想研究方法，完全可以借鉴到《政事论》等印度传统论著研究领域：（1）根据当代国际关系学知识谱系的框架来解读《政事论》等传统经典的国际政治思想，将其中的概念表达与当代国际关系学的概念进行对接，从而将国际关系学领域对《政事论》的研究与东方学（尤其是梵文研究）、历史学、思想史学和哲学等领域的研究区分开来。（2）将《政事论》中所涉及的国际政治思想进一步系统化和理论化。（3）将印度传统国际政治思想与当代西方国际关系理论进行比较，寻求二者之间的异同点。（4）将印度传统国际政治思想与当代印度外交实践和国家安全理念相联系，寻求其在当今世界的现实解释力和生命力（王日华《先秦国家间政治思想的研究纲领与理论建构——兼论阎学通等著〈王霸天下思想及启迪〉》，《当代亚太》2010年第2期）。这些研究路径在这本《〈政事论〉国际政治思想研究》中也有不同程度的体现。

三、不足之处

可以理解的是，由于原著主题广泛、内容庞杂，作为国内首部专门研究《政事论》的学术专著，《〈政事论〉国际政治思想研究》一书在对原著进行引介和研究时也难免会显得内容繁杂、术语众多，初涉此领域的读者可能会觉得阅读难度较大。此外，全书在语言的精练方面似乎还可继续提升，以提高阅读的流畅程度。这里也要特别指出，目前国内外的已有研究普遍存在对原著核心术语的翻译和解读不一致的问题。造成这一情况的客观原因是《政事论》原著为梵文写作，在翻译成英语的过程中就出现了不同译本。国内直到 2020 年 12 月才有首个《政事论》完整中译本公开出版，学界的研究大多是以英译本为依据，因此对于核心术语出现了各种不同的中译名和存在出入的解释。这些复杂各异、古奥难懂的术语常常让初学者摸不着头脑。这可能正是本书花了较大篇幅对具体术语和背景知识进行专门介绍的原因。

此外，《〈政事论〉国际政治思想研究》设定的研究目标之一是"将《政事论》国际政治思想与西方国际关系理论进行比较研究，探索国际关系理论的新路径"。但在实际操作中，作者主要是从"国际安全悲观论""权力政治观""道德淡漠主义"等 7 个方面对《政事论》思想和西方现实主义国际关系理论进行了横向比较，甚至有从西方国际关系理论视角解读《政事论》的倾向，在理论探索上仍然有所缺憾。当然，这一点也是研究者将来可以继续深入探究的方向。

最后，在分析《政事论》对当代印度外交的影响时，此书遭遇到一个普遍瓶颈的制约，即如何确定憍底利耶思想对印度外交真正产生了影响、影响有多大以及如何影响的问题。总体来看，学界的已有研究大多强调憍氏思想对当前印度的外交实践与安全理念确有影响，甚至直接用憍氏思想来解读印度当前的外交行为。在这方面，此书主要采取了举例论证，通过列举印度重要领导人对憍底利耶的评价、印度对外政策中的圈层式思维、印度外交实践中某些符合憍氏思想的做法来论证《政事论》思想的影响力。在笔者看来，这种分析方法仍然欠缺经验上的可验证性，理论说服力仍有不足。其实，《政事论》的众多观点本来就与西方现实主义国际关系理论较为契合。因此，评价憍氏思想对印度外交政策产生影响时，就必然存在"难以界定和区分"的问题：印度某些外交政策是受到西方现实主义思想的影响，还是受到侨氏思想的影响，抑或二者都有，这些都是值得进一步探讨和商榷的。

结语

    中印两国都是具有重要影响力的亚洲大国，而且都是处于崛起中的人口和经济大国。中印关系的良性互动对两国的和平发展非常重要。但是由于边界争端、战略互信不足等一系列问题，中印关系仍然处于机遇与挑战并存、冲突与合作交织的局面。由于中印关系复杂而敏感，对印度内外政策加强研究也就变得越发重要。《政事论》是古代印度战略思想的丰富宝藏，也是当今印度战略文化和外交理念的重要源泉。由于中印关系的重要性不断上升，对《政事论》的研究也将越来越凸显出重要的学术价值和现实意义。总体而言，《〈政事论〉国际政治思想研究》一书的开拓性研究为国内《政事论》研究形成了坚实基础。相信通过此书的介绍和分析，有更多的读者会被《政事论》的深刻思想所吸引，进而对原著进行阅读和精研。也希望在不久的将来，会有更多的学者加入《政事论》和印度战略文化的研究中，并产生更多高质量的研究成果。

"金色孟加拉"经济发展的成效与走向
——《"一带一路"国别经济研究——孟加拉国》书评

袁梓芯 [①]

孟加拉国位于南亚次大陆东北部，三面与印度毗邻，东南与缅甸接壤。中国国家主席习近平2016年对孟加拉国进行国事访问时表示："过去十年中，孟加拉国GDP增幅都在6%以上。"这一成绩来之不易。孟加拉国1971年独立之初的贫困率高达75%，不仅面临着沉重的历史包袱，资源禀赋也先天不足，但此后的经济发展却表现出强劲动力。因此，我们更应该深究数字背后经济增长的长期驱动力。同时，随着全球形势的剧烈变化，各国经济的深层问题不断显现，疫情时代乃至后疫情时代的全球经济增速放缓，在新的条件下构建新兴的对外开放与合作格局已成为各国经济发展的现实路径。《"一带一路"国别经济研究——孟加拉国》一书对孟加拉国的经济进行了系统深入的研究，分析了孟加拉国在贫困、交通、产业结构等方面的问题，并就这些问题分析了孟加拉国政府的有关举措。这有助于从理论上深化对中孟合作的思考与前瞻，更有利于在实践层面促进中孟产业合作。

《"一带一路"国别经济研究——孟加拉国》由教育部人文社科重点研究基地四川大学南亚研究所李建军老师撰稿。作者深耕孟加拉国研究，对孟加拉国的政治、经济、对外关系等领域的发展情况极为熟悉。该书立足前沿数据、政府文件、刊物报告等原始资料，对孟加拉国的经济运行概况以及财政、货币与金融等具体领域进行了基础性介绍与系统分析，花费了很大精力进行数据汇总与归纳，独创性地整理与翻译了孟加拉国接受国际援助组织与国家、主要进口商品种类、外汇储备情况等累计70份原始数据表格，平均每章约有6张表格。该书兼顾专业性与大众性，既可作为专业研究人员的基础性工具书籍，也能够满足广大读者对孟加拉国加深了解的阅读兴趣。此书给予了笔者多方面的启迪，特借此机会与广大读者分享探讨。

---

① 袁梓芯，教育部人文社科重点研究基地四川大学南亚研究所硕士研究生。

看发展：立足数据，建设成就显著

此书由十二章构成，从孟加拉国经济的发展基础、运行概况、国民生产总值、储蓄与投资等多方面进行了梳理，每章节都以翔实的数据为支撑，以清晰的图表向读者展示。如第十章和第十一章，通过发电量情况、各类型电源发电量占比、天然气消费情况、公路里程、铁路线路千米数、客车数、机场旅客运输量、国内河运运输局航运里程、客运情况等表格数据，直观展示了该国以火力发电为主的能源消费结构、以公路为主的客运货运交通方式。由此，本书通过大量的图表和数据帮助读者对孟加拉国的能源结构与交通情况迅速形成总体性认识。管中窥豹，由此可见本书研究方法之一斑。

此书聚焦孟加拉国经济，其清晰的编排方式既便于读者"按图索骥"迅速找到某一方面的经济数据，又向读者提供了"精练"的孟加拉国的经济信息；既是对该国经济的百科全书式介绍，又着眼产业结构、粮食生产等微观经济问题深入挖掘。在横向勾勒孟加拉国经济整体轮廓的同时，进一步对其经济政策进行历时性梳理，展示了第七个"五年计划"将实现国民生产总值增长7.4%、贫困率降至18.6%等重要目标。基于对外经济、国民生产总值增长、消费水平表现、投资储蓄等领域的具体情况，深入分析孟加拉国宏观经济持续向好的总体格局。

尤其值得一提的是，该书第十二章对孟加拉国的减贫事业进行了梳理，在该国预计于2024年从"最不发达国家"名单毕业的背景下，从历史的角度观照了孟加拉国为减贫工作所做出的努力，回顾了其减贫过程中采用的不同测量指数，既有人类发展指数、食物能量摄入、直接卡路里摄入，也有基本需求成本、家庭收入与支出调查等测量手段。该书通过不同测量指数来展示孟加拉国的减贫工作成效，同时认为，孟政府实施多元贫困测量无疑表明了其减贫的决心与毅力。

贯穿全书的大量数据表格通过直观的数据，展示了孟加拉国人民发展经济、创造美好生活的不懈努力。积极采取各种有效措施应对本国的先天不足，具体包括不断优化创汇产品结构，实施关税改革，提升粮食产量并成为"世界上第四大水稻生产国"和"世界上第三大淡水鱼生产国"，推动蓝色经济蓬勃发展，作为"世界第二大服装生产基地"并以名牌服饰畅销全球等。通过经年累月的探索与改革，其经济发展已取得了亮眼成就。总之，年届"知天命"之年的孟加拉国正朝着"金色孟加拉"的目标不断迈进。

谈问题：结合政策，深入剖析国情

本书既注重数据准确清晰，又结合孟加拉国政府政策，对减贫、电力供应、交通运输、产业结构等关键问题进行剖析，梳理了孟加拉国本身的结构性矛盾。笔者对以下几个问题感触较深。

产业结构跳跃，支柱产业单一。孟加拉国产业结构比重呈现倒序，服务业比重远超工业。尽管第三产业能够有效地缓解就业压力，但没有第二产业作为支撑的第三产业的发展是不牢固的，主要依靠服务业并不能从根本上解决就业问题，制造业才是经济增长与创需消费的根本动力。尽管孟已建立了初步的工业体系，但特定的人口红利与自然条件决定了孟加拉国的产业优势仍然集中在纺织服装方面这一劳动密集产业。这一布局帮助实现了妇女赋权，创造了大量就业机会。但随着人造纤维等新面料的使用，孟加拉国的优势产业附加值逐渐下降，短期又难以培育高附加值特色产业，重工业方面缺口大，工业化水平低，尤其是在钢铁、金属等重要产品方面仍然依赖进口，经济发展抵抗力弱。

减贫不平衡，优先规模受阻。孟加拉国的政府采取了大量措施来推进减贫事业，成效突出，从独立到 2018 年贫困率下降了 52.5 个百分点。但通过直观数据，发现其减贫过程也暴露了诸多问题。依据减贫率数据，孟加拉国的农村减贫效果不佳（城市减贫率为 4.68%、农村减贫率为 1.97%）；依据基尼系数，孟加拉国的贫富差距呈现出扩大趋势。城镇居民收入差距扩大；财富不断集中到少数人手中；"东部－北部"贫困鸿沟依然存在，居民收入与地区发展差距悬殊。总之，地区减贫工作效果不一、减贫工作失衡成为突出矛盾，将阻碍孟经济持续健康发展。

交通运输紧张，电力能源匮乏。在交通方面，孟加拉国综合运输体系亟须建设。公路是全国客货运输的主要载体，而运输能力低下的乡村公路覆盖面是国家公路的 3 倍；铁路、航运、航空等其他运输方式状况也不容乐观。目前，孟加拉国的公路、铁路、航运、航空建设一度陷入停滞状况。此外，受洪涝灾害的影响，公路和铁路的里程数不仅没有增加，甚至出现了倒退

（1981-1982 财年，孟加拉国的铁路总里程为 2884 千米；2015-2016 财年孟加拉国的铁路总里程为 2877 千米）。交通运输是经济结构中的基础产业，紧张的交通运输限制了孟加拉国经济格局拓展。同时，在能源领域，该国在煤炭、石油等资源禀赋相对匮乏的基础上，一直存在电力供应紧张甚至短缺的问题。自产的天然气是其发电的主要能源，但随着大部分气田产量即将进入平台期，能源供给缺口将持续扩大。能源作为其他工业部分的基础，突出的能源供需矛盾无疑严重制约了孟加拉国的经济发展，更对其未来前景构成严重挑战。

出口商品单一，出口市场集中。在孟加拉国的出口创汇商品中，纺织品和服装占绝对优势，主要出口商品还处于国际产业链比较低端的位置，附加值较低，商品出口结构有待优化；而目标市场则高度集中于北美，新兴出口市场开拓有限，出口布局不均衡带来了较大的依赖性和波动风向。无论从扩大市场份额还是维护经济安全考虑，孟加拉国构建多元化、多层次、多渠道的出口市场格局迫在眉睫。

需要注意的是，中国读者在关注孟加拉国经济发展持续向好的同时，也需要认识到其经济发展所存在的问题。由此针对孟加拉国的重要关切开展合作，充分发挥中方产业优势与基建优势，优化双边贸易结构。如在电力方面，中国企业可以聚焦孟加拉国对电力的旺盛需求，在该国大力发展新能源发电，积极参与孟加拉国电力工程建设和运营，抢抓孟方鼓励私人企业进入并实行 15 年免税待遇、对电力设备免征增值税和关税等重要机遇，让中国电力设备产能和"中国标准"共同走出去。

说展望：提升思考，纵深拓展思维

该书全面梳理了孟加拉国的基本情况、产业结构、货币政策、金融市场等内容，更深入剖析了电力供需矛盾、交通供需矛盾、对外经济发展等关键问题。从深化研究的角度考虑，研究似还可在以下三方面进行拓展，从而进一步丰富本书内容，拓宽研究视野。

首先，增添商务风俗，拓展书籍参考性。本书对孟加拉国经济发展的基本情况做了较为清晰的梳理。若能在勾画基本情况的基础上，进一步增加塑造孟加拉国经商环境的风俗习惯、社会文化等方面内容，就能够更好地为中孟企业的投资合作提供参考，从而大大增加本书的实用性，助力中国企业"走进"孟加拉国。

其次，梳理经贸往来，回顾共建成果。中孟 1975 年建交，两国经贸合作领域持续深化。尤其是近年来，孟加拉国自中国进口逐年增长，中孟共建项目蓬勃开展。本书的立意侧重最新情况，但如能同时以适当篇幅介绍中孟两国在 40 多年来的经贸合作概况、贸易协定、金融投资等经济往来，从历史角度审视中孟合作存在的深厚传统、机遇与挑战，就可为政府机构和研究人员的决策和研究提供更有力的智力支持。另一可供参考的思路是，可以借助本书丰富的数据资料，深度评估"一带一路"倡议背景下中孟共建项目的成效与问题，透视其在水电、能源、道路交通等社会经济方面促成的发展与变化，最终又借助丰富的图表以可视化的形式系统呈现研究成果。这样一来，本研究就能够对共建项目成果进行总结，也能对存在问题进行反思，更能将"中孟共建"的成果作为典型进行宣传。

最后，立足长期经济发展，把握未来合作走向。"一带一路"倡议已迈入新阶段，需对第二阶段的合作方向进行前瞻性思考。从技术上说，相关规划可以立足于国民生产总值增长、国内融资的年度发展计划占比、公共支出等基本数据，对孟加拉国的投资环境、贸易环境、金融环境等经济状况进行总结。研判孟加拉国的短期与中长期经济态势，分析中孟新阶段合作面临的风险及挑战，为中资企业投资提供评估性建议，思考中孟共建新阶段的新方向，助力中孟关系飞跃式发展。其实，该书作者近年来的相关论文（如《孟加拉国经济发展的现状与前景》《孟加拉国财政改革及成效》《中孟经贸关系的现状与前景》）已较多地涉及以上许多内容。本研究如以其已掌握的最新数据进行重新预判，或许能更有力地助推中孟两国的发展和双边合作。

随着世界局势的不稳定性进一步凸显，各方都迫切需要加强经贸合作以有效应对百年未有之大变局带来的挑战与风险。孟加拉国是"一带一路"倡议中"21 世纪海上丝绸之路"的重要节点，更是新"丝绸之路经济带"的重要参与者。中孟共建了卡纳普里河河底隧道、帕德玛大桥等重点项目，对改善孟加拉国民众生活、提升其工业产能等方面都有显著作用，更进一步带动了两国的经济增长。近年来，国内出版了一套"一带一路"沿线国家经济丛书，囊括了印度、哈萨克斯坦、土耳其、巴基斯坦等 14 个国家的经济发展情况，但孟加拉国并未纳入丛书，不得不说是一大缺憾。其实，在"一带一路"倡议下的孟加拉国经济研究有重大的研究价值和广阔的研究空间。而这本《"一带一路"国别经济研究——孟加拉国》是作者立足自身研究专长与研究经验，参阅了相关专家学者的论文专著和政府文件，在深入掌握原始数据的基础上，对孟加拉国的经济最新情况进行了较全面的介绍与研究，为中孟经贸往来发展提供了重要的智力支持。相信通过一大批同类研究和相关学者的刻苦钻研，"一带一路"建设必然可以建立在更扎实的基础之上，必然表现出更蓬勃、更强劲的发展态势，必然能够更好更有力地助推中华民族伟大复兴的梦想早日实现。

艰难的合作——评《中印海上安全合作研究》

解斐斐 ①

中印同为海洋大国，且海洋经历颇为相似。遭受殖民侵略的不幸历史和海上门户洞开的惨痛后果使两国都意识到海洋对国家安全的重要性；同为陆海复合型国家的地缘政治属性使两国都能体会到维持海陆平衡的艰难；全球化浪潮下经济实力及综合国力的迅速提振又都为两国走向海洋提供了深层次的内在驱动力。在中印两国共同崛起的大背景下，中印海洋战略转型、中印海军现代化建设、中印海洋互动、中美印海洋互动及中印与周边国家的海洋互动都成为各界关注和讨论的话题。就中印海洋互动而言，讨论中印海洋竞争及冲突者多，探讨中印海洋合作者则相对较少；而在近期中印关系遭遇困难的背景下，理性探讨中印之间的海洋安全合作更显弥足珍贵，兼具独特的理论价值和重大的现实意义。

四川大学南亚和中国西部合作与发展研究中心邹正鑫撰写的《中印海上安全合作研究》一书详细论述了中印海上安全合作中的若干重要问题，涉及这一合作的背景、现状、特点、影响因素以及加强合作的对策建议等重要内容，在附录部分详细探讨了印度"海洋花环"项目及印度海军的最新发展。本书还详细探讨了影响中印海上安全合作的各项因素，并对进一步加强中印海上安全合作提出了较为完备而新颖的建议。笔者通读书稿之后，感到颇受启发，借此机会与各位读者分享一些读书感悟。

一、合作与海洋安全

合作（Cooperation）与海洋安全（Maritime Security）是本书的两大核心概念，对这两个概念做一个简要辨析，有助于从宏观层面把握中印海洋安

---

① 解斐斐，四川大学中国西部边疆安全与发展协同创新中心博士研究生，四川大学南亚研究所印度洋研究项目科研助理，主要从事印度海洋战略、海洋安全和中印关系等研究。

全合作。合作既是一种重要的国际现象，也是国际关系理论中的一个重要概念，新自由制度主义的代表人物罗伯特·基欧汉（Robert O. Keohane）对合作的阐释颇为经典。基欧汉将国际交往模式分为和谐、合作、争端三类，认为合作是介于利益完全一致的和谐与利益完全冲突的争端之间的一种模式，是国际关系的实质。基欧汉指出，合作是指行为体之间有着利益冲突，但在政策协调之后双方行为符合相互的利益，合作只有在双方既有利益冲突又有利益趋同的复杂情况下才会出现。基欧汉同时指出，无政府状态下国际合作的困境在于行为体在国际交往中的信息失衡及欺骗行为，而国际制度可以通过提供有效信息、降低欺骗的可能性来协调行为体行为，增强国际合作。

海洋安全是"安全"概念在海洋领域的具体延伸。海洋安全大体可分为两类，即传统海洋安全（主要涉及政治军事等"高政治"领域）和非传统海洋安全（具体涉及海洋恐怖主义、海盗、海上走私、海洋环境等问题）。若从具体领域划分，海洋安全又可细分为海洋政治军事安全、海洋经济安全、海洋社会安全、海洋环境安全等。这些安全议题与海权、蓝色经济、海上安宁及沿海地区的人口活力等概念密切相关，共同构成了海洋安全的不同侧面。对这些概念的理论化辨析虽然并不能完全对标实践性很强的中印海洋安全合作，却有助于构建海洋安全合作的思维框架，深入理解中印海洋安全合作中"合作困境""机制建设"等具体问题。

二、印度海洋安全战略视角下的中印海洋互动

共同的海洋利益是中印海洋安全合作的基点，而具体的海洋安全合作则需在中印各自海洋安全战略框架的指导下进行。作者从印度洋海洋安全态势入手，分析了中印海洋安全战略的异同及中印海洋安全合作的可能性。作者在正文部分对印度海洋安全战略着墨不多，但在附录部分另辟一章专门论述印度海军的最新进展，亦可将其视为作者对印度海洋安全战略的某种透视。近年来，印度海洋意识显著提升，海洋战略加速转型，海军现代化建设持续推进。尽管资金、技术、海陆协调等方面的问题依旧严重制约着印度走向海洋的步伐，但印度在海洋领域（尤其是海军现代化建设方面）取得的成效仍极为显著。正如作者所言，当前印度海军积极调整战略意图，努力打造一支均衡、合理的"远洋型"蓝水海军；采取自研与仿制相结合的模式，加快推

进海军装备的现代化与国产化；积极推进海军外交，努力拓展印度的战略空间。印度维护自身海洋利益、加速建设海洋强国的种种举措本无可厚非，但是其中浓厚的"中国因素"却为中印开展海洋安全合作蒙上了一层阴影。印度战略界对中国与缅甸、巴基斯坦、泰国、斯里兰卡等国的正常交往与合作颇为忌惮，认为中国试图运用将"马汉"与"麦金德"的理念相结合的方法从海陆两个方向同时进入印度洋。还有印度专家将中国进入印度洋、维护自身战略利益、加强与印度洋沿岸国家联系的举措解读为"中国试图从印度洋上对印实施'战略包围'"。尽管印度海军近年发布的海洋战略文件不像印度战略界那样大张旗鼓地宣称中国从海上"威胁"印度，但其对中国海军在印度洋上的存在看法颇为负面。在这一背景下，中印海洋安全合作的艰难性及曲折性可想而知。

作者在书中颇为详尽地梳理了近年来中印各个层面的海洋安全互动，包括两国政府高层间、科研机构间的海洋安全对话交流，舰艇互访、联合演习及反海盗护航等海军层面的海洋安全联合行动以及科技、海洋基础设施开发方面的海洋安全技术合作。单从形式上来看，作者对中印海洋互动的论述已涉及两国政府高层、外交部、海洋部门、海军、智库、高校、社会组织、企业、个人的多个维度和多个层面；但是从整体上看，中印海洋安全互动在互动频次、互动规模和互动内容等方面均不尽如人意，作者也颇为犀利地指出当前中印海洋安全合作呈现出一种矛盾态势，即互动频繁但合作基础薄弱，合作领域广泛但实质内容有限，海洋合作框架脆弱且发展不充分，两国海洋安全合作易受国际政治环境及两国政治关系波动的影响。中印两国政治高层有关海洋事务的宏观规划本来就少，而已签署的相关海洋文件及海洋科技合作项目也迟迟得不到落实，两国海洋安全合作停留在"只说不做"的层面。相比两国政府和海军层面在海洋安全合作问题上的踌躇不前，近年来中印智库和高校之间的海洋交流对话活动明显增加。但受2020年以来中印边界局势紧张、印度对华态度趋冷及政府政策收紧等因素的影响，中印这一层面的海洋安全互动逐渐遇冷也是可以预见的。

三、借用"印太"视角透视中印海洋安全合作？

作者将有关"中印海洋安全合作"的讨论集中于印度洋地区。就笔者的理解，一方面这有利于作者集中思考论述印度洋上的中印海洋安全互动，另一方面这也是中印在其他地区的海洋安全合作相对较少所致。考虑到目前的情况，思考中印海洋安全合作的时候，也可扩大地域范围，将"印太"作为中印海洋安全合作的地理范围。这种思路似乎也有一定可取之处。

诚然，"印太"概念由于美国的兜售和推广而大火，中国也无须"随美起舞"，但中国完全可以从自身战略考量出发，以"印太"视角来透视中印海洋安全合作。一方面，中印海洋利益交集涵盖从印度洋到太平洋的广阔区域，从"印太"范围来考虑中印之间的海洋安全合作有利于通盘考虑中印之间的海洋问题，有利于确保中印海洋安全合作的地域平衡性，避免因完全"聚焦"印度洋而引起印方的极度警惕。另一方面，中印在整个"印太"地区（尤其是太平洋地区）的海洋安全合作相对较少，但这并不意味印度不关注太平洋水域。近年来印度将其"东看"政策升级为"东向行动"政策，其"印太"倡议正逐步规划成型，印度关注甚至逐步增加在太平洋水域的存在已显露头角。在这一背景下，中国在关切印度合理海洋利益的同时，通过双边或多边方式推动太平洋上的中印海洋安全合作可在一定程度上引导塑造印度的印太观，加深双方对海洋问题的共同理解。

四、中印海洋安全合作及其未来

中印两国在海洋领域有共同合作的必要性、有海洋安全治理方面的迫切需求且两国在海洋领域有一定的互补性和互助性，但为何两国的海洋安全合作历经十多年的发展仍然处于初级阶段，且后续深度合作缓慢乏力？这是困扰笔者的一个问题，也是作者在书中重点分析的一大问题。这里仅以海军演习为例来说明中印海洋安全的"合作困境"。作者在书中梳理了 21 世纪以来为数不多的几次中印海军联合演习，最近一次双边联合演习为 2007 年双方舰艇编队在黄海海域举行的联合演练，演习内容为灯光通信、旗语交流、队形变换等项目，中方的"青岛"号导弹驱逐舰和印方的"拉纳"号、"兰吉特"号导弹驱逐舰参加演习，演习规模小且演习内容相对基础。而进入 21 世纪的第二个十年，双方鲜有单独联合演习，演习大都在多边框架下进行。相较而言，印度与美国、新加坡等国的海军演习不仅次数频繁，而且规模大、演习内容精细复杂。譬如，2018 年 11 月印度与新加坡举行的第 25

次"新印海上双边演习"（SIMBEX-18）在安达曼－尼科巴群岛首府布莱尔港、安达曼海及维沙卡帕特南多地举行。演习内容包括武器实弹演练（涉及多种型号的导弹发射、重型鱼雷、中程火炮及反潜火箭的发射）、先进的反潜作战演习、潜艇救援演练以及水面及防空联合作战演练。

对于中印海洋安全合作面临的"合作困境"，作者用一章内容详细分析了影响中印海洋安全合作的各项因素，指出印度洋地区安全环境复杂、中印两国海洋战略各异且互信不足、海洋安全合作机制及理论缺失以及美国、日本、东盟等外部因素是困扰中印海洋安全合作的关键问题。同时，也应该认识到中印两国海洋安全合作在对接方面的具体问题。譬如，有印度专家认为中印两国海军交流仍处于非常初级阶段的一大原因是，两国海军在发展方向、作战学说和战争思想方面极为不同，且两国海军在沟通交流及装备互通性方面也有一定障碍。这一论断虽未必全面，仍可帮助我们思考中印海洋安全合作中的一些具体问题。

作者在书中详细论述了加强中印海洋安全合作的对策建议，该建议系统完备且不少具体措施颇为新颖，是本书的一大亮点。作者强调通过加强海洋沟通对话、建立全面系统的海洋安全合作机制、推动海上合作倡议与政策的对接、大力发展海洋经济、充分利用多边平台和国际组织等推动中印海洋安全合作。在建立海洋安全合作机制方面，作者系统阐述了海洋安全问题中从预警到处理的高层磋商机制、预警机制、应急处理机制、亚丁湾联合巡航机制及海洋信息共享机制。作者的大体思路是在充分利用现有机遇和平台的基础上，以多边推动双边，以非传统安全问题、海洋经济问题及港口等基础设施建设问题为重点突破口、通过一种"自上而下"的政策引导方式加强中印之间的海洋安全合作。毫无疑问，这种思路有其可取之处，但在中印关系屡遇波折、中印海洋安全合作裹足不前的大背景下，要尽快推行这种全面方略似乎颇有难度。

笔者认为，可以"重点突破""自下而上"两种思路作为补充。一方面，印度社会复杂多元，各方利益诉求亦有区别，战略界对中国海洋战略的发展、中国海军在印度洋地区的存在及中印海洋安全合作等问题的认知并非铁板一块。尽管批评质疑的声音居于主流，但也有学者认为"印度应充分考虑中国在印度洋上的利益关切"，"中国海军的加入可有效补充印度洋地区的集体安全力量"，甚至有学者指出，"为缓解中国的忧虑，印美可在恰当时机将中国拉入'马拉巴尔'海军演习"。这种声音的存在为中印海洋智库和研究机构联合研究论证相关问题，进而推动中印在具体海洋领域开展合作提供了可能。另一方面，针对中印海洋利益多元、各方诉求多样的特点，中印可积极培育有各种行为体参与的海洋安全共同体（Maritime Security Communities）。海洋安全共同体由一体化理论家卡尔·多伊奇（Karl Deutsch）首倡的安全共同体（Security Communities）概念演化而来，用于描述海洋领域各个参与方之间的一种理想合作形式。海洋安全共同体中的行为者通过日复一日的海洋参与、信息共享及行动协调来增进成员间的共同理解、培育成员之间的互信感及集体身份意识。海洋安全共同体成员之间的关系不同于国家之间的结盟关系，其认同感和集体身份意识是在实践性强的海洋互动中发展起来的，不失为安全治理的一种有效形式。此外，海洋安全共同体虽会涉及高层次的政治外交活动，但其主要关切为中下层海洋安全从业人员与专家以及他们之间的互动方式。海洋安全共同体虽是一种理想化的模式，但仍有助于扩大中印之间共同的海洋利益、培育海洋认同感，从而夯实中印海洋安全合作的基础。

Special Topic: Sino-Indian Maritime Exchanges

Sino-Indian Maritime Exchanges:
A Brief History

Zeng Xiangyu & Zhu Yufan, translated by Zheng Zirou[①]

Abstract: This paper presents the Sino-Indian cultural exchanges via maritime routes, focusing on the prehistoric connections, the spread of Buddhism via maritime routes, the medieval seaborne trade between China and India, and the Chinese/Indian communities and antiquities in ancient India/China. The marine interaction between China and India, especially between Southwest China and the Bay of Bengal Region started from the prehistoric age, which indeed catalyze the evolution of both civilizations. In medieval times, the sea route has significantly promoted the introduction of Buddhism to China. It also facilitated the subsequent trade that underpinned the prosperity of both countries. In the context of frequent cultural, material, and personnel exchanges, coastal communities in both China and India mushroomed with residents from the other side, leaving a mass of cultural relics. It has laid a historical foundation for the two countries to re-expand maritime exchanges and jointly develop a maritime community with a shared future in the 21st century.

Key Words: Sino-Indian Cultural Exchange; Maritime Civilization; Maritime Silk Road; The Spice Road

---

① Zeng Xiangyu is associate research fellow at the Institute of South Asian Studies at Sichuan University, a key research institute for humanities and social sciences of Ministry of Education of China. His research interests cover South Asian security and diplomacy, maritime affairs and Chinese diplomacy. Zhu Yufan is an associate professor at the Central Institute of Socialism. Her research interests include neighborhood diplomacy, maritime security, and the study of China's overseas interests. Zheng Zirou studies International Relations (South Asian Studies) at the Institute of South Asian Studies at Sichuan University.

China and India are close neighbors and great civilizations enriched by mutual learning. The exchanges between China and India have a long history and far-reaching influence. For years, studies on Sino-Indian exchanges have been concentrated on exchanges through land route, that is the Silk Road linking hinterland China and Western Regions (Xiyu) and the ancient Tibet–Nepal passage. One can find just a few academic research on Sino-Indian exchanges via maritime routes. However, it must be noted that both civilizations have profound maritime tradition and long-time mutual maritime exchanges. This is of very big social significance. This article made a tentative discussion of Sino-Indian cultural exchanges via maritime routes, focusing on prehistoric connections, the spread of Buddhism via maritime routes, the medieval seaborne trade between China and India, and the Chinese/India communities and antiquities in ancient India/China.

I. Sea Passage and the Beginning of Sino-Indian Exchanges

The earliest surviving written evidence concerning Sino-Indian exchanges as was recorded by *Shih Chi* (*Historical Records*, by Sima Qian) indicates that Zhang Qian (164–114 BCE) had visited the Western Region (Xiyu) and saw Qiongzhu Zhang (a cane made of a special bamboo called Qiongzhu) and Shubu (a special cloth originated from ancient Shu, roughly the present

Sichuan Province) circulating in the market of Bactria.[①] Moreover, *Arthasastra* (believed to be written at the end of the 4th century BCE in ancient India) also mentioned that silk cloth and garments were produced in Cinabhumi (Kauśeyaṃcīnapaṭ ṭāśca cīnabhūmijāḥ).[②] Cinabhumi is generally regarded as a reference to China. In the summer of 1986, along with other excavations, some seashells were found in Sanxingdui, Guanghan, Sichuan Province, Southwest China. Among the discoveries, researchers find some monetria

---

① According to the *Historical Records–Record on Dayuan*, Zhang Qian said, "When I was in Daxia (Bactria), I saw Qiongzhu Zhang and Shubu (commodities from Sichuan). To my question on how they could have such items, the locals in Daxia replied that 'our business-men purchased such items from Juandu (India), which is thousands of li (1 li is 500 meters) southeast from here. The custom and people there are roughly identical to Daxia, while it has a lower latitude and more humid climate. Its people ride elephants for warfare, while its territory borders very big rivers.' According to my estimates, Daxia is 12 thousand li from Han and lies on its southwestern side. Juandu must not be far away from Shu (Sichuan) as it lies thousands of li to the southeast of Daxia and has products from Shu." *Historical Records–Record on Southwest Barbarians* also indicates that after he came back in the first year of Yuanshou (122 BCE) from his diplomatic trip to Daxia Zhang Qian said he saw Shubu, Qiongzhu Zhang in Daxia. He asked an agent to inquire sources of such items. The reply was "they are from Juandu, a place located in the southeast thousands of li away where I can do business with merchants from Shu." It is heard that Juandu lies 2000 li west of Qiong (a place inside Shu). Zhang Qian thereby proactively asserted that Daixa lied in the southwest of China. He claimed that Daxia admired China but was separated with China by Xiongnu (an ancient nomadic people in northern China and central Asia). He believed a route via Juandu would be beneficial and harmless as it would be shorter and more convenient, if a linkage with Shu could be explored. The emperor therefore ordered Wang Ranyu, Bo Shichang, Lü Yueren and others to find a way from west of Xiyi (western barbarians) in order to visit Juandu.

② Ji Xianlin, "The history of Sino-Indian cultural exchanges" in *Ji Xianlin Complete Works (Volume 13)*, Foreign Language Teaching and Research Press, 2010, p. 375. See also R. Shamasastry (translated), *Kautilya's Arthasastra*, Bottom of the Hill Publishing, 2010, p. 83. R. P. Kangle (translated), *The Kauṭilīya Arthaśāstra (Vol. 2)*, Motilal Banarsidass Publishers, 8th Reprint: Delhi, 2014 (Second Edition, Bombay University, 1969), p. 105. Zhu Chengming, Kauṭilīya Arthaśāstra, PhD Thesis in Peking University, 2016, p. 102. Several studies have suggested that the cīnabhūmi mentioned is not China, but rather somewhere like Baltistan in present-day Pakistan-controlled Kashmir, but the majority of studies indicate that this is China. Scholars who support this reference to China are divided into two schools of thought, with one proposing that this is evidence of the late date of the *Arthasastra* and the other proposing that this is evidence of Sino-Indian interaction well before the existing literature.

annulus, or ring cowrie (see Fig.1), which is one third the size of Cypraea tigris with tooth-shaped grooves on their central parts. They only live in the deepwater of the Indian Ocean instead of the coastal areas or rivers/lakes. These amounts of tooth shells found in inland Sanxingdui must be transported directly from the northern littorals of the Indian Ocean, mainly the areas between the Bay of Bengal and the Arabian Sea.[①] Moreover, these unearthed seashells in Sanxingdui were collected not indirectly from Yunnan but directly through economic and cultural exchanges between peoples in ancient Shu and the Bay of Bengal.[②] With archaeological methods, this earliest evidence of the communication between China and South Asia dates roughly to the 11th century BCE, about 1,000 years earlier than literature records. Obviously, such exchanges must be synergy of sea and land transportation, with people landing straightly along the coast of the Indian Ocean and then moving to inland China, rather than sailing from the Indian Ocean to the Pacific coast.

In addition, some studies suggest that the Qiongzhu Zhang and Shubu as was witnessed by Zhang Qian in Bactria, were not transported from southwest China to India by land route, but by the route of Shu–Yelang–Nanyue–South China Sea.[③] The land part of this route is about the same as the Zangke Route of later years, while the sea part is roughly the same as the Maritime Silk Road. If this is true, the first documentary evidence of the Sino-Indian passage would refer to the passage of the sea, instead of the land.

---

① Duan Yu, "Sino-Foreign Communication in Southwestern China via the Southern Silk Road during the Pre-Qin/Han Dynasty period," *Historical Research*, 2009 (01), p. 15. Xue Keqiao, *A History of China–India Culture Exchange*, Encyclopedia of China Publishing House, 2017, pp. 13–14.

② According to Duan Yu, the earliest age of sea shells excavated on the Shu-India Road from Yunnan to Sichuan is the Spring and Autumn Period, whereas the age of Sanxing-dui is early in the middle and late Shang dynasty, almost a thousand years earlier, and no sea shells were excavated in Yunnan during this period. See also Duan Yu, "Sino-Foreign Communication in Southwestern China via the Southern Silk Road during the Pre-Qin/Han Dynasty period," *Historical Research*, 2009 (01), p. 17.

③ Lü Zhaoyi, "view on Sino-Indian transportation during the Western Han Dynasty," *South Asian Studies*, 1984 (02), pp. 64–67.

II. The Spread of Buddhism via Sea Routes

It is generally believed that Buddhism entered China mainly via the land route. Buddhism's journey to China is believed to start from northwest India, then go to Central Asia, the Western Regions (Xiyu), the northern part of inland China, and the eastern and the southern part of inland China. However, a sea route for the spread of Buddhism also deserve academic attention. Following Liang Qichao's first discussion of Buddhism's journey to China via sea route, Ji Xianlin claimed that the Buddhism in China "may first come through sea route, or from land route".[1] He made this judgment because Buddha, the core concept of Buddhism, had two translations in Chinese at the very beginning: "Fo"and "Futu". The former should come from a language from Western Regions (Xiyu) such as Tocharian, while the latter should be directly imported from Sanskrit. However, it was "Futu" that became popular in China at first. [2]

Certain archaeological discoveries in recent years have revealed a possibility that Buddhism could enter China through maritime routes. The Kongwang Mountain cliffside carvings are located on the coast of Jiangsu Province in eastern China. The earliest carvings here can be attributed to the reign of Emperor Huan and Emperor Ling in late Eastern Han Dynasty (late 2nd century CE). Some of the carvings are deemed as the Buddha statue, as they have a mass of hair arranged in a bun or chignon on top of the heads, with the right hand in Abhaya-mudra, a gesture signifying "no fear"; those on padamasana had the hands placed on the chest (see Fig.2, Fig.3, and Fig.4). Some suggested that this could be the earliest Buddha statues in China, much

---

[1] Ji Xianlin, "Futu and Fo," in *Ji Xianlin Complete Works (Volume 15)*, Foreign Language Teaching and Research Press, 2010, p. 11. The original manuscript was written on October 9, 1947.

[2] Ibid.

earlier than the statues in the grottoes along the westbound Silk Road.[1] Generally speaking, local statues are made in a date later than the introduction of a certain religion. That is to say, the arrival of Buddhism at Qingzhou and Xuzhou (nowadays Shandong Province and surroundings) should be much earlier than the birth of Kongwang Mountain cliffside carvings. This indicates that Buddhism arrived at the easternmost coastal areas earlier than the west-to-east land road could do. This could be made possible only via a sea route. Existing documents also reveal important signs of the spread of Buddhism by sea. It is recorded that Liu Ying, the Prince of Chu under the reign of Emperor Ming of the Eastern Han Dynasty, developed a favor to Futu (possibly Buddhist) Teachings. The princedom of Chu was located in coastal areas covering modern-day Jiangsu Province with its capital located at Pengcheng (now Xuzhou City in Jiangsu). Obviously, this region have a disposition to cultural influence from overseas. It is worth noting that the Buddhism believed by the Prince of Chu used the word "Futu" which is proximate to the Indian expression, rather than "Fo", a word indirectly learned from the Western Regions. This in fact imply that the Buddhism Liu Ying practiced was directly from India, obviously imported through sea route.[2]

Although there are some disputes about the sea route by which China encountered Buddhism at an early time, there is no doubt about the Buddhist exchanges between China and India through the sea route (the Buddhist Road

[1] Yu Weichao, Xin Lixiang, "Chinese Journal Articles on An Examination of the Dating of the Cliff Statues at Kongwang Mountain," *Cultural Relics*, 1981 (07), pp. 8–15.

[2] Wu Tingmiu, Zheng Pengnian, "A Study of Buddhism's Maritime Introduction to China," *Historical Research*, 1995 (02), pp. 30–31. As is recorded in *Biographies of Ten Princes as the Sons of Emperor Guangwu* in *The History of Late Han Dynasty*, Liu Ying, Prince of Chu...was fond of chivalrousness and engagement with clients and guests when he was young. He became even more interested with teachings of Huanglao school and tried to learn Futu (Buddhist?) vegetarianism and rites...The emperor in his royal decree said: "The Prince of Chu cherishes the sublimed teachings of Huanglao school and the benign worshiping of Futu (Buddhism?) ...Let him be absolved in order to facilitate offerings to Yipusai (Upāsaka?) and Sangmen (Sramana?)."

via the South China Sea) in later periods. Renown Buddhist monks followed
the Maritime Silk Road, opened in the Western Han Dynasty (202 BCE–8 CE),
to travel between China and India, in a duration started from 2nd century CE
to mid-14th century CE. Faxian, a prominent monk of the Eastern Jin Dynasty,
went to India by land in 399 CE. After years of study in Northern India, he
traveled along the Ganges to a place not far from today's Kolkata and sailed
to Lion Country (now Sri Lanka). He departed from Sri Lanka in the autumn
of 411 CE. The ship was caught in a storm two days later. After repairing the
ship, they continued for 90 days before arriving at Yavadvipa (now east of
Sumatra Island). In the spring of the following year, Faxian set sail again but
was caught in another storm. He finally landed on the coast of present-day
Shandong on 412 CE.[1]

It is worth noting that many of those moving between China and India
took the sea route—monks departing from China often traveled westward by
the traditional overland route but returned home via the sea route. One example
was Zhiyan. He went to Kashmir, and then set sail to China with a local
monk named as Juexian (Bodhibhadra?). A Youzhou (nowadays Beijing and
surroundings) resident called Li Yong took the land route to India for his study,
and then "embarked on a ship in southern India and arrived in Guangzhou." In
the Northern and Southern Dynasties (420–589 CE), many foreign monks came
to China by sea. For example, Guṇabhadra, a Buddhist monk from Central
Tianzhu (Central India), "took a journey along the sea route" and arrived in
today's Guangzhou in 435 CE. The Kashmiri prince Gunavarma first went
to the Lion Country (Sri Lanka), arrived at Java Island by ship, and sailed to
China. In 546 CE, Gunarata (Paramartha) of West Tianzhu (West India) took
the sea route from Funan (near present Cambodia) to Nanhai County (present
Guangzhou). A Tianzhu (India) monk Nagasena sailed home from Guangzhou
on a Funan ship, according to *the Historical Record of the Southern Qi Dynas-*

① Liu Yingsheng, *The Silk Road*, Jiangsu People's Publishing House, 1st edition, September 2014, p. 356.

ty.[①] All these indicate that after the Han Dynasty (202 BCE–220CE), the sea channel was of growing importance in the context of communication between China and South Asia.

Maritime Buddhist cultural exchanges between China and India took a great leap forward in the Tang Dynasty (618–907 CE). In 671 CE, 44 years after Xuanzang's journey, Yijing (I-Tsing) set off from Guangzhou to India by sea to study the Buddhist teachings. In his *Biographies of the Elegant Monks*, Yijing recounts the deeds of 61 monks in their pursuit of Buddhist teachings in India during the 46 years and mentions that 37 monks reached India by sea route. According to his records, the first 7 monks traveled both way by land. After that, some started to take the sea route and the last 41 monks almost all chose to go by sea, indicating the increasing popularity of sea routes and a tendency of replacing the land route as the first choice.[②] Some argues that Yijing was more familiar with travelers who chose the sea route as he himself traveled by sea. He thereby inadvertently exaggerated the influence of sea routes. However, it is unreasonable to speculate Yijing's tendency to highlight the sea passage intentionally or unintentionally. Despite Yijing's personal experience, he also recorded the 24 travelers who took the land routes. He spent 12 years studying in India, traveled around East and North India, and stayed for a long time in Nalanda Monastery. With sufficient time/ space conditions, and interpersonal communication opportunities, Yijing could collect information about all traffic methods.

Comparing Yijing's accounts with earlier Buddhist monks' transportation methods between China and India, we can find that, the convenience of maritime transportation between China and India has been gradually improved, from the Han Dynasty to the Northern and Southern Dynasties and then to

---

① Liu Yingsheng, *The Silk Road*, Jiangsu People's Publishing House, 1ˢᵗ edition, September 2014, p. 357, 383.

② Meng Liang, "Culture Exchanges between China and India in the Early Tang Dynasty—Taking YI Jing's Master Works as the Center," *Journal of Chongqing Jiaotong University* (Social Sciences Edition), 2019 (01), p. 46.

the Tang Dynasty. Accordingly, the first choice to move between China and India changed over time. Overland route used to be the first preference in the early age. Later on, it developed into a going-by-land and returning-by-sea transportation in the Northern and Southern Dynasties (420–589 CE), and a traveling-back-and-forth by sea in the middle of the Tang Dynasty (618–907 CE).

III. Sino-Indian Maritime Trade in the Mid-ancient Times

Existing documents indicate that direct maritime exchanges between China and India were established as early as the Western Han Dynasty (2nd century BCE to earliest years of Common Era). This passage of more than one-thousand-year old is called "the South Sea Passage". *The History of Han—The Geography*, written in the early years of the East Han Dynasty (late first century), depicts a maritime silk road stretching from today's Guangdong, to Southeast Asia and South Asia, with access to "Jibucheng"and "Huangzhi"in South Asia.[1] The location of Huangzhi is generally considered to be Kanchipurram of Tamil Nadu in southeast India. About 100 km from the south of Kanchipurram is Arikamedu, an important port bordering the Bay of Bengal.[2] The word "Huangzhi" was mentioned 4 times in *the History of Han*. According to the description, Huangzhi had a vast territory and a large population, and its folk customs were similar to Hainan Island at that time. It would take about 10 months to travel from Huangzhi to Rinan (northern part of present-day Vietnam). Despite the remote distance, there were frequent

---

① As is recorded in *The History of Han—The Geography*, "Sailing from Rinan (northern Vietnam)... one encountered with Huangzhi (Kanchipuram?). With custom somewhat similar to Zhuya (Hainan), Huangzhi enjoys sizable territory and big population, as well as product particular to this region. They come to China from time to time from Emperor Wu of Han's time (141–87 BCE). About 8 months are needed sailing from Huangzhi to Pizong. Another 2 months will be enough to sail to Rinan..."

② Xiong Zhaoming, "An Archaeological Observation of the Maritime Silk Road Route in the Han Dynasty," *Social Scientist*, 2017 (11), p. 38.

interactions between China and Huangzhi. Since the time of Emperor Wu of the Han Dynasty (156–87 BCE), it has sent emissaries to China many times. *The History of Han—The Biography of Emperor Ping* suggested, "In the spring of the second year of Yuanshi (2 CE), the State of Huangzhi proffered rhinoceros". *The History of Han—The Biography of Wang Mang* mentioned that "the State of Huangzhi paid tribute with rhinoceros from 30,000 li (about 15,000 kilometers) away". [1] Rhinoceros was rare in China. Wang Mang himself was keen on creating "good fortune" in order to build public opinion for his throne legitimacy. Therefore, the official historical records especially depicted the event of Huangzhi's gift of rhinoceros. Frequent exchange of common items between Huangzhi and China, despite lack of written evidence, would not be surprising.

Then in the Southern and Northern Dynasties (420–589 CE), China was split into the North and the South for more than 200 years. The Southern Dynasties controlled a much smaller territory with hardly any access to overland Silk Road, while its maritime linkage with ancient India were maintained so that the communication remained unimpeded. *The History of Song—Records of the Barbarians* was written in the sixth year of the Yongming Period (488 CE). It recorded that the State of Kapili of Tianzhu (India)[2] sent envoy to China in the fifth year of the Yuanjia Period (428 CE), presenting treasures including diamond rings, violet gold ring, a red parrot and a white parrot. More importantly, his diplomatic correspondence to Emperor Wen of the Song Dynasty said, "May there be continuous bilateral communications and hopefully my messenger could come back with an

---

[1]   Liu Yingsheng, *The Silk Road*, Jiangsu People's Publishing House, 1st edition, September 2014, p. 345.

[2]   According to the credentials, this state "has Jiabi river and borders the sea... and enjoys the protection of Shouluotian (Ishvara?)." Xue Keqiao believed that the Jiabi river refers to Kaveri river in South India where Shaivism or worship of Ishvara was most popular. Xue Keqiao, *A History of China–India Cultural Exchange*, Encyclopedia of China Publishing House, 2017, p. 39.

envoy."[1] Yet no sign indicates whether Emperor Wen sent emissaries to ancient India or not. If so, they had to go there by sea. Besides, it is impossible to confirm whether the two sides frequently sent emissaries (if so, they would have traveled by sea), but it is not until the second year of Taishi (466 CE) that Kapili's envoy and tributes were recorded in the historical records.[2]

The maritime trade between China and India upsurged in the Tang and Song Dynasties. The maritime route earned its name of "Road of Porcelain" or "Road of Spices" as China's porcelain and India's spices became the staple commodity along this route. According to *A Record of the Eastern Expedition of the Great Monk from Tang*, "there were ships from Brahman state, Persia, Kunlun and so on, carrying mountains of spices, medicine, and treasures, in the river" outside Guangzhou on the ninth year of Tianbao or 750 CE.[3] In 1974, an ocean ship of the Song Dynasty (sunk no later than 1274 CE, see Fig.5, and Fig.6) was excavated in Quanzhou Bay off the coast of Fujian Province. Several precious cultural relics were found in the vessel, among which are spices and medicines (weighing about 2350 kg without dehydration) from Southeast Asia or South Asia (see Fig.7, Fig.8, Fig.9, and Fig.10).[4] This is a rare surviving testimony to the ancient trade of spice. On the southwest coast of India, Cochin used to be one of the trade (spice trade in particular) hubs with China. The city had been flourishing until the Ming and Qing Periods (1368–1911 CE). A local Jewish businessman made a fortune through engaging in the bilateral trade. He ordered a batch of Chinese-style blue tiles for the floor of a local synagogue which has been well preserved (see Fig.11 and

---

[1] *The History of Song (Volume 97)*. Also in the fifth year of Yuanjia, the state of Shizi sent an envoy and "commissioned four Taoists to send two men in white to deliver the statue of the Toadai as an oath", and again in the twelfth year of Yuanjia (435 CE) .

[2] *The History of Song (Volume 57)*.

[3] Genkai(authored), Liang Mingyuan(checked and annotated), *A Record of the Eastern Expedition of the Great Monk from Tang*, Guang Ling Press, November 2010, p. 71.

[4] According to the author's visit at the Quanzhou Maritime Museum Shipwreck Hall on June 19, 2016.

Fig.12).[1] Kollam (or Quilon) in Kerala, an important port on Malabar coast, developed a close trade contact with China in the Song Dynasty (960–1279 CE). According to *the Gazetteer of Foreign Lands* written at the end of the Southern Song Dynasty (1127–1279 CE), "Kollam could be reached by boat from Namburi within 5 days... The local customs are roughly the same as the Namburi... Many Taziks lived in the area."[2] In recent years, over 500 pieces of porcelain fragments and more than 1,300 pieces of copper coins (or coin fragments) have been found in archaeological excavations.[3] The former was from Zhejiang, Jiangxi, Guangdong, Fujian, and other Chinese provinces, dated between the 10th and 14th centuries, while the latter can be attributed to a period between the 8th to 14th centuries. Porcelain fragments were discovered in great quantity in the Patnam site in Kerala as well. They were largely from Jiangxi and Fujian provinces in a period from 15th to 19th centuries.[4] All these witnessed a very prosperous trade between India and China.

Besides, large quantities of fragments of Song and Yuan porcelain have been found along the Coromandel coast in the southeast of India. Archaeological investigations in Arikamedu site in the 1930s discovered fragments of the Yue Kiln dishes from the 9th to 10th century, Yue Kiln porcelain, Longquan Kiln celadon and Cizhou Kiln pottery from 11th to 12th century, elegant celadon bowls, deep bowls and small jar pieces produced by Longquan Kiln, white porcelain and celadon dishes in the Southern Song Dynasty (1127–1279 CE), as well as the "Xuanhe Tongbao" Coins, circulated at the Xuanhe Period (1119–1125 CE) of the Northern Song Dynasty. It demonstrated that from the 9th to 13th century, shipping of Chinese porcelain to this place has never ceased. The Korimedu site nearby is scattered with

---

[1] According to author's visit in Cochin on March 19, 2014.

[2] Zhao Rushi(authored), Yang Bowen(annotated), *Zhu Fan Zhi(Collation and Explanation)*, Zhonghua Book Company, April 2004, p. 68.

[3] Ji Luoyuan, "Investigation and harvesting of two excavated Chinese heritage sites in Kerala, India in 2014," *Forbidden City*, 2017 (05), p. 70.

[4] Ibid., p. 68.

pieces of Chinese porcelain from the Song and Yuan Periods (960–1368 CE), including pieces of pearly celadon bowls and pale blue-and-white glazed pots from Zhejiang and Fujian during the 12ᵗʰ–13ᵗʰ centuries in the Southern Song Dynasty (1129–1279 CE), and blue-and-white porcelain from Fujian and Guangdong after the 14ᵗʰ century.[1]

The prosperity of the Maritime Silk Road after the Tang Dynasty and rapid upgradation of the economic status of Southeast China happened at the same time and were correlated closely. Xue Keqiao pointed out that the South Sea Road had played a unique role in the Sino-Indian exchanges. It facilitated the communication between the east coast of China and India. It supplemented the overland road (blocked sometimes) and eliminated various taxes imposed on commerce along the land routes.[2] These views are quite reasonable and persuasive.

IV. The Chinese/Indian Communities and Antiquities in Each Other's Territory

Both China and India have a very long history of sailing. During the long-time maritime activities, people moved across the sea and settled down in each other's territory, constituting some large communities while leaving many historical relics. Malabar Coast on the west of India for a long time seems to be the westernmost boundary of the westward Chinese voyage. For example, Zhao Rushi in late Southern Song Dynasty said in *Gazetteer of Foreign Lands* that Namburi (generally believed to be along the Malabar Coast) was "at the southwest extreme... it is the most distant country and few ships can reach there".[3] He also stated that there is "a father and a son called Shiluoba

---

[1] Xue Keqiao, *A History of China–India Cultural Exchange*, Encyclopedia of China Publishing House, 2017, pp. 211–212.

[2] Ibid., pp. 25–26.

[3] Zhao Rushi(authored), Yang Bowen(annotated), *Zhu Fan Zhi(Collation and Explanation)*, Zhonghua Book Company, April 2004, pp. 66–67.

(Quanzhou dialect: Silopa) and Zhiligan (Quanzhou dialect: Tilatkan). Their compatriots are now living in the south of Quan."[1] The word "Quan" here refers to the modern-day Quanzhou, an important port in southeast China at that time. Zhao Rushi specifically recorded their names, since Shiluoba and Zhiligan must be important figures among the long-staying Indians in Quanzhou at that time. His manner of speaking indicated that he thought the contemporaries must be very familiar with the two and thereby no bother with further introduction. Since the 20th century, a number of relics characterized with distinct Indian culture colour have been discovered in Quanzhou, Fujian Province of China. The discovery of over 300 Hindu stone carvings and a broken Tamil stone tablet has been turned into collections of Quanzhou Maritime Museum, Museum of Archeology in Xiamen University, Kaiyuan Temple of Quanzhou (see Fig.13), Tianhou Temple, etc...[2] Some pillar carvings at the rear side of the Great Buddha's Hall of the Kaiyuan Temple, a famous ancient temple, were identified as Hindu images like Naramsinha and Krishna as Gopala (see Fig.14, Fig.15, and Fig.16).[3] A most typical Vishnu sculpture (115 cm tall, unearthed in 1934 in the south drill ground of Quanzhou, see Fig.17) and the ruins of some temples are now exhibited at Quanzhou Maritime Museum, while many "Lingam" images were also found. These remains reflect how Indian migrants lived their daily lives in China in medieval times, suggesting that in the Yuan Dynasty (1271–1368 CE), a large population in Quanzhou believed Hinduism.[4] The number of Hindu temples and altars also indicates that there used to be a large Hindu community comprising Indians who have been gradually turned into residents of Quanzhou before the Yuan

---

[1]   Zhao Rushi(authored), Yang Bowen(annotated), *Zhu Fan Zhi(Collation and Expla-nation)*, Zhonghua Book Company, April 2004, pp. 67–68.

[2]   David Yu, Wang Liming (translator), "A Comparative Study of Hindu Stone Carv-ing Art in Quanzhou," *Journal of Maritime History Studies*, 2017 (01).

[3]   Qiu Yonghui, *An Introduction to Hinduism*, Social Sciences Academic Press (China), 2012, pp. 363–364.

[4]   Wang Liming, "Review and Reflections on the Study of Hindu Stone Carvings in Quanzhou," *Journal of Maritime History Studies*, 2016 (01), p. 123.

Dynasty.[1] Both Vaishnavism and Shaivism appeared in Quanzhou, while Hinduism to some extent, was integrated into folk beliefs.[2] Many studies claim that the Hindu heritage in Quanzhou is characterized with distinct South Indian style,[3] considering the description of Malabar family that corroborated it. This is not an isolated example. As a matter of fact, Guangzhou, a major city to the south of Quanzhou, had three Hindu temples as early as the Tang Dynasty (618–907 CE). According to *A Record of the Eastern Expedition of the Great Monk from Tang*, in the 9th year of Tianbao (750 CE), Guangzhou had "three Brahmanical temples, providing residence for foreign monks as well" and "peoples from many countries, such as Lion Country... lived here"[4]. The foreign monks and those from Buddhist states mentioned here should all come from India, Sri Lanka, and other parts of South Asia.

Similarly, there was once a sizeable group of Chinese dwellers in India. According to the records of Yijing, 40 courier-station distance east of Nalanda Temple, there was a Deer Park Temple and not far from it was the Cīna Temple. It is said that more than 20 Guangzhou monks came here in the time of Maharaja Sri Gupta (late 3rd century CE). Up to the Tang Dynasty, there

---

[1] Wang Liming, "Review and Reflections on the Study of Hindu Stone Carvings in Quanzhou," *Journal of Maritime History Studies*, 2016 (01), pp. 134–136.

[2] Qiu Yonghui, *An Introduction to Hinduism*, Social Sciences Academic Press (China), 2012, p. 364.

[3] Wang Liming, "Review and Reflections on the Study of Hindu Stone Carvings in Quanzhou," *Journal of Maritime History Studies*, 2016 (01), pp. 131–132, 134–135.

[4] Genkai(authored), Liang Mingyuan(checked and annotated), *A Record of the Eastern Expedition of the Great Monk from Tang*, Guang Ling Press, November 2010, p. 71.

were still people of three villages belonging to the Deer Park Temple.[①] These monks reputedly "took the Shu-Zangke Road ," namely trekking from Sichuan Province to India, passing through Zangke Commandery (covering present-day Yunnan and Guizhou).[②] However, according to *Historical Records–Records on Southwest Barbarians*, Guangzhou can be reached directly by boat from Zangke River in southwest China. The "Zangke Road" in history was in fact a waterway from the Southeast China to Guangzhou, instead of an overland road from the Southwest China to India. Therefore, it is more likely that the monks traveled by water from Sichuan to Guizhou before going to Guangzhou, and then sailed via the South China Sea to India.[③]

In the Song and Yuan Periods (960–1368 CE), a Chinese community emerged on the southeast coast of India and built a Chinese-style pagoda.

---

① Liu Yingsheng, *The Silk Road*, Jiangsu People's Publishing House, 1st edition, September 2014, p. 355. As is recorded in *Buddhist Monks' Pilgrimage of the Tang Dynas-ty–Biography of Hunlun* (Authored by Yijing (or I-ching), a Chinese monk active in late 7th Century), "not far away from this temple (Mriga-sthapana), there is an old temple with only its brick base remained. It has been named as Cheena Temple. It was told that, the temple was constructed by Maharaja Shri Gupta (240–290 CE?) for Buddhist monks from Cheena. A group of 20-plus Chinese monks came from Sichuan via Zangke Route (river linkage between Southwest China and Guangzhou?) to pay a pilgrimage to the Mahabhodi. The king, out of a desire to honor the monks, decided to donate this land so as to render a place of rest. 24 villages were ordered to subordinate to the temple. Such villages were later subordinated to others as the presence of Chinese monks gradually diminished. 3 of such villages are subordinated to Mriga-sthapana at present. Looking back to the emergence of Cheena Temple, that was more than 500 years ago." See Yijing (authored), Wang Bangwei (checked and annotated), *Buddhist Monks' Pilgrimage of the Tang Dynasty–Biography (with Annotation)*, Beijing: Zhonghua Book Company, September 1988, p. 102.

② Wang Luping, "A Discourse on Buddhism in Guizhou during the Tang Dynasty," *Guizhou Social Sciences*, 1998 (02), p. 49.

③ Wu Chao, "Misconceptions about the Study of the Southwest Silk Road," *Historical Research*, 1999 (01), pp. 43–44. Some researches refer to the Zangke Route as a land route as the monks from Guangzhou can travel westward from Sichuan after finished the first section of their westward trip from Guangzhou to Sichuan. The route might be too complicated and illogical if the monks first traveled westward to Sichuan and then traveled back to Guangzhou before made a sea voyage to India. However, it would no longer be a dilemma if the phrase of "Guangzhou monk" is understood as monks departing from Guangzhou.

Wang Dayuan in the Yuan Dynasty (1271–1368 CE) personally visited India and in his book *Foreign Islands and Countries* he depicted an "earthen pagoda"(Tu Ta) in South India. It is recorded that "the pagoda lies in a plain of Badan and is surrounded by woods and rocks, brick-made, several zhang (1 zhang is about 3.33 meters) in height. Chinese characters inscribed on it said, it was built in August of the 3rd year of Xianchun (1267 CE). Rumor has it that Chinese people came here that year and carved the words in the stone. Yet it is not eroded".[①] The word Badan shall be the homophonic transliteration of a Tamil word Pattinam, or Patam, a walled town. It is generally believed to be Nagapatam (presently Nagapattinam).[②] This indicates that by the end of the Southern Song Dynasty (1127–1279 CE), there used to be a large number of Chinese people living on the east coast of India. The site was preserved for nearly 600 years by locals and was even documented by subsequent westerners. In the 16th century, a Portuguese named Gasparo Balbi described "the Seven Pagodas of Cīna" he had seen at Nagapatam, which were built by ancient Chinese seafarers.[③] In 1615, Portuguese Jesuit Manuel Barradas recorded that the locals "believed (the pagoda) have been built by a (Chinese) Business Leader in India: the brick structure of this ownerless building, despite centuries of disrepair, still stood tall in good condition." Franqois Valentijn, an employee of the Dutch East India Company in the 18th century, called it "Pagood China (Chinese Pagoda)". In 1846, an Englishman called Walter Elliot made a detailed description and drawing of this pagoda (see Fig.18),

---

① Wang Dayuan(authored), Su Jiqing(checked and annotated), *Foreign Islands and Countries*, Zhonghua Book Company, May 1981, pp. 285–287. According to Su Jiqing, the book also mentioned Tu Zhu (Zhu means pearl), Tu Bu (Bu indicates cloth) and Tu Fen (Fen refers powder). The "Tu" in such phrases in fact indicates indigenousness (from China) like that in Tu Chan (indigenous product) instead of "earth." That is to say, the Tu Ta here in fact indicates "China pagoda" instead of "earth pagoda."

② Liu Yingsheng, *The Silk Road*, Jiangsu People's Publishing House, 1st edition, September 2014, p. 433.

③ Ji Xianlin, The history of Sino-Indian cultural exchange in *Ji Xianlin Complete Works (Volume 13)*, Foreign Language Teaching and Research Press, 2010, p. 471.

saying that it was about 30 meters high with three square stories and brick construction, which tightly fitted and ensured a snug fit without cement. The first and second stories are in the shape of cornices with a door or window in the middle of each side.[1] John Guy thought "as for the pagodas of this style, the direct prototype is the Chinese pagoda of the Song and Yuan Dynasties."[2] This edifice should be the brick pagoda mentioned by Henry Yuer in his notes on *the Travels of Marco Polo*, about a mile away in northwest of Nagapatam in South India, commonly known as "the Chinese Pagodaa".[3] The pagoda still survived in 1866 (see Fig.19)[4] but was demolished after August 1867. The purpose for building this pagoda is unknown, but in the concept note of "Project Mausam", India's Ministry of Culture points out that it has been a major navigation landmark in the 17th to 19th century.[5] This explanation is plausible, considering that the Portuguese Gasparo Balbi saw the pagoda while circling the island of Ceylon and that Manuel Barradas heard that it was built by a Chinese businessman.

Until Yuan and Ming Dynasties (1271–1644 CE), center of the Sino-Indian maritime exchanges seemed to be gradually shifted from the Coromandel Coast, southeast of India, to Malabar Coast of the southwest coast. When Yang Tingbi, a Guangdong official of Yuan Dynasty, was sent to India as an envoy, his destination was Malabar.[6] In the Ming Dynasty (1368–1644 CE), Zheng He's voyage fleets arrived in places like Kezhi (Kochi) and

---

[1] Walter Elliot, "The Edifice Formerly Known as the Chinese of Jaina Pagoda at Negapatam," *Indian Antiquary*, Vol. 7(1878), p. 64.

[2] Tansen Sen, "The Maritime Interaction Between China and India: The Rise of Chinese Naval Power along Indian Coast during the Song Dynasty to the Early Ming Dynasty," *Fudan Journal* (Social Sciences Edition), 2014 (02), p. 16.

[3] Wang Dayuan(authored), Su Jiqing(checked and annotated), *Foreign Islands and Countries*, Zhonghua Book Company, May 1981, p. 286.

[4] The authors hereby thank Sun Li, Liu Bingxue, both are Associate Research Librarian, National Library of China for assistance in locating Figures 18 and 19.

[5] Ministry of Culture, Government of India, Concept Note: Mausam/ Mawsim: Maritime Routes And Cultural Landscapes, p. 5.

[6] *The History of the Yuan Dynasty, Biography No. 97 (Volume 210).*

Guli (Khozikode) many times. *The History of the Ming Dynasty—Biography 214* said that Kochi had paid tribute in Song, Liang, Sui and Tang Dynasties. In the 9th year of Yongle (1411 CE), Kochi King sent an envoy to pay tribute, and asked for a title of his crown and the mountain in his kingdom. Zheng He started his fifth voyage in the winter of the 15th year of Yongle (1417 CE). This time, he was ordered to convey Emperor Yongle's Decree to Kochi and monumentalize the decree as well. The inscription reads, "The emperor now makes Keyili the King of Kochi, confers his rule on the people with the seal, and names the mountain of his kingdom the Country Guarding Mountain. The momentum is set up on it so as to demonstrate its infinite authorization."[①] For specific inscriptions, please refer to *Analects of the Ming Dynasty and History of the Ming Dynasty.*[②] The monument has not been found so far. However, the people of Kochi have long used a type of "Cheena vala" (Chinese fishing net, see Fig.20, Fig.21, Fig.22), which is generally believed to be closely related to trade with China in the 13th and 14th centuries. *The History of the Ming Dynasty* also described another important maritime town Khozikode on the Malabar Coast, also called the Great Country in Western Ocean. It embraces the sea in the west and from Kochi... it's only three days away by water and ten days away by land, traversing Mount Ceylon. Zheng He's fleet attached great importance to Khozikode and used it as a vital stopping point for his several voyages to the western seas. According to Ma Huan's *The Oversea Travel Stories*, Zheng He set up a stele in Khozikode with the inscription saying that "Being one hundred thousand li away from China, this is a country which shares similar customs, goods, and lifestyles with China. Today I set up a monument at this site so posterity may know it forever!" Unfortunately, this tablet has not been found, leaving enough room for imagination.

---

① Liu Yingsheng, *The Silk Road*, Jiangsu People's Publishing House, 1st edition, September 2014, p. 501.

② *The History of the Ming Dynasty, Biography No. 214.*

Conclusion

The following conclusions are made after a brief historical review of Sino-Indian maritime exchanges before modern times. Firstly, maritime exchanges between China and India started from ancient times and took various forms. Sino-Indian maritime exchanges began from prehistoric times. These routes have been established before the Common Era as indicated in documented records. After that, the maritime exchanges kept pace with the land exchanges for a long time and even surpassed the land exchanges in late Middle Ages. These Maritime communications were active in terms of economic, social, and cultural fields, covering personnel, material, and idea exchanges. This could be rightly defined as a landmark of civilization exchanges in the human history. Secondly, Sino-Indian maritime exchanges are of great and far-reaching significance. The exchanges promoted the communication between Chinese and Indian civilizations in the spiritual field and propelled the spread and development of Buddhism in eastern Asia, especially in coastal areas. In terms of economic field, it enhanced the material exchange across the western Pacific Ocean and eastern Indian Ocean in the whole eastern Asia as well as the exchanges of crops. The main ports of the two countries also prospered due to overseas trade (with each other in particular), thus laying a sound material foundation for the economic advantage of China's southeast coast over the north, as well as the long-term prosperity of several regimes in southern India. Some researchers believe the maritime trade is of great importance for China and India to take a long-time lead in the world economy in the mid-ancient times when they even accounted for nearly half of the world's GDP at one time. This indicates that the maritime exchanges between China and India is of great importance in bilateral, regional (Eastern Asia), and world economic landscape. Finally, it should be the common task for China and India to rejuvenate the maritime civilization and develop a harmonious ocean. Both China and India have profound maritime traditions. However, both countries have lost this ancient tradition in various degrees and have been reduced to semi-colonies and colonies since the advance of western colonialism to Asia and Oceans in early modern times. Both countries learned from the lesson when they lost their autonomy because of the loss of maritime rights. And both have the tradition of effectively utilizing maritime endowments for the benefit of their people. In the 21st century, China and India are committed to reviving their maritime traditions and developing themselves into sea powers. It should be the shared proposition for China, India, and other countries of the world to develop a harmonious ocean that serves the common interests of all peoples and effectively addresses common challenges. We are convinced that China and India, endowed with a impressive tradition of friendly exchanges through the sea, will join hands in this field and make effective contributions.

Attached Figures

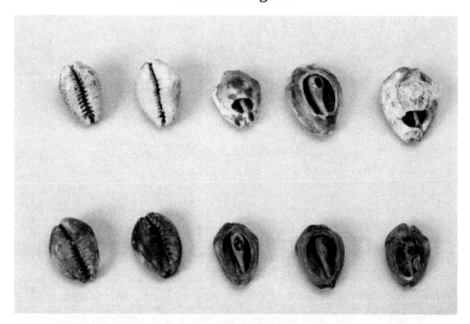

Fig.1 Sea shells excavated at Sanxingdui (more than 3,000 years ago, about 1.5 cm long, roughly divided into a black group and a white group, slightly ovoid, photo from the website of the Sanxingdui Museum)

Fig.2 Buddhist cliff statue at Kongwang Mountain (Lianyungang City, Jiangsu Province, photo from the Internet)

Fig.3 Buddhist cliff statue at Kongwang Mountain (Lianyungang City, Jiangsu Province, photo from the Internet)

Fig.4 Buddhist cliff statue at Kongwang Mountain (Lianyungang City, Jiangsu Province, photo from the Internet)

Fig.5 The excavation site of the Song Dynasty shipwreck at Houzhu Port in Quanzhou Bay in 1974 (Photo from an exhibition board in the Shipwreck Hall of Quanzhou Maritime Museum)

Fig.6 Restoration display of Song Dynasty shipwrecks in Quanzhou Bay (Shipwreck Hall of Quanzhou Maritime Museum, photo by author, June 19, 2016)

Fig.7 Spices and other goods on a Song Dynasty shipwreck in Quanzhou Bay (Photo from an exhibition board in the Shipwreck Hall of Quanzhou Maritime Museum)

Fig.8 Spices and other goods on a Song Dynasty shipwreck in Quanzhou Bay (Photo from an exhibition board in the Shipwreck Hall of Quanzhou Maritime Museum)

Fig.9 Spices on a Song Dynasty shipwreck in Quanzhou Bay (Shipwreck Hall of Quanzhou Maritime Museum, photo by the author, June 19, 2016)

Fig.10 Spices on a Song Dynasty shipwreck in Quanzhou Bay (Shipwreck Hall of Quanzhou

Maritime Museum, photo by the author, June 19, 2016)

Fig.11 Synagogue in Cochin (Photo by author, March 19, 2014)

Fig.12 The Chinese floor of the Cochin Synagogue (photography is not allowed inside the synagogue, photo from the Internet)

Fig.13 Main Hall of the Kaiyuan Temple in Quanzhou (Photo by author, June 19, 2016)

Fig.14 Hindu-style stone pillars on the back side of the Kaiyuan Temple in Quanzhou (Photo by author, June 19, 2016)

Fig.15 Hindu-style stone pillars on the back side of the Kaiyuan Temple in Quanzhou (Photo by author, June 19, 2016)

Fig.16 Hindu-style stone pillars on the back side of the Kaiyuan Temple in Quanzhou (Photo by author, June 19, 2016)

Fig.17 Statue of Vishnu unearthed in Quanzhou (Collection of Quanzhou Maritime Museum, photo by author, June 19, 2016)

Fig.18 The "Chinese Tower" at Nagapatam in 1846 [from the catalogue at the end of Indian
Antiquary Vol. 7 (1878), drawn (at the request of Walter Elliot) by an unknown draughtsman of
the Public Works Department of the Madras Administration of British India]

Fig.19 The "Chinese Tower" at Nagapatam in 1866 [from the catalogue at the end of Indian Antiquary Vol. 7 (1878), photo by Middleton Rayne]

Fig.20 "Chinese fishing nets" in Cochin (Photo by author, March 19, 2014)

Fig.21 Galle Trilingual Inscription Stone Slab of Zheng He (Colombo National Museum Collection, photo by the author, January 17, 2020)

Fig.22 Modern rubbing of the Galle Triling Inscription Stone Slab of Zheng He (The original is in
the Colombo National Museum in Sri Lanka. The modern rubbing is displayed in the Stele Gallery
of Nanjing Treasure Ship Shipyard Ruins Park, photo from the Internet)

Blue Economy in China: Present and Future

Liu Jiawei, translated by Zheng Zirou[①]

Abstract: In the context of China, the blue economy is not only inseparable from the marine economy, but also signifies the organic integration of the marine economy with sustainable development and circular development. This paper examines the current state, challenges, and future development prospects of China's blue economy from two perspectives: marine economic development, marine ecological environmental protection and circular economy development, respectively. As an essential component of China's modern economic system, the marine economy has experienced significant growth in recent decades. In addition to significantly increasing its investment in the marine economy, the Chinese government has also scientifically formulated the general principles and strategic objectives for the development of the marine economy. However, due to the objective environment and the limitations of people's perception of the marine economy, the rapid development of China's marine economy has simultaneously revealed a number of problems. China's marine ecological environmental protection and circular economy development have simultaneously evolved through environmental protection–marine ecological environmental protection–sustainable marine development–circular economy. China, as a large marine nation, will promote the scientific development of the blue economy in accordance with its own economic development and economic development

① Liu Jiawei is Executive Director and Associate Professor at the Center for South Asia–West China Development and Cooperation Studies, Institute of South Asian Studies, Sichuan University. His research interests cover Chinese economy and Indian economy, Indian domestic politics, Indian energy policy, and public diplomacy. Zheng Zirou studies International Relations (South Asian Studies) at the Institute of South Asian Studies at Sichuan University.

153

law, and contribute its own strength to the socioeconomic advancement of humanity.

Key Words: blue economy; marine economy; sustainable development; circular economy; China

Gunter Pauli, a Belgian economist and entrepreneur, is generally referred as a pioneer of "Blue Economy" as a concept and a business model. Since the publication of his book *The Blue Economy* (Chinese edition) in February 2012, the idea of "Blue Economy" has attracted extensive attention and discussion among Chinese scholars, businessmen and even within the government. Gunter Pauli believes that Blue Economy is an organic combination of the ecological and the economic systems with foci on natural resources, environmental protection and sustainable development. China accepted but redefined the "Blue Economy" concept to suit its specific national conditions and cultural traditions. Thus, the term in China is used as Gunter Pauli suggested in a broad sense, or is used to refer to the marine economy. Based on available studies of the conceptual framework of "Blue Economy" in China, this paper aims to highlight how Chinese are recognizing and applying the concept of Blue Economy in both theoretical and practical ways.

I. What Is Blue Economy?

The concept of Blue Economy is relatively new. In China, government or academic authorities have not yet reached a consensus of its definition as it basically has two meanings in a broad or narrow sense. As for the broad sense, *Management Dictionary* (Chinese Edition) by Shanghai Dictionary Publishing House defines Blue Economy as the circular economy characterized by resource-conserving and recycling utilization, an environment-friendly economic development pattern, which embeds the "resources–products– renewable resources" feedback into the economic activities and underlines low exploitation, high utilization and low emissions. In an interview, Gunter Pauli acknowledged the similarities between his Blue Economy Theory and circular economy. Meanwhile, the narrow sense of Blue Economy specifically refers to marine economy. It hereby encompasses the production activities conducted for marine resources or in marine space and relevant service-centered industrial activities conducted directly or indirectly for the exploitation of marine resources and the use of marine space. According to *Outline of the National Plan for Marine Economic Development*, a report released in May 2003 by the State Council (central government of China), the conceptions could be defined as the summarization of all kinds of marine industries exploiting and utilizing marine resources and relevant economic activities.[1]

Several factors attributes to such a two-layer definition of Blue Economy in China. First, the theoretical system of Blue Economy, especially its connotation and denotation, remains vague. As an interdisciplinary study, it requires understanding in economics, sociology, politics and natural sciences. When Gunter Pauli expounds his idea of Blue Economy based on his economic practice, it is in fact more focused on micro-economic level and thereby did not develop a theoretical system. Secondly, the blue economy as a more advanced economic development and management model, is in fact in line with the future reform orientation for China as it is trying to steer its economy to a more advanced stage. However, this job will have to be implemented in a gradual way with steps from parts to the whole and from elementary to advanced level, as it is almost impossible to completely alter the development mode for Chinese economy in a short time. Thirdly, against the backdrop of China's booming marine economy, the newly-introduced concept of "blue economy" and marine economy inextricably overlapped and interwove in the analyses of the government officials and scholars.

As a major maritime economy, China is endowed with enormous potentials for maritime economic development. In the new millennium, along

---

[1] The State Council, *Outline of the National Plan for Marine Economic Development*, May 9, 2003, http://www.gov.cn/gongbao/content/2003/content_62156.htm.

with the further improvement of comprehensive national power of China and the comprehensive development of its economy, an increasing importance has been attached to marine economy. The first edition of *Outline of the National Plan for Marine Economic Development* issued by the Chinese government in 2003 defined the development strategy and objectives of China's marine economy for the decade from 2001 to 2010. This has been regarded as the beginning of the rapid growth of maritime economy in China. In 2012, the 18th National Congress of the Communist Party of China specified the strategic goal and major task of "developing China into a major maritime power", highlighting an extension from land economy to maritime economy. Considering the great attention attached to maritime economy at that time, the introduction of blue economy concept is naturally regarded as a supplement, development and evolution of maritime economy by scholars and government. Ocean University of China, a top institution for the study of maritime issues in China, believes that blue economy is a socio-economic phenomenon occurring at a certain stage of the development of marine science and technology, marine economy and marine culture. It is an economic modal that put maritime economy at its core and characterized with mutual promotion, combination and coordination of land and sea economies.[①] It is worth mentioning that in January 2011, the State Council agreed to build in Shandong Province a blue economic zone, where maritime economy will be developed as pillar industry in order to ensure the comprehensive development covering social, economic, ecological, scientific and technological dimensions. This is similar with the maritime economy by definition.

It can be inferred from the discussion above that China's understanding and cognition of blue economy differ quite a lot from the definition of Gunter Pauli or any developed western countries. In China, the word "blue" is usually associated with concepts relevant with ocean. Blue economy, thereby, is intertwined with maritime economy. Moreover, it is deemed as an organic

---

①   The official website of Ocean University of China, http://www.ouc.edu.cn/lsjj/list.htm.

integration of maritime economy, sustainable development and circular development. In March 2016, Chinese government published *Outline of the 13ᵗʰ Five-Year Program for the National Economic and Social Development of the People's Republic of China*. Chapter 41 of this document, entitled as "Expand the Blue Economy Space", called for strong commitment to "coordinate land and sea, drive maritime economy development, scientifically exploit maritime resources, protect marine ecology and environment, safeguard marine rights and interests, and construct China as a sea power".[1] As a guideline for China's development from 2016 to 2020, it indicated two primary elements of blue economy: maritime economy and scientific exploitation of marine resources as well as the marine ecological and environmental protection. Therefore, such two elements are employed in this paper as two perspectives to help illustrate the current situation and future development of blue economy in China.

Ⅱ. Current Situation and Development of Maritime Economy in China

Since ancient times, China has been abundant in marine resources. From the perspective of natural resource, China's marine economy has great potential.

1. The Status Quo of Marine Economy in China[2]

According to the Department of Marine Strategic Planning and Economics of the Ministry of Natural Resources of the People's Republic of China, China's marine economy contributed about 8.3415 trillion RMB, accounting

---

[1]   The State Council, "Outline of the 13ᵗʰ Five-Year Program for the National Economic and Social Development of the People's Republic of China," March 17, 2016, http://www.gov.cn/xinwen/2016-03/17/content_5054992.htm.

[2]   The data in this part are from *Statistical Bulletin of China on Marine Economy 2018* released by the Ministry of Natural Resources of China, April 11, 2019, http://gi.mnr.gov.cn/201904/P020190411338141849830.doc.

for 9.3% to the nation's gross domestic product (GDP) in 2018. Marine gross domestic product (marine GDP) grew 6.7% from 2017 to 2018, close to the 6.6% GDP growth. The marine economy has generated 36.84 million jobs, with the primary industry generating nearly 364 billion yuan, the secondary industry 3.0858 trillion yuan, and the tertiary industry 4.8916 trillion yuan. Obviously, the service sector accounts for over half of the marine economy, contributing around 58.6% to marine GDP.

The Department stipulates that the marine GDP is a monetary measure of the market value of all the final marine goods and services produced in a specific time period by permanently residential units in coastal areas. It is the sum of marine industries and marine-related industries. In 2018, China's gross product of marine industries was 5.2965 trillion yuan while the marine-related industries reached 3.0449 trillion yuan. Coastal tourism, marine transportation and marine fishery are still the pillar industries of China's marine economy, with the respective output value of 1.6078 trillion yuan, 652.2 billion yuan and 480.1 billion yuan.

Marine GDP in 2018

	Total (hundred million yuan)	Growth rate (%)
Marine GDP	83415	6.7
I. Marine industry	52965	6.2
1. Major marine industry	33609	4.0
Coastal tourism	16078	8.3
Marine transportation	6522	5.5
Marine Fishery	4801	−0.2
Marine construction	1905	−3.8
Marine oil and gas	1477	3.3
Marine chemical industry	1119	3.1
Marine shipbuilding	997	−9.8

	Total (hundred million yuan)	Growth rate (%)
Marine bio-pharmaceuticals	413	9.6
Marine power generation	172	12.8
Marine minerals	71	0.5
Sea salt	39	−16.6
Seawater utilization	17	7.9
2. Marine research and education	19356	10.2
II. Marine-related industry	30449	—

Note: The data was collected from *the Statistical Bulletin of China on Marine Economy 2018*. When rounding the numbers, the total differs from the sum of all listed.

As can be seen in the table, emerging industries such as marine bio-pharmaceutical, marine power generation and seawater utilization are leading much of the growth. Traditional industries, including sea salt, marine shipbuilding, marine construction and so on, are declining despite their high output value. China's Marine economic structure is upgrading step by step.

2. Three Stages of Marine Economy Development in China

At the outset, marine economy came to the foreground in western countries in 1960s. In order to maintain rapid economic growth and tackle the foreseeable depletion of traditional natural resources, people turned to the resourceful oceans and embedded the marine economy into their national economy. In the late 1960s and early 70s, to provide essential theoretical foundation for the marine economic development, American scholars initiated the concept of marine economics, paving the way for its perfection and rapid development in the golden 70s. In the meantime, China was in its incipient shift to the reform and opening up policy, both marine exploitation and utilization were still at a relatively preliminary stage and the marine economic development remained unsystematic and fragmented. The last two decades of the last century witnessed the smooth implementation of the reform and opening up policy, which brought China into the scientific track of rapid economic development. With the continuous enhancement of the comprehensive national strength, China has been attaching more importance to the marine economy. In general, the development of China's marine economy can be roughly divided into three stages.

2.1. Startup phase (1949–2000). Since the establishment of the People's Republic of China in 1949, Chinese government has always incorporated the development and utilization of marine resources into its overall economic development plan. However, due to the inadequacy of overall economic strength and insufficient theoretical understanding of the issue and slow progress in science and technology, the development and utilization of the ocean remained at the primary stage, confined to traditional fields such as fishery, mining industry and transportation for a long time. Overall planning for the development of marine economy was neglected. After adopting the reform and opening up policy, China determined to attach greater importance to the ocean. In 1998 (International Ocean Year as defined by the UN), the White Book on *The Development of China's Marine Undertakings* was issued by the Information Office of the State Council (Central Government of China). It illustrates the developing progress of China's marine career and proclaims the ocean as one of the paramount themes. Despite that, the lack of scientific knowledge and systematic planning hindered the development of marine economy, which toddled and stayed immature.

2.2. Expansion phase (2001–2010). During this decade, great progress has been made. On the one hand, marine economy was formally designated as a national plan. In May 2003, the State Council issued *Outline of the National Plan For Marine Economic Development*, which clearly states the great significance of marine economic development in promoting the economic layout and industrial restructuring in coastal areas, as well as keeping national economic growth sustainable, healthy and rapid. Based on the principle of developing marine economy, the general objective for Chinese marine economy was first proposed as the following:"For marine economy, we shall further raise its proportion in the national economy, optimize its structure and industrial layout. We need to rely more on marine science and technology utilization in order to accelerate the development of marine pillar industries and emerging industries and further strengthen the international competitiveness of marine industries. We need to significantly improve the quality of marine ecology and environment as well. We shall build marine economic regions with their own characteristics, make marine economy a new growth pole, and gradually develop China into a strong marine country."[1] On the other hand, marine GDP was shooting up. *The Outline* stipulates the increase target in certain numbers:"to gradually make marine industry one of the pillar industries in China's domestic economy, the proportion of marine industrial increase in GDP should stand at around 4% in 2005 and over 5% in 2010." Actually, China's marine economic development has far exceeded these targets. Marine GDP recorded a year-on-year increase of 13%, rising from 951.9 billion yuan to 3.8439 trillion yuan during 2001–2010. In 2010, it surpassed China's overall increase rate of 10.7% in the same period. In 2010, the marine GDP accounted for 9.7 percent of China's GDP. Third, industrial distribution was promoted and marine economy achieved orderly development. By 2010, China's marine economy has formed a relatively complete industrial system. With a declining portion of primary industry, a more reasonable structure of tertiary industry–secondary industry–primary industry began to take shape, and China's marine economy started to achieve high and steady growth.

2.3. Scientific development phase (2011–2020). At this stage, the Chinese government and scholars were gaining new insights of the marine economy and get more conversant with the concepts of sustainable development and circular development. First of all, the development of marine economy has

---

[1] The State Council, "Outline of the National Plan for Marine Economic Development," May 9, 2003, http://www.gov.cn/gongbao/content/2003/content_62156.htm.

been further upgraded from a national plan to a major national strategy. According to the Report to the 18th National Congress of the Communist Party of China in 2012, it was proposed that China should improve its ability to exploit marine resources, develop the marine economy and protect the marine ecology and environment, resolutely safeguarding China's maritime rights and interests and building China into a strong marine player.[1] In September, the State Council issued *The 12th Five-year Plan for the Development of China's Marine Economy*. Based on the comprehensive analysis of the development trend of China's marine economy, this document put forward the main marine economic development aiming for the next five years. In March 2016, the State Council issued *the Outline of the 13th Five-Year Program for National Economic and Social Development of the People's Republic of China*, which brought forward the concept of "blue economic space" and confirmed the marine economic development strategy during the 13th Five-year Plan period. In 2017, in the report to the 19th National Congress of the Communist Party of China, the indication on accelerating the development of a strong marine country and formally incorporating the marine economy into China's modern economic system was involved in the section on "Developing a Modern Economic System".

Second, the marine industrial structure has been more integrated and the development of marine economy has been more reasonable. China dismissed the idea of "speed first" and gradually lowered and smoothened the marine GDP increase. Government and enterprises have invested huge in the marine ecological and environmental protection, with technological innovation in marine industry strikingly advancing. As ecological conservation, sustainable development and circular economy played a more and more significant role in driving marine economy, the high-tech industries and the sustainable-

---

[1]   Hu Jintao, *Firmly March on the Path of Socialism with Chinese Characteristics and Strive to Complete the Building of a Moderately Prosperous Society in All Respects*, Beijing, People's Publishing House, 2013, p. 17.

development industries grew rapidly and have been more and more important for the marine economy.

3. Major Problems

For the past decades, marine economy has achieved great progress as one of the key components of China's modern economic system. While Chinese government has greatly increase its input in marine economy, the major principle and strategic targets were designed in a scientific way. However, due to the objective environment and limitation of people's understanding of marine economy, four major problems have occurred as the marine economy was rapidly developed.

3.1. Marine economy does not offer enough support for the overall economic development. As planned, marine economy has been expected to act as a pillar industry for China's economy and to play an important role in its modernized economic system. However, compared with the 15% to 20% contribution of marine GDP to the whole in developed countries, China's marine GDP only accounted for 9.3% of the GDP in 2018. Obviously, there is still a long way to go to realize the initial strategic goal.

3.2. Traditional industries has been dominating the marine industry. The emerging industries like marine bio-pharmaceutical industry, power generation, seawater utilization, etc. witnessed a rapid growth, but accounted for a relatively low percentage of the total revenue compared with traditional industries. The whole marine economy deeply relies on traditional industries such as coastal tourism, marine transportation, marine fishery, etc., which would be a huge burden for the structural adjustment and upgrading of China's marine economy in the future.

3.3 Marine ecology and environment are under great pressure. Chinese government has long prioritized environmental protection at the same level of the development of marine economy. However, due to the problems of technical capacity, operation guidelines, etc., marine economy development is still operating in a poor-quality way. Some local authorities failed to implement the environmental-friendly policies made by the central government and upheld the idea of "speed first". Besides, the negative effects of predatory exploitation in the past decades can't be eliminated in a short term. That is to say, China's marine environmental protection, especially that of the paralic areas, is still under great pressure and will remain so for a certain period.

3.4. The understanding of marine economy remained un-comprehensive. With greater attention being paid to marine economy within China, governments at all levels and both public and private enterprises now have regarded marine economy as a priority for the future. Financial investments and the input of material resources have been increasing in recent years. Nonetheless, coastal or offshore areas are in the spotlight, but there is not much attention to pelagic areas, the deep sea and ocean development design, which will be key areas for global marine economic development. The resultant flop could range from hindering concept innovation to impede the progress of building a world-class marine economy.

III. Marine Ecological and Environmental Protection and Circular Economy in China

1. A Brief History

In general, the evolution of China's understanding of Marine ecological and environmental protection and circular economy can be roughly divided into four stages, comprising environmental protection, marine ecological and environmental protection, sustainable marine development, and circular economy. Since the founding of the People's Republic of China, environmental protection had been one of the foci of the government. However, due to objective problems such as underdeveloped economy, imperfect system, and cognitive limitations, China's environmental protection, including the marine ecological and environmental protection, for a long time had been devoid of systematic and scientific approach. Till 1989, the 11th session of the standing committee of the 7th National People's Congress passed the first Environmental Protection Law of the People's Republic of China. In the Law, the ocean was regarded as an important part of the environment, and in the following years, marine ecological and environmental protection gradually evolved into a complete and independent concept and was reflected in the process of China's policy formulation and implementation. In 1996, the State Oceanic Administration of China published the China Ocean Agenda 21, further perfecting the concept of marine ecological and environmental protection. For the first time, it's an official work that listed the protection idea into the sustainable marine development targets. In 1998, The State Council Information Office issued a white paper entitled *the Development of China's Marine Programs*, of which six chapters are "Sustainable Development Strategy of Marine Programs", "Reasonable Development and Utilization of Marine Resources", "Marine Environmental Conservation and Preservation", "Development of Marine Science, Technology and Education", "Implementation of Comprehensive Marine Management" and "International Cooperation of Ocean Affairs".[1] It elaborated the position, attitude and specific measures of China on the marine ecological and environmental protection and sustainable development in a more systematical way.

With the rapid development of marine economy in China in recent years, the concepts of marine ecological and environmental protection and sustainable development have been incorporated into the scientific framework of marine economy with greater attention. In 2000, *The Law on the Protection of Marine Environment of the People's Republic of China* was formally promulgated and put into effect, beginning to provide an independent judicial guarantee for marine ecological and environmental protection. In 2003, *The Outline of the National Plan for Marine Economic Development* clearly

---

① The State Council Information Office, "The Development of China's Marine Programs," September 10, 2000, http://www.scio.gov.cn/zfbps/ndhf/1998/Document/307963/307963.htm.

stated that, upholding the guiding principles for the development of marine economy, "we should prioritize the protection of resources and environment while developing economy and ensure the sustainable development of marine economy. We should strengthen the protection and improvement of marine ecology and environment, coordinate the scale and speed of marine economic development with the bearing capacity of resources and environment, and take the road of sustainable development characterized by the coordination of industrial modernization and ecology and environment."[1] Protection of marine ecology and environment and resources has been added to the development goals of marine economy as well. In the same year, the Ministry of Ecology and Environment began to publish the annual Bulletin on the Environmental Quality of China's Coastal Waters. It is worth mentioning that in 2018, the communique was officially renamed *Bulletin of Marine Ecology and Environment Status of China*. Since then, marine ecological and environmental protection and sustainable development began to frequently appear in all of China's important marine policies and plans.

In 2012, the blue economy concept was introduced to China and circular economy was written in the ocean-related policy document for the first time. In September 2012, circular economic development was mentioned in *The 12ᵗʰ Five-year Plan for Marine Economic Development* issued by the State Council. In terms of the basic principle, the Plan aimed to "comprehensively consider the marine ecological and environmental protection and terrestrial pollution prevention and control, vigorously develop marine circular economy, enhance effectiveness of marine resources use, stride toward an energy-saving and low-emission marine industry and promote clean production, and reinforce marine ecological and environmental protection and disaster prevention and mitigation. The Plan called for continuously strengthen the sustainable

---

[1] The State Council, "Outline of the National Plan for Marine Economic Development," May 9, 2003, http://www.gov.cn/gongbao/content/2003/content_62156.htm.

development capacity of marine economy".[1] In Chapter Eight, "Developing a Green Marine Economy", it further expounds how to develop the circular economy, including "advocate marine enterprises' investment in marine resources recycling technology research, development and application, and guide the industrial parks and enterprises to carry out demonstrating projects in marine circular economy. Focusing on mariculture, seawater utilization, marine salt industry and salt chemical industry, the state shall explore and build a circular industrial system in coastal areas, actively improve information consultation and technology promotion services, give support to sea-related enterprises in participating in international exchanges and cooperation, and import advanced technologies and models of circular economy".[2] In *The 13th Five-year Plan for Marine Economic Development* (2016–2020), circular economy is mentioned again.

From the stage above we could see that on the one hand, the concept of circular economy has been embedded in China's economic development strategy and evolves and develops over time. On the other hand, based on China's basic national conditions and cognitive habits, the circular economy is now still classified into marine field and has become an important component of China's marine economy.

2. The Present and the Future

Since the implementation of *The Law on the Protection of Marine Environment*, China has been pursuing marine ecological and environmental protection via a large amount of human and material resources input for the past more than 10 years. With the most advanced technologies and scientific concepts around the world, exalting achievements have been made. According to *The Bulletin of Marine Ecology and Environment Status of China in 2018*,

---

[1] The State Council, "The 12th Five-year Plan for the Marine Economic Development," September 16, 2012, http://www.gov.cn/xxgk/pub/govpublic/mrlm/201301/t20130117_65866.html.

[2] Ibid.

China's Marine ecology and environment was stable with good momentum, the water environment quality was improved, the sea area of first category accounted for 96.3% of the total, the ratio of high-quality offshore water was 74.6%, the health condition of the typical marine ecosystem and lives in the marine conservations remained basically stable, the environmental quality of the marine dumping areas and oil and gas exploitation areas generally conformed to the protection requirements of marine functional areas, and the overall water quality for fishery was good.[1]

In China, the whole responsibility for marine ecological and environmental protection lays on the Ministry of Ecology and Environment, while specific responsibilities are assumed by local governments and local ecological and environmental departments. In addition to deployment and guidance, in order to effectively fulfil the protection task, the Ministry of Ecology and Environment has set up "a central monitoring group for ecological and environmental protection" to go straight to the front line to supervise and promote the smooth progress of environment-related protection work. To empower the ecological and environmental departments in protecting the marine ecology and environment, the Standing Committee of the National People's Congress sets up law-enforcement inspection teams to do fieldwork, supervising and inspecting the implementation of *the Law on the Protection of Marine Environment of the People's Republic of China* from time to time. At a higher level, the central government established the National Inter-ministerial Conference on Marine Economic Development to coordinate the marine economy development, marine ecological and environmental protection and circular economy.

For now and in the future, "Give Priority to Ecology and Green Development" will always be the basic principle for China in the protection

---

[1] The Ministry of Ecology and Environment, "The Bulletin of Marine Ecology and Environment Status of China in 2018," May 2019, http://hys.mee.gov.cn/dtxx/201905/P020190529532197736567.pdf.

of marine ecology and environment and the development of circular economy, which means that both development and protection should be paid equal attention to, intensive and economical utilization of marine resources should be improved, source control of the marine environmental pollution should be enhanced, and the ecology and environment should be effectively protected.[①] It will be the mainstream of future development to conserve and utilize marine resources and promote low-carbon development of marine industry. Chief measures are listed as follows.

Upgradation of traditional marine industries. China needs to promote the transformation and upgradation of fisheries, oil and gas, shipping, transportation, and marine salt and chemical industries related to sea, introduce greener and safer production technologies, strictly control the intensity of opening-up, and strengthen the protection and restoration of environments that were affected by industries.

The rapid development of emerging marine industries should be promoted. For doing so, investment in marine pharmaceuticals and biological products, seawater utilization and renewable energy need to be increased; resource conservation and regeneration need to be emphasized; an organic synergy of emerging industries with the circular economy model need to be encouraged.

The protection and restoration of marine eco-systems should be enhanced. Compulsory protection and strict control need to be practiced; red line system for marine ecological protection shall be established; supervision system and conducting regular supervision shall be guaranteed. At the same time, ecological restoration and biodiversity conservation shall be carried out in major regions.

The Chinese government is also enhancing marine research on climate change, strengthening marine disaster monitoring, risk assessment and disaster

---

① National Development and Reform Commission, State Oceanic Administration "The 13th Five-year Plan for Marine Economic Development," May 2017, http://images.mofcom. gov.cn/www/201709/20170907170048332.pdf.

prevention and mitigation capabilities, improving strategic precautions of marine disaster relief and promoting marine emergency response capabilities.

To sum up, blue economy is an inevitable mode of economic development in the future. However, the timing and measures to promote the development of blue economy are intimately relevant to the conditions of any particular country. China will promote the development of blue economy in accordance with its own development stage and the objective law of economic development, and thereby contribute its own strength to the social and economic progress of mankind.

Impact of Climate Change on Maritime Security: China and India

Zou Zhengxin, translated by Zou Zhengxin[①]

Abstract: Climate change and its subsequent effects represent a significant threat to China and India's maritime security and growth. This study contends that, in terms of maritime economic security, the changes in ocean hydrographic components produced by climate change and the resultant secondary disasters represent significant threats to the safety of SLOC(Sea Lanes of Communications), marine fisheries, and marine resource development. As to maritime sovereignty security, under the combined influence of sea level rise, changes in marine meteorological, hydrological, and atmospheric conditions, and extreme weather, some islands and reefs beyond the continental shelf of the two countries are facing submergence or contraction, which also affects coastal and island military arming and places greater demands on maritime military operations. In terms of maritime public security, large-scale migration caused by climate change, the prevention and mitigation of maritime disasters, and pollution prevention and control have brought new challenges. In terms of maritime geo-security, the alterations in maritime geography brought by climate change would heighten the game of great powers, resulting in a more complex maritime competition between China and India. As two largest developing countries, in the process of transitioning from a large maritime power to a strong maritime power, China and India must address the relationship between maritime security and development and take

---

① Zou Zhengxin, PhD in Department of Political Science, University of Delhi, India. Director Assistant, Center for South Asia–West China Cooperation and Development Studies, Institute of South Asian Studies, Sichuan University. His research focus on Indian Ocean security, Indian politics and China–India relations.

joint actions to effectively respond to the deteriorating maritime environment in the context of climate change.

Key Words: climate change; China–India maritime security; climate migration; SLOC

As one of the most important environmental issues for humanity, climate change constitutes a serious challenge to maritime security, social/economic development, living conditions of mankind and ecosystem. However, the secondary problems caused by climate change proved to be major impediment for the development of sea power in both countries. In this context, it will be of important practical and strategic significance to analyse from ocean perspective an effective response to climate change and its impact on maritime security and development for both China and India. Research in this regard remains insufficient while the exploration to the relations between climate change and maritime security remains incomprehensive. This article tries to explore the impact of ocean climate change on China and India's maritime economic security, maritime sovereignty security, maritime public security and maritime geo-security on Pacific Ocean and the Indian Ocean. It also made an exploration of countermeasures.

The ocean and the entire atmosphere are interconnected systems with constant energy inter-exchanges. From 1971 to 2010, ocean has absorbed 93% of all excess heat stored by air, sea water, land, and melting ice. Therefore, the climate change has a significant impact on the ocean. The Technical Summary of The First Global Integrated Marine Assessment released by the United Nations in 2017 indicates that ocean changes relevant to climate change are mainly manifested in: ocean warming, sea level rise, ocean acidification, sea salinity augmentation, ocean stratification, ocean circulation transformation, storms, frequent extreme weather events, and de-oxygenation.[1]

The ocean is of practical significance to both China and India in light of economic interests, national security, and even the pursuit of great power status. Both countries have realized the disadvantage of climate change to the marine ecosystem as well as the negative impact on their respective pursuit of sea power. In recent years, the two countries have actively participated in multilateral discussions on global climate change. In 2015, China and India introduced a Joint Statement on Climate Change, acknowledging that climate change and its adverse effects is a common concern for mankind and one of the greatest global challenges for the 21st century, and thereby needs effective countermeasures through international cooperation under sustainable frameworks like *United Nations Framework Convention on Climate Change (UNFCCC)* and its *Kyoto Protocol*. Both countries agreed to work together with other parties to advance the multilateral negotiations to achieve a comprehensive, balanced, equitable and effective agreement under the UNFCCC in 2015, ensuring the full, effective and sustained implementation of the UNFCCC.[2] The two countries are active participants and contributors to climate change governance with fruitful cooperation at the government level and multilateral levels. However, it should be noted that with the maritime interests extension and sea power evolution of both, the adverse effects of climate change to ocean will consistently challenge the maritime security of the two countries and thereby deserves greatest attention.

---

[1] UN, "The Technical Summary of The First Global Integrated Marine Assessment— The Impacts of Climate Change and Related Changes in the Atmosphere on the Oceans," 2017, https://www.uncclearn.org/sites/default/files/inventory/1705753-c-impacts-of-climate-change_print-body.pdf, pp. 3–6.

[2] The State Council, the People's Republic of China, "Joint Statement on Climate Change between India and China," May 15, 2015, http://www.gov.cn/xinwen/2015-05/15/content_2862749.htm?gs_ws=tsina_635675440362130507.

I. The Impact of Climate Change on the Maritime Economic Security of China and India

Ocean has become an important foundation for the economic development of littorals, thanks to its vastness, convenience and resource abundance. Both China and India are big littoral countries with great importance attached to coastal areas and development of the "blue economy". However, the marine climate and hydrological change as a consequence of climate change as well as other secondary disasters are posing new challenges to socio-economic development of littoral areas and to the safety of sea lines of communication (SLOC), marine fisheries, and marine resource exploitation.

1. Impediment to the Economic Development of Coastal Areas

In the context of global climate change, the overlap of multiple natural disasters has caused extremely complex impacts on coastal areas. The rising sea level can result into higher tide levels, erosion of coastal lowlands and islands, and weakened protective capacity of coastal embankments. Storm surges may cause drastic tide-surge in coastal area, an destroy of seawalls. Rise of sea-level and insufficiency in fresh water have resulted in pollution of fresh water in coastal areas and salinization of farmland in addition to saline water intrusion in estuary region. This might damage the ecological balance and make it more difficult for pollution discharge control. Most of the economically-developed cities of both China and India are located in coastal areas.[1] They can be immediate victims of climate change.

India has a coastline of about 7,500 km along with 12 major ports and over 200 minor ports. The ports and its surrounding coastal communities are cornerstone for India economic development. However, many Indian ports

---

[1] Li Xin, Zhang Ren, Li Qian, et al., "The Effect Evaluation of the Climate Change on the National Maritime Strategy," *Defense Technology Review*, 2012(03), p. 53.

have the relatively backward infrastructure, and thereby are highly vulnerable to secondary disasters caused by climate change. For example, the consistent rise of sea level can change the shape of the land-based sediment near the coast, resulting in insufficient water depth in the harbor basin and channel which will affect the port's throughput. The movement of sediment may cause siltation or even abandonment of available transnational channels. This might increase transportation costs. The coastal community development in India's "Sagar Mala Project"[1] has a reference to fishery, fish product processing, value-added product development, coastal agriculture, handicrafts, small businesses and marine leisure tourism among other integrated development. All of the above industries rely heavily on a favourable maritime environment. However, the rising sea level has compressed the living room for people in coastal communities while the backflow of acidified and saline seawater has polluted the seashore and inland rivers, resulting in serious salinization of farmland and a sharply decline in agricultural output. The changes of acidification, salinity, stratification and circulation of seawater have led to a shortage of fishery resources and the risk of fish products safety. In addition, the frequent occurrence of extreme weather has also led to the slowdown of the development of marine tourism and associated facilities.

Due to its dense population and eco-environmental fragility, the coastal areas of China are sensitive to the impact of climate change. *Blue Book on Climate Change and Its Impact on Ocean in China 2019* indicated that from 1980 to 2018, sea surface temperature in China's coastal areas increased by an average of 0.23 Celsius degree every 10 years, coastal sea levels increased by an average of 3.3 millimeters per year, and coastal EHWL (extreme high water levels) increased by an average of 4.5 millimeters per year, the coastal

---

[1] Ministry of Shipping, Government of India, "Concept Note on Sagar Mala Project: Working Paper," October 28, 2014.

temperature rised by an average of 0.37 Celsius degree every 10 years.[1] Moreover, the above changes are increasing year by year, and the increment in recent years has reached a record high level. Five major megalopolis areas stretch over the coastline of China, constituting major locomotives for the economic development and foreign trade of China. However, climate change has posed a serious threat to the functioning of megalopolis areas and the safety of residents' lives and properties. For example, Tianjin, Shanghai, Guangzhou and other cities are facing very big risks of flooding and submerge of its lowlands due to the combined effects of sea level rise, storm surge, typhoon, and heavy rain; the Yangtze River, Pearl River and Yellow River are encountered with the danger of seawater intrusion and water pollution due to sea level rise during dry seasons; the storm surge, typhoon, and sea level rise will also cause severe erosion of coasts and deltas; the sea level rise will lead to abandonment of ports and watercourses to reduce transportation capacity.

2. Challenge to the Security of Maritime Energy Channels

Maritime energy channels mainly refer to sea line of communication, strait waterways and cargo ports. The changes of the marine environment caused by climate change is threatening the navigation of cargo ships and the safety of key hub waterways, further exacerbating the transportation risks of traditional energy channels for China and India. Maritime transportation is of central significance for foreign trade due to geographical location of the two rising economies. The neighboring Pacific and Indian Oceans are important international transportation routes, and the Strait of Malacca and the Strait of Hormuz are strategically located at the key hub to connect the oceans. However, sea level rise has changed the width, depth, and distribution of reefs and submerged reefs in the channel. Changes in marine meteorological and

---

[1]　Academy of Ocean of China, "The Ministry of Natural Resources released *Blue Book on Climate Change and Its Impact on Ocean in China 2019*," October 1, 2019, http://aoc.ouc.edu.cn/2019/1001/c9828a270601/pagem.psp.

hydrological attributes have caused frequent occurrences of extreme weather such as storms and typhoons, while changes in sea temperature and salinity have increased ocean stratification and disordered circulation mechanism. All of such might reduce the safety of navigation.

Piracy is another serious security challenge to SLOC. As an important transportation route and strategic channel, the Indian Ocean carries 90% of the world's cargo trade and 60% of the oil transportation. More than half of China's exports to the Middle East, Africa and Europe, and 80% of its oil imports need to pass through the Indian Ocean.[1] The Indian Ocean is relevant to the security of India's maritime transport as well as its maritime sovereignty security, since India is located in the centre of the region. The strategically significant Strait of Malacca and the Gulf of Aden at the east and west ends of the Indian Ocean are high-risk areas of piracy, where pirates earned economic benefits by armed robbery of merchant ships passing-by. The emergence of piracy is the result of a set of comprehensive factors with climate change as a major one. Global warming and reduced precipitation have led to inadequate food and water supply in some areas. Natural disasters such as tropical cyclones and floods, as well as the depletion of offshore fishery resources and marine pollution, have caused coastal residents to fall into extreme poverty and thereby encouraged preference to piracy as a method for livelihood. The continuous deterioration of the living environment may lead to more serious piracy and maritime terrorism, bringing about major challenges to the safety of maritime transportation.

3. Threats to the Security of Marine Fisheries and Marine Resources Exploitation

Marine fishery is an indispensable element of the marine economy. Both China and India have a heavy dependence on seafood, as the seafood output

---

① Xu Ke, "The Threat of Maritime Piracy in the Indian Ocean and China's Indian Ocean Strategy," *South Asian Studies*, 2011(01), pp. 2–9.

is relevant to the food supply and food security of both countries. However, global ocean currents, water salinity and acidity changes as caused by climate change have seriously threatened the security of marine fishery resources. The rising sea temperature and the irregular alteration of global ocean currents have caused large-scale migration or extinction of fish. Fishing grounds are encountered with resource depletion. This is harmful to domestic aquatic economy and nutrition balance of citizens. At the same time, it will make fishing grounds crowded and a large number of fishermen under the pressure of unemployment and economic burden. Changes in the salinity and acidity of water bodies, as well as marine pollution directly lead to pollution of fish, which finally cause food safety issues and additional economic costs. In addition, the depletion of marine fishery resources will also cause the rupture and closure of the capital chain of fishing companies. Resource disputes among littoral countries might be aggravated. Contradictions among economy, resources and marine ecosystems are becoming increasingly prominent. This is a common challenge for the world as well as both China and India.

The exploitation of marine resources is a linked process that includes resource exploration, extraction, processing and transportation. Both China and India attach importance to marine scientific research and oil & gas exploration. The two countries have deployed a large number of offshore drilling platforms in their respective seas to provide the necessary momentum for national economic development. However, under the background of global climate change, offshore exploration, mining and transportation are bound to face huge risks. For example, sea level rise directly threatens the safety of offshore drilling platforms and personnel; meteorological and hydrological changes of seawater salinity, acidity, and ocean currents need robust marine scientific research so as to reassess the exploitability of marine resources. The increase of extreme weather such as offshore storms and typhoons will be a serious test for the stability of offshore drilling platforms. Higher technical requirements are needed in this regard. All of the above will definitely increase the technical difficulty in the investigation and exploitation of marine resources and increase the economic cost. China and India have a relatively successful experience of cooperation in scientific research of the Indian Ocean. However, as the adverse effects of climate change become increasingly prominent, it may restrict the scope and profundity of maritime economic cooperation for the two countries, and thereby bring about a negative affect on the development of the maritime economy of both China and India.

II. The Impact of Climate Change on Maritime Sovereignty Security of China and India

Climate change and its negative effects constitute a challenge to the sovereignty security of maritime powers. Under the combined influence of sea level rise, changes in marine meteorological and hydrological conditions, as well as extreme weather, islands and reefs outside the continental shelf of China and India are likely to be submerged or contracted. This might increase the risk of sovereignty disputes over some islands and reefs. Climate change has also deteriorated the marine ecosystem, affecting the military defense of coasts and islands, and putting higher demands on maritime military operations.

1. Rising Sea Level will Inundate Islands and Reefs and Increase the Risk of Sovereignty Disputes

The continuous rise of sea level will reduce mainland coastline, while certain islands might be submerged or reduced into reefs. The territorial waters, contiguous zones, and exclusive economic zones of China and India as demarcated in accordance with the United Nations Convention on the Law of the Sea, will undergo major changes. The islands of extreme low-altitude of the two countries will be submerged by seawater. For islands generating territorial waters, contiguous zones, exclusive economic zones and continental shelves, they will lose a large part of sea areas under jurisdiction once the islands are completely submerged. Lower-altitude islands or coastal highlands

179

might be partially submerged and thereby be more vulnerable to events related to extreme sea level rise. It will result into great damage to the population, resources and facilities of these islands and even survival conditions. Jurisdiction over large exclusive economic zones and continental shelves will be lost.[①]

More than 6,700 islands play an important role for the economic development, national defense as well as political & diplomatic efforts of China. It is relevance to China's maritime jurisdiction as well. The continuing rise of sea level may submerge islands in South China Sea. Some islands will permanently disappear while others might shrink day by day. It is not only relevant to China's maritime sovereignty, but also relevant to the conflicts among sovereign claimants. For example, disputes over island sovereignty and economic interests between China and Vietnam have a long history. The reduction or disappearance of some islands will inevitably increase the maritime friction between the two countries and make the current maritime situation more complicated.

Another example is the sovereignty dispute between India and Bangladesh over the New Moore Island (referred as South Talpatti by the Bangladesh). New Moore Island is located in the Bay of Bengal covering an area of about 10.5 square kilometers. For nearly 30 years, India and Bangladesh have argued over the control of this tiny rock island because of its abundance in oil and gas resources. However, the island was submerged in 2010 as a consequence of the impact of global warming and rising sea levels. The demarcation of the maritime boundary—and who controls the remaining islands—remains an open issue between the two South Asian neighbors, despite the disappearance of New Moore, said an official from India's Ministry of External Affairs. Both countries claimed sovereignty over the island and disputed over the exclusive

---

① Li Xin, Zhang Ren, Li Qian, et al., "The Effect Evaluation of the Climate Change on the National Maritime Strategy," *Defense Technology Review*, 2012(03), p. 54.

economic zone (with rich oil and gas resources) over this island.[1]

2. Rising Sea Levels and More Frequent Extreme Weather will Affect the Military Deployment on Coastal Areas and Islands

Sea level rise and extreme weather caused by climate change will affect military deployment of the coastal areas and islands. A prominent example is that in October 2014, Vishakhapatnam, a city accommodating the headquarter of Indian Navy Eastern Command, was hit by hurricane Hudhud. Severe damage to the entire city in general as well as the naval base's airport and other military facilities in particular was made.[2] Both China and India have large number of coastal ports. Superior geographical location and hydrological conditions have made the ports centers for international trade and logistics as well as ideal spots for naval stationing, ship construction, berthing and maintenance. However, rising sea levels and extreme weather will lead to changes in coastline and thus loss of ideal berthing bases. The coastline moving to the mainland have changed the depth of the water and the shape of the bottom sediment. The changes in seawater flow, salinity and acidity have presented new challenges to the berthing of warships, and therefore the military strategic deployment had to be adjusted including the redeployment or transfer of personnel and military facilities. In addition, Changes in meteorological and hydrological conditions also require corresponding adjustments in naval combat parameters.

Rising sea levels and increasing extreme weather will also threaten the military deployment and defence over islands and reefs, especially when these islands are used as important defense bases. It will bring about a direct

---

① "Island claimed by India and Bangladesh sinks below waves," *The Guardian*, March 24, 2010, https://www.theguardian.com/world/cif-green/2010/mar/24/india-bangla-desh-sea-levels.

② "Vizag first Indian city directly hit by cyclone Hudhud," *The Times of India*, October 18, 2014, https://timesofindia.indiatimes.com/city/visakhapatnam/Vizag-first-Indian-city-directly-hit-by-cyclone-Hudhud/articleshow/44864271.cms.

impact on military installations and the surroundings in terms of relocation of personnel, changes over naval deployment for battle, and impairment on maritime defense. This will cripple maritime sovereignty in a indirect way.[1] Islands and reefs can work as important strategic bases as is illustrated by the case of US military bases overseas. The US naval base in Guam and overseas enclaves in fact constitute a "bridgehead" and "outpost" for military operations. They have been used for preemptive strike in overseas operations and maintenance of strategic advantages over neighboring regions. Located in eastern Indian Ocean, between the Bay of Bengal and Myanmar Sea and north of the Ten Degree Channel, the Andaman Islands, as a guard for the Strait of Malacca and the Indian Ocean, is of great strategic significance to India. Indian former navy commodore Anil Jai Singh pointed out that about 120,000 ships pass through the Indian Ocean each year and nearly 70,000 of them pass through the Malacca Strait. He added that "if we have to really monitor China's movements, we need to be adequately equipped in the Andaman islands."[2] However, in the context of global climate change, environmental changes on these islands will inevitably lead to the adjustment of national maritime strategies and increase the cost of military defense spending on islands and reefs.

3. Climate Change Will Raise the Requirements for Maritime Military Operations

The global geostrategic center has further shifted to the Western Pacific and Indian Ocean regions. Ocean-centered military preparedness constitutes a major element of international politics. However, climate change and its adverse effects is making higher requirement on maritime military operations.

---

① Li Xin, Zhang Ren, Li Qian, et al., "The Effect Evaluation of the Climate Change on the National Maritime Strategy," *Defense Technology Review*, 2012(03), p. 54.

② "Indian Navy Opens Third Andaman Islands Air Base to Monitor China's Movements," Guan Cha, January 24, 2019, https://www.guancha.cn/military-affairs/2019_01_24_488080.shtml.

Some experts pointed out that global melting of snow and ice may cause changes in seawater density, thereby reducing the density of seawater in northern latitudes. In warmer low-latitude regions where strong evaporation and increased seawater density prevails, changed seawater salinity may cause changes in the buoyancy of submarines and the performance of underwater weapons.[1] The change of sea water density may change the underwater acoustic characteristics with an adverse affect on sonar performance. A recent study concluded that by the middle of this century, future carbon dioxide emissions from fossil fuels might lead to increased acidification and a significant decrease in low-frequency sound absorption.[2] In addition, seawater operations may be affected by constantly changing thermoclines, there might be major transformation in the flow patterns of hot and cold water. In fact, the Indian Ocean current may be easily affected by the change of ocean monsoon patterns.

Future extreme weather occurrences could impede the deployment of navy surface combatants. Inclement weather can affect the physical and emotional health of a ship's military crew. In warmer climes, for instance, surface temperatures on aircraft carrier decks can reach high levels, which can inflict a major burden on deck employees' usual duties. High temperatures can also have detrimental effects on ships that operate with a high frequency. Diverse ranges of bad weather also place obstacles for crews and sailors' underwater training. Lastly, climate change may have a negative impact on the performance of shipboard combat systems, particularly certain weapons with a high degree of precision. All of these negative consequences of climate change on military personnel and ships will increase the difficulty of naval military operations. With the continued implementation of India's Indian Ocean strategy

---

① National Development Council, "National Security Implications of Climate Change for U.S. Naval Forces," Washington DC: National Academies Press, 2011, pp. 107–108.

② Hester, Keith C., Edward T. Peltzer, William J. Kirkwood and Peter G. Brewer, "Unanticipated Consequences of Ocean Acidification: A Noisier Ocean at Lower pH", *Geophysical Research Letters*, Vol. 35, 2008.

and the strengthening of China's strategic position in the Indian Ocean, India and China must consider the influence of climate change and other variables on their maritime security while negotiating their security ties.

III. The Impact of Climate Change on Maritime Public Security of China and India

Public security is an integral constituent of maritime security. Climate change and the resultant large-scale migration can be a major challenge to national security and marine public security of China and India. In addition, marine disaster prevention & mitigation and marine pollution control are crucial for marine public security.

1. Climate Migration

Climate change will trigger large-scale population migration in the Indian Ocean region. Studies indicate that desertification in littoral countries like those on Africa and South Asia may trigger a vicious circle of environmental degradation, migration and conflict. In April, 2019, the United Nations High Commissioner for Refugees (UNHCR) released data showing that the number of people displaced by climate change-related disasters since 2010 has risen to 21.5 million. And Australian think tank Institute of Economic and Peace (IEP) predicts that at least 1.2 billion people could be displaced by such climate-related events by 2050.[1] In Indian Ocean region, South Asian countries may be more vulnerable. Climate migration also challenges the governance capacity of weak countries. It is conceivable that if the people of the island countries in Indian Ocean and Pacific Ocean migrate to the mainland on a large scale to escape the deteriorating environment, extreme weather, political turmoil and

---

[1] Tetsuji Ida, "Climate refugees—the world's forgotten victims," Economic Forum, June 18, 2021, https://www.weforum.org/agenda/2021/06/climate-refugees-the-world-s-forgotten-victims/.

military conflicts, littoral countries like China and India are undoubtedly their best choice. In this case, on the one hand, it will increase the risk of conflicts in coastal communities and destroy the original economic and ecological balance in coastal areas; on the other hand, it will require the state to increase the deployment of coastal and offshore defense forces to prevent the influx of large-scale climate refugees and deal with possible conflicts. All these will increase the pressure on public security at sea and coastal areas.

Available researches indicate that the Indian Ocean is warming in a faster speed than that in other tropical seas. It is constituting a "warm pool" and changing the intensity of the southwest monsoon. In the future, abnormal weather and extreme events will be more frequent.[1] It can be expected that extreme weather and rising sea levels will inevitably put island residents into disease and famine, while the acidification and seawater pollution will damage farmland and freshwater systems to an extent that they may finally disaggregate the living environment. Residents of some island countries such as Tuvalu, Maldives, Seychelles, Nauru and Samoa are suffering the risk of homeless one day as they are gradually losing their land territory due to the continuous rise of global sea levels. In the 1990s, Tuvalu has lost 1% territory due to rising sea levels. The extreme high tide in February 2000 almost engulfed the whole Tuvalu. During each high tide, about 30% of Tuvalu's land has been submerged by sea water. In 2001, Tuvalu announced that all its efforts had failed. The country would disappear from the world map after 50 years. The country's 11,000 citizens would have to abandon their homes and move to New Zealand with which the country signed an agreement.[2] As emerging regional powers, both China and India have a responsibility for regional maritime security. In fact, climate migration and the resultant public security

---

[1]　Roxy, M.K., Ritika Kapoor, Terray Pascal and Masson Sabastien, "The Curious Case of Indian Ocean Warming," *Journal of Climate,* 27(22), pp. 8501–8509.

[2]　Wang Hui, Li Tingting, "New Challenges of Maritime Security in the Context of Climate Change," *Journal of Zhejiang Ocean University* (Humanities Science), June 6, 2014, Vol. 31 No. 3, p. 4.

issues would be major test for the governance capabilities and sense of international responsibilities of rising powers such as China and India.

2. Maritime Disaster Prevention and Mitigation

The economic prosperity in Indian and Pacific Oceans has led to an increase in maritime activities in the region. Activities ranging from the development of marine resources to the sea and air transportation of goods and people are conducive to the smooth flow of goods around the world, but they at the same time also increase the personnel safety risks caused by maritime and aviation accidents. The Malaysia Airlines flight MH-370 in 2014 and South Korea's Sewol ferry disaster are vivid examples that help illustrate the relevance of maritime disaster prevention and mitigation to the safety of marine personnel and facilities as well as regional marine public security. In the future, marine public security like disaster prevention and mitigation will become more urgent, due to increasingly harsh maritime climate, rising sea levels and evolution of the regional security situation.

In the context of global climate change, the general performance of maritime disaster prevention and mitigation is far from satisfactory. It is estimated that the urban population exposed to the risk of tropical cyclones will increase from 310 million to 680 million before 2050. By 2070, urban assets exposed to rising sea levels and flooding will reach 35 trillion US dollars, which is ten times the current level. The economic losses caused by earthquakes, tsunamis, hurricanes and floods will severely affect key sectors such as infrastructure, energy, agriculture, environment, water resources, health and education.[1] For China and India, the two countries have long coastlines with large number of economically developed cities and large populations. Coastal communities are also important supports for the future development

---

① UN News, "International Day for Disaster Reduction: Special Representative of the Secretary-General Robert Glasser highlights the close relationship between natural disasters and climate change and the achievement of sustainable development goals," October 12, 2017, https://news.un.org/zh/audio/2017/10/1001341.

of the two countries. Affected by rising sea levels, seawater meteorological and hydrological factors, and increasingly frequent extreme weather caused by climate change, the construction of coastal and maritime disaster prevention facilities, water resources protection, and marine ecosystem developments in both countries are encountered with challenges. The two countries have a relatively successful experience of cooperation in maritime disaster prevention and mitigation. Through bilateral visits, meetings, joint researches and military exercises, both countries have strengthened the cooperation in marine disaster prevention and mitigation, marine scientific research, marine environmental protection, and polar scientific research.[1] Whether it is maritime-related agreements, scientific research surveys or naval exercises, the main themes are about maritime disaster prevention and mitigation, which indicates that the two countries have recognized the importance of the ocean to their respective strategies, and they also realized that marine problems are beyond the control of one country alone so that cooperation is the most effective way to resolve issues.

International cooperation is a desirable way to solve problems considering the globality of climate change and the borderless nature of the ocean. Despite certain competition between the two countries, China and India have huge potential for maritime cooperation, especially in the Indian Ocean, driven by shared interests in dealing with common challenges. China and India have been coordinating their policies and naval operations since 2008, including through the Contact Group on Piracy off the Coast of Somalia (CGPCS) to carry out escort missions in the Gulf of Aden-Somali. High-level military officials of the two countries have held dialogues on joint combat against piracy on many occasions. Cooperation plans and implementation rules have been drafted. In recent years, the two countries have coordinated their positions on bilateral

---

[1] State Oceanic Administration, "Deputy Director Chen Lianzeng led a delegation to visit India," April 23, 2015, http://www.soa.gov.cn/xw/hyyw_90/201504/t20150423_37103.html.

and multilateral occasions to seek joint actions such as joint anti-piracy escort, maritime disaster prevention and mitigation as well as maritime rescue.[1] Under the circumstance of climate change, the two countries will have more opportunities for cooperation in maritime field. The anti-piracy platform is a useful exploration for maintaining marine public security. The information sharing and cooperative actions established during the said cooperation provide convenience for maritime disaster prevention and mitigation in which both navies play a major role. At the same time, we must also be aware that climate change and its secondary problems hinder the smooth development of maritime disaster prevention and mitigation, and further aggravate the inherently fragile security environment at sea.

IV. The Impact of Climate Change on Maritime Geo-security of China and India

Maritime security is a major objective for major maritime powers. The opening of the new Arctic waterway will reshape the current world economic structure. It will bring about a serious impact on the Asia-Pacific countries and other lowland countries. The maritime interaction between China and India is manifested as a complex relationship of both competition and cooperation. Changes in the marine geographic environment will bring about transformation of the maritime relationship between the two countries.

1. Arctic Waterway

Historically, there were two Arctic routes connecting the Pacific and Atlantic. One is the famous "Northwest Passage" across a wide range of islands in western Canada; the other is the "North Sea Passage" along the northern coastline of Asia. Due to ice meltdown in Arctic region as a consequence of

---

[1]   Xin Hua, "International Escort Seminar held in Nanjing on Feb. 23," February 23, 2012, http://news.xinhuanet.com/mil/2012-02/23/c_111560746.htm.

global warming, it is estimated that the "Northwest Passage" will be navigable for at least one month in summer within 10 years. After another 15 years, the "Northwest Passage" will be available for several months each year. It will be navigable whole-of-the-year by 2080 at the earliest.[①] Once the Arctic Ocean become fully navigable, it will have a profound impact on world geopolitics and change the existing global power structure. It will become the fastest route between North America, Northern Europe and Northeast Asian countries as it could shorten to a great extent the voyage distance. Under such circumstances, whoever controls the Arctic Ocean will have much say over the new corridor of the world economy.

Although China and India lie far away, the opening of the Arctic waterway has an impact on the maritime security of both countries because of its far-reaching significance in changing the world geopolitics. India tries to expand its participation in Arctic affairs by taking a number of measures such as expanding Arctic research, seeking observer-ship in the Arctic Council, strengthening energy cooperation with Arctic countries and active Arctic diplomacy. The white paper titled "China's Arctic Policy" indicates that as a responsible major power, China is willing to work with all relevant parties to seize the historic opportunities of Arctic development and actively respond, in line with the basic principles of "respect, cooperation, mutual benefit, and sustainability," to the challenges brought about by changes in the Arctic. By learning, protecting, using and participating in the governance of Arctic, China aims to actively advocate Arctic cooperation associated with the "Belt and Road" initiative and actively promote the development of a community with shared future for mankind. In such a way, it will contribute to the peace, stability and sustainable development of the Arctic. China and India's attention to the Arctic will, to a certain extent, lead to the adjustment

---

① Wang Hui, Li Tingting, "New Challenges of Maritime Security in the Context of Climate Change," *Journal of Zhejiang Ocean University* (Humanities Science), June 6, 2014, Vol. 31 No. 3, p. 2.

of the maritime security strategy of both countries. Future competition of the two countries may not only be limited to the region covering west Pacific and India ocean, but also extend to the Arctic region in terms of energy and economic development. It might further complicate the Indo-China relationship concerning maritime security.

2. China–India Maritime Interaction

Both China and India attach great importance to the development of the concept on sea power and maritime capabilities. The increasing maritime power of the two countries has obvious intersections. The rise of the two countries has a huge impact on the regional (even global) maritime space in general and manifests a more competitive relation in Indian Ocean region in particular. In the context of climate change, the possibility of competition on a broader and deeper level cannot be ruled out. This will undoubtedly pose a new challenge to the geographic security of the two countries. Climate change has exacerbated the fragility of the marine environment, which may make it difficult to deepen the original bilateral cooperation and eradicate the original foundation for cooperation. For example, in terms of maintaining the safety of sea lines of communication, both China and India might lose much influence if climate change leads to international routes moving away from two countries. This will reduce the depth and breadth of the two countries' participation in maritime affairs.

However, climate change can be a new dimension for China–India maritime security cooperation. At present, the two countries mostly put their own national security in the first place and regard each other as competitors from the perspective of realist international politics. As the marine environment is deteriorating, the two rising powers are bound to explore possible ways of cooperation to deal with climate issues. A prominent example is the competition and cooperation between the two countries in the Arctic. The impact of climate change on strategic channel of the Arctic is more serious, while the strategic game among major players in this region has been intensified. As major maritime powers, China and India naturally set their sights on this region. This is the inevitable development as a result of the two countries' maritime strategies and is also closely relevant to the evolution of the international political environment. China and India are still making their own strategy over sea lanes of communication. In comparison, China's vision is mainly based on marine scientific research combined with other methods, while India's interest appeals are much more obvious and immediate. At the same time, both countries have expressed their willingness to cooperate and made active efforts. Therefore, from the perspective of geo-security, climate change may have both positive and negative effects. China and India should proceed from the overall situation to maintain a fair and just ocean order and safeguard their legitimate ocean areas. The two countries can work together to make a response to the increasingly severe maritime security environment in the context of climate change.

Conclusion

As major security challenges for mankind, the interplay of Climate change and maritime security has worsened the living conditions of mankind. Climate change has dampened the economic development of coastal areas, as it has impeded the safety of maritime communication lines and the development of marine resources. Rising sea levels and changes in marine meteorological and hydrological conditions have increased the risk of disputes over island sovereignty on the one hand, and complicated the military defense of coastal/ islands / reefs and maritime military operations on another hand. Climate change has generated many public security issues such as climate migration, maritime disasters, and marine pollution. In terms of maritime geo-security, climate change may shift the global geopolitical center and thereby trigger maritime competition and worsen certain maritime security issues among major powers.

In light of the severe climate challenge and its relevance to maritime affairs, it is a great urgency for all countries to take active measures and joint actions. As the two major developing countries in Indian ocean and Pacific ocean region, China and India need to balance the relations between maritime security and development so as to upgrade themselves from major maritime players to maritime powers. They need to take joint actions to deal with the deteriorating marine ecological environment in the context of climate change. Specifically, the two countries should take actions in terms of legislation, education and scientific research, industrial cooperation, and international exchanges in this regard. Both governments need to introduce legislation to formulate maritime development plans and action plans in order to ensure the implementation of policies. China and India need to enhance scientific research on marine hydrology and meteorology so as to establish a seawater detection and analysis platform in order to provide reference for policy formulation. Both countries need to enhance cooperation in marine-related industries and encourage the participation of people for a joint effort for security of the marine ecological environment. New models of international cooperation need to be explored while maritime cooperation systems and mechanisms need to be optimized. All in all, in terms of effective response to climate change and maritime security threats, both China and India should play a leading role in safeguarding maritime security and development interests and developing a green, harmonious and sustainable marine ecological security environment.

Book Review

Exploring Effective Approaches for Sino-Indian Cooperation

Zeng Xiangyu, translated by Wang Qing and Liu Shichai[①]

The summed-up population of China and India (2.746 billion) is equivalent to 36.16% of the world population (7.593 billion). The combined territory of China and India (12.58 million square kilometers) takes 28.22 percent of Asia, 22.97 percent of Eurasia, or 8.44 percent of the world land area. The combined GDP of the two countries reaches 16.327 trillion dollars in 2018, equivalent to 19.00% of the world total (US $85.931 trillion). One can easily conclude from the above that both China and India are major developing countries while the relations between them is of great significance to the interests of the two countries, the stability of Asia and even the peace and development of the world.

Research on the Interactive Mechanism of Win-Win Development between China and India, edited by Prof. Yang Wenwu, a senior research fellow at the Institute of South Asia Studies at Sichuan University, is an important effort for exploration of the win-win development involving China and India. This book offered some very useful inspirations in terms of both theory and practice.

I. China–India Cooperation via Institutional Development

Over the years, researchers have fully discussed the need for China–India cooperation to achieve win-win development, but the potential of

---

① The author is associate research fellow at the Institute of South Asian Studies at Sichuan University. Wang Qing and Liu Shichai study International Relations (South Asian Studies) at the Institute of South Asian Studies at Sichuan University. Wang focuses on India–Vietnam relations research and Liu's main research is on the development of India's satellite.

such evolution has not been fully exploited. Sino-Indian disagreements and even frictions have surfaced from time to time. Ups and downs seem to be a regularity of China–India relation. Since 2020 India has introduced a series of measures to restrict Chinese investment in India. The two countries were involved with the most grave stand off in western section of LoC after the Docklam incident. Remove China Apps targeted against Chinese mobile apps emerged in Indian market in 2020. During outbreak of the COVID-19, some Indian institutions and think tanks made provocative remarks and measures against China. This was very regrettable in 2020, the 70th anniversary of the establishment of diplomatic relations between China and India. This also prompted us to reflect on the reasons for and solutions to the slow progress of the win-win cooperation between China and India.

To this question, the book gives its own answer from the perspective of international regimes. Drawing some essence from the neo-liberalism theory in international relations, this book advocates ensuring the stabilization, normalization and comprehensiveness of China–India cooperation from system or mechanism development. It made comprehensive suggestions for the development of a win-win interactive "quaternity" comprising political, economic, security and cultural exchanges in order to make full use of the leading role of the political trust, economic benefit, security stability and cultural mutual learning, so as to develop the China-India win-win cooperation to a higher level. The author does not simply regard mechanism as omnipotent, as he objectively points out that China–India interactive institution is in a "low-intensity cooperative institution based on interest generalization"stage at present. It is in a transformation to a "moderate cooperative institution based on development of system". However, it is anyhow far away from a "deep cooperative institution based on value solidification". This is in fact a pragmatic and realistic conclusion.

II. Need to Develop Engagement between Political Parties

Prof. Yang's book presents a panoramic view of the engagement mechanism for the win-win development involving China and India from four aspects comprising political, economic, security and cultural exchanges. The discussion offers much details. For example, 5 tables in chapter 3 list information on communication between heads of state and heads of government (1949–2018), the international or regional multilateral organizations which both China and India enjoy membership, information on sister provinces/cities involving the two countries (excluding information involving Hong Kong, Macao and Taiwan of China), engagements between the National People's Congress of China (NPC) and the Indian Parliament, as well as the information of exchanges between top echelon of the Communist Party of China and the Indian National Congress. This informative discussion will be helpful for further discussion.

However, as an observer, I am more interested in some non-existents rather than established institutions. For example, the third chapter (contributed by Wang Juanjuan) makes a comprehensive sum-up of the interaction mechanism between China and India at the political level from the three aspects of government communication, parliamentary/NPC diplomacy and party diplomacy. Her opinions on parliamentary/NPC diplomacy and party diplomacy are quite innovative. She points out by comparison that China has more inter-party contacts with left-wing parties represented by the Communist Party of India, the Communist Party of India (Marxist), and traditional national parties represented by the Indian National Congress. However, the Chinese side has not established a robust communication institution with the Bharatiya Janata Party (BJP), which is the current ruling party, and the local political parties. In fact, in terms of the number of party members, the Bharatiya Janata Party has become the largest political party in the world. In terms of its ruling status, the Bharatiya Janata Party has been in charge of the central government for 3 times in May 1996 for 13 days, March 1998–May 2004, and from May 2014 till today. Importantly, BJP at present is the ruling party in 19 Indian states and territories (in addition, the so-called "Arunachal Pradesh" in eastern section of the China–India disputing area is also under its ruling). Uttar Pradesh, among them, has a population of more than 230 million, surpassing most countries. What's more, the Hindu nationalism as represented by the Bharatiya Janata Party and its parent organization Rashtriya Swayamsevak Sangh (RSS, or National Volunteer Service) has become a social and political decisive force for India. Obviously, development of party diplomacy towards the Bharatiya Janata Party is in fact an urgent need. That is also the case for local political parties in India. As a federation, the ruling party in central government may not be in charge of local authorities. In fact, India has powerful regional parties in West Bengal, Maharashtra, Telangana, Tamil Nadu, Bihar, Odisha, Uttar Pradesh and other places. Such places are ruled by regional parties or coalitions of regional parties and national parties. Inter-party contacts with regional parties will help broaden the contacts between Chinese and Indian parties and help implementation of all cooperation programs. Needless to say, this work deserves more attention from both sides.

III. Developing a Health Exchange Mechanism

Chapter 6 (authored by Yang Wenwu and Sun Shalan) of this book offers another interesting example. In addition to a comprehensive discussion of China–India exchange mechanisms on science, technology, education and culture, this chapter highlights the noteworthy void of an effective cooperative mechanism for public health between the two countries. In fact, this absence is not only detrimental to inter-state relations between China and India, but also against people's livelihood and public security in both countries. Thanks to its advantage in generic drugs, India has established a competitive pharmaceutical industry. Even if it is difficult for China to import generics from India on a large scale as a result of patent reasons, entrepreneurs from the two countries can still share experience with each other and exchange what they need. Considering the fact that China is moderately encouraging the production of some generic drugs and the globalization of the generic drug industry, it is more necessary for Chinese producers to communicate with Indian counterparts. Medical tourism to India has become a major element of Indian tourism, as some well-known private medical organizations in India can offer health care services with high standards and reasonable cost. Compared with more than half a million medical tourists to India every year, only a few Chinese people visit India for medical tourism. Obviously, cooperation in this field enjoys great potential with direct benefit to the two peoples and related industries. In contrast to some of the leading private medical institutions mentioned above, a large number of public medical institutions in India are underinvested, underfunded, understaffed and suffer from insufficient medicine. This in fact constitute a big risk for public health in India. The contacts and cooperation between China and India in health sector and reasonable learning from some effective practices of China and other countries will certainly help to improve public health in India. During the COVID-19 pandemic, the negative effects of these gaps are proved to be grave. Needless to say, it should be a major task for policymakers in both countries to timely fill this gap.

IV. Improving the Micro-dynamics of Cooperation

Senior leaders of the two countries has attached great importance to the win-win cooperation between China and India and come up with many plans and projects. Despite numerous interaction mechanisms, China–India exchanges can hardly be termed as a close engagement with strong momentum. One of the reasons is what is called "micro-dynamic insufficiency" in this book. It means that despite promotion from the top level, companies, industry associations and entrepreneurs are absent during the practical implementation, resulting in insufficient impetus for effective communication and cooperation.

Therefore, the authors of this book propose to develop a multi-level and multi-subject interactive mechanism which focuses on encouraging the participation of local governments and enterprises, civil organizations, non-governmental organizations and even families and other economic entities, and to strengthen the operability of some micro-mechanisms so as to avoid a situation of "mechanism without progress".

Emphasis of micro-dynamics is not to diminish the importance of the macro-dynamics, but to solidify the weak points. Looking forward, the mechanism and system of interaction for win-win development between China and India must be a synergy of top-level design and effective implementation in grass-root level. Only in this way can win-win development between China and India become a reality.

Understanding *Arthashastra*, A Book of Governance in Ancient India

Gao Gang & Nan Ping, translated by Zeng Weiwei[①]

Arthashastra is an ancient Indian treatise on statecraft, economic policy and military strategy and a representative work of classical realism in India. Kauṭilya, generally referred as the author of *Athashastra*, was regarded as a famous politician and strategist in Indian, as he is believed to be an important adviser and the first prime minister for Chandragupta, the founding emperor of Maurya Dynasty. He has been often referred as "Machiavelli of India" by later generations because of his strong preference to political realism, as was reflected by detailed discussion of governance, foreign policy and hegemony in *Arthashastra*. This masterpiece in fact touched upon a number of disciplines such as political theory, political system, law, economy, diplomacy and military affairs. In recent years, the research on *Arthashastra* and Kauṭilya's thoughts has received increasing attention as researchers have been trying to reach a better understanding of India with the help of understanding its diplomatic traditions and strategic cultures.

It is under this backdrop that the recent publication of a book *Arthashastra: Conceptualizing Its Thought on International Politics*, co-authored by Zeng Xiangyu, Associate Research Fellow at the Institute of South Asia Studies at Sichuan University, and Wei Chuxiong, Professor at Beijing Normal University-Hong Kong Baptist University Joint International College,

---

① Gao Gang is an assistant professor at the Institute of South Asian Studies, Sichuan University, mainly engaged in research on Indian diplomacy and security, India–Sri Lanka relations, The Politics and India's strategic culture. Nan Ping, a researcher of South Asian affairs based on Sichuan. Zeng Weiwei studies International Relations (South Asian Studies) at the Institute of South Asian Studies at Sichuan University, mainly on the research separatism and nationalism in Northwest India.

deserves a further attention and discussion. This is the first Chinese academic monograph that systematically introduces the international political thought of *Arthashastra* to Chinese audience and offers a comprehensive study in this regard. For researchers on strategic culture and classical diplomatic thoughts of India, this book may constitute a valuable reference.

I. Academic Contributions

Arthashastra: Conceptualizing Its Thought on International Politics has made a number of academic contributions in a step-by-step way. First, it elaborates on the basic research situation of *Arthashastra*, so that beginners can have a quick and tentative understanding of the work. The authors discuss in a systematic way about available researches at home and abroad in recent years, which provides important reference materials for domestic researchers in related fields. The authors' summarization of the "existing research approaches" in the first chapter can be a valuable reference and guidance for further research by domestic scholars. Secondly, this book makes an in-depth analysis of *Arthashastra*'s discussion on international politics, such as "Seven Elements of the State", "Mandala International System", "Six Foreign Policies", "Espionage" and "War and Military Thoughts". This part can help readers to have instant location of the content that they have an interest in and thereby have a systematic command of the international political thoughts in *Arthashastra*. The third is to make a horizontal comparative study of *Arthashastra* and the western realism international relations theories by further deepening the theoretical aspect after a preliminary introduction. For students majoring in international relations but unfamiliar with traditional political thoughts of India, this book will help them develop a more accurate understanding of the international political thoughts of *Arthashastra*. The fourth is to analyze and explore the relationship between the thought of *Arthashastra* and India's diplomatic practice, focusing on the influence of "Mandala" thought on India's history and contemporary India's diplomatic practice.

It is especially worth mentioning here that *Arthashastra*: *Conceptualizing Its Thought on International Politics* advocates a "holistic view" in its research methods: it advocates a comprehensive investigation and evaluation of various or even contradictory views in the original work. As a matter of fact, the original work of *Arthashastra* is full of numerous and self-conflicting contents. Kauṭilya often listed various viewpoints and refuted them one by one before drawing out his own points. It is not easy to grasp the whole picture of *Arthashastra*'s thoughts as beginners in many cases might be confused with a conceptual ocean in Arthashastra. They are likely to focus only on some elements of the original work, and interpret some core terms in a rigid way or deviate from their true meaning in the original work. This tendency is not uncommon in interpreting the works of *Arthashastra* from the perspective of international relations. In light of this, "integrity" as a research method is of big significance.

II. Inspiration for Future Research Directions

In the conclusion part, this book points out the difficulties and future research directions in the research of *Arthashastra*. The authors discuss several possible directions. Firstly, there is an urgent need for a reliable and detailed Chinese translation of *Arthashastra* at home to lay a foundation for in-depth research. The second is to strengthen the comprehensive and interdisciplinary study of *Arthashastra*. The third is to expand the scope of research on India's traditional international political thoughts, involving various epics, dharma shastras, puranas and other political works in addition to *Arthashastra*. The fourth is to strengthen the comparative study between the thought of "political affairs" and India's history and current diplomatic practice. All such possible directions are of great value for the in-depth study of *Arthashastra* in China.

In addition to the above-mentioned aspects, another possible research apporach is to compare *Arthashastra* with the treatises of politics in ancient

China. In fact, strategic treatises in classical period around the world often share robust similarities. Here is a brief example. *Arthashastra* put forward the seven elements of a state (Prakrti) comprising monarch (swami), ministers (amatya), land and residents (janapada), fortresses (durga), wealth (kosa), army (danda) and allies (mitra). For these elements, we can compare the similar analysis of Jia Yi (200–169 BCE), a political commentator in the Western Han Dynasty (202 BCE–8 CE), in *Treatise on the Fault of Qin*. Jia Yi's analysis of the development of Qin's national power during the period of Shang Yang (390–338 BCE) Reform is as follows: (Qin Xiaogong, the ruler of Qin) "occupies the terrain guarded by Mount Xiao and Hangu, and owns the entire Yongzhou area. The Qin was firmly guarded by monarchs and ministers, coveting for the power of the Zhou regime. He has the intention to unify the world and annex all countries. At that time, he, assisted by Shang Yang, established a domestic legal system, devoted himself to farming and textiles, building defensive and offensive weapons, and carrying out continuous tactics to make rulers of other states fight each other. Finally the Qin people effortlessly acquired a large area of land west of the Yellow River." This involves many factors such as forts, lands, monarchs, ministers, strategic intentions, legal systems, economy, armaments, diplomacy and so on, which coincides with Kauṭilya's idea of seven elements of the state.

Of course, there have been some exploratory studies in this regard in the West and India. However, the available researches are generally speaking hardly satisfactory as they are mostly based on English translation of ancient Chinese works. In comparison, Chinese scholars may have more advantages in terms of language and cultural understanding. Moreover, thanks to a systematical analysis of international political thoughts in pre-Qin classic works, Chinese scholars have produced a number of high-quality academic works and a large number of journal articles in the past decade. This provide an important support for the comparative study of international political thoughts in Chinese and Indian classical canon works. More importantly, the research approaches used by such studies can provide important reference for the research of *Arthashastra* as well. (1) To interpret the traditional international political thoughts such as those in *Arthashastra* in accordance with the framework of contemporary international relations, and thereby distinguish the research on "Political Affairs Theory" in international relations from the research of Indology (especially Sanskrit research), history, intellectual history and philosophy. (2) To systematize and theorize the international political thoughts in *Arthashastra*. (3) To compare India's traditional international political thoughts with the contemporary western international relations theories to seek the similarities and differences between them. (4) To link India's traditional international political thoughts with the contemporary diplomatic practice of India and national security concept, while seeking its explanatory applicability and vitality in today's world (Wang Rihua's "Research Program and Theoretical Concepualization of Pre-Qin Political Thoughts," Contemporary Asia Pacific, No. 2, 2010). These research approaches have in fact been partly applied in Arthashastra: *Conceptualizing Its Thought on International Politics*.

III. Inadequacies

Understandably, due to the wide range of themes and numerous and jumbled contents of the original work, as the first academic monograph specializing in the study of *Arthashastra* in China, this book inevitably appears complicated. Readers who are new to this field may find it difficult to have a quick understanding. The writing can also be furthur refined to help the readers to have a better reading experience. This is to an extent understandable as the available translation and interpretation of the core terms in the original work are generally inconsistent in the existing researches at home and abroad. The objective reason is that the original work of *Arthashastra* was written in Sanskrit, and different versions appeared when translating it into English. Most of the academic research on *Arthashastra* in China is based on English translation, as there is no complete Chinese translation of *Arthashastra* published until December 2020. Therefore, there are various Chinese translated terminology and different explanations for the core terms. These complicated, different, archaic and abstruse terms often confuse beginners. This may be the reason why this book devotes a large amount of space to the specific terminology and background knowledge.

In addition, one of the research objectives set by the book is to "compare the international political thoughts in *Arthashastra* with the western international relations theories and explore a new approach of international relations theory". However, in the actual operation, the authors mostly make a horizontal comparison between the thoughts in *Arthashastra* and the realism of the western international relations theories from seven aspects such as "pessimism on international security", "political view of power" and "moral apathy". The book seems to incline to interpret *Arthashastra* from the perspective of western international relations theories. There are still some defects in theoretical exploration.

Finally, when analyzing the influence of *Arthashastra* on contemporary Indian diplomacy, the book encountered a bottleneck that may also be a headache for every researcher. That is how to determine the real influence of Kauṭilya's thought on Indian diplomacy, how much the influence is and how it influences the diplomacy. Generally speaking, most of the existing researches emphasize that Kauṭilya's thought do have an impact on India's diplomatic practice and security concept. They even directly use Kauṭilya's thought to interpret the current diplomatic behavior of India. In this regard, the book mainly takes examples to demonstrate the influence of the *Arthashastra* thought by listing the evaluation of Kauṭilya by important Indian leaders, the mandala-like concept in India's foreign policy, and some of India's diplomatic practices that conform to the thought. In my opinion, however, this analysis method has a shortcoming of insufficiency in empirical verifiability and theoretical persuasiveness. In fact, many viewpoints in *Arthashastra* are in good agreement with available western realism theories of international relations. Therefore, when the influence of Kauṭilya's thought on India's foreign policy is evaluated, there must be a problem of distinguishing one from another: whether some Indian foreign policies are influenced by western realism or by Kauṭilya's thought or both. All of them are worthy of further discussion.

Conclusion

Both China and India are rising populations as well as economic powerhouse in Asia. A benign interaction between China and India is very important to the peaceful development of the two countries. However, due to a series of problems such as border disputes and lack of strategic mutual trust, Sino-Indian relations are still in a situation where opportunities and challenges coexist and conflicts and cooperation are intertwined. Due to the complexity and sensitivity of Sino-Indian relations, it is very important to enhance studies on India's internal and external policies. As a rich treasure of ancient India's strategic thoughts, *Arthashastra* is an important source of India's strategic culture and diplomatic ideas today. As the importance of Sino-Indian relations rises, the study of *Arthashastra* will increasingly highlight its academic value and practical significance. Generally speaking, the pioneering research as was made by *Arthashastra: Conceptualizing Its Thought on International Politics* has laid a solid foundation for the further research on *Arthashastra* in the future. I believe that through the introduction and analysis of this book, more readers will be attracted by the profound thoughts of *Arthashastra* and then read and carefully study the original work. It is hoped that in the near future, more scholars will join in the research of *Arthashastra* and Indian strategic culture and produce more high-quality research results.

Economic Development of "Golden Bengal"— A Book Review on *BRI Partner State Economy: Bangladesh*

Yuan Zixin, translated by Yuan Zixin[①]

Bangladesh is located in northeast South Asia Sub-Continent. It is surrounded by India on three sides except a section on its southeast neighboring with Myanmar. During a state visit to Bangladesh in 2016, President Xi Jinping in his speech highlighted the growth performance of Bangladesh as "its GDP growth reached over 6 percent averagely in the past ten years". This is indeed not an easy job, considering its starting point. When it earned independence in 1971, the poverty rate in Bangladesh was as high as 75%. It not only confronted a historic burden but also suffered from resource shortage. However, the economic development of Bangladesh indicated strong vitality. Therefore, we need to study the long-term driving force for this impressive economic growth. At the same time, it is a realistic path for each country to develop new cooperation patterns and structures of opening to the outside world in the backdrop of a drastically changing global situation, constant eruption of deep-rooted economic problems, a global economic slowdown during and after the COVID-19 pandemic. In such a backdrop, the recently published *BRI Partner State Economy: Bangladesh* made an valuable discussion in this regard as it attempted an in-depth study on the economy of Bangladesh in general and its poverty reduction, transportation, industrial structure well as policy measures of Bangladeshi government on these issues in particular.

BRI Partner State Economy: Bangladesh is authored by Li Jianjun from

---

① Yuan Zixin studies International Relations (South Asian Studies) at the Institute of South Asian Studies at Sichuan University.

the Institute of South Asian Studies of Sichuan University, an experienced researcher for Bangladesh studies familiar with the political, economical and diplomatic affairs of Bangladesh. Based on recent data, government documents, latest publications, reports and other firsthand materials, the book makes a comprehensive discussion on the economic development of Bangladesh including fiscal, monetary, financial areas and other issues, with the help of more than 70 tables on, for example, organizations/states offering international assistance to Bangladesh, imported commodities and foreign exchange reserves. All such tables (6 for each chapter on average) were worked out by the author with great effort to collect, summarize and translate the rawdata. The book can be a valuable reference for both professionals and public.

I. Focusing on Development: Eminent Progress as Indicated by Data

The book consists of 12 chapters, covering the foundation for economic development, operation of the economy, GDP growth, savings and investment, etc. Each chapter is supported by detailed data and graphs. Chapter 10 and Chapter 11 will be good examples to highlight this methodology. The two chapters offer a number of figures covering power generation, natural gas consumption, mileage of highways and rail lines, the number of passenger cars, air passenger traffic, mileage of inland shipping, etc. Such tables offer a detailed description of Bangladesh's energy consumption structure with thermal power generation as the main supplier as well as a highway-centered transportation mode for both passengers and freights. This is of particular convenience for readers who wish to have a quick and comprehensive understanding of the energy structure and transportation mode in Bangladesh.

Thanks to its clear arrangement of chapters, readers can have a quick understanding of the economic situation in certain aspect. The book not only makes an encyclopedic introduction to Bangladeshi economy, but also explores certain micro-economic issues such as industrial structure and grain production among others. While drawing the overall outline of Bangladesh's economy, the analysis of its economic policy and performance indicates that the seventh five-year plan will realize its targeted economic growth comprising a GDP growth rate of 7.4% and a poverty rate under 18.6%. Based on discussions on the export-oriented economy, GDP growth, consumption performance, investment & savings and other indicators, the book provides an in-depth analysis of the reasons behind Bangladesh's good macroeconomic performance.

Based on the background that Bangladesh will graduate from the list of "Least Developed Countries" in 2024, Chapter 12 analyzes the poverty reduction effort of Bangladesh from a historical perspective. It reviews all major poverty reduction indicators such as human development index, food energy intake, direct calorie intake, basic demand cost, household income and expenditure survey, etc. After a discussion of its poverty reduction achievement by various measures, the author points out that Bangladeshi government proves its determination and perseverance to reduce the poverty through implementing mutiple poverty measures.

The book illustrates Bengal people's unremitting efforts to develop the economy and create a better life. Bangladesh takes various effective measures to cope with its own deficiency, including optimization of export products structure and tariff reform. At the same time, The country improves food production as it has developed itself as the world's fourth largest producer of rice, while develop a flourished blue economy since it has been the third largest producer of freshwater fish around the world. It is also the second largest garment producer in the world. Through years of exploration and reform, Bangladesh's economy has made remarkable progress. In short, the 50-year-old Bangladesh is on track to become a "golden Bangladesh".

II. Examining the Problems: An Exploration to the Basic Condition of Bangladesh with the Help of Policy Analysis

This book not only focuses on the accuracy and clarity of data, but also analyzes key issues such as poverty reduction, energy contradiction, transportation and industrial structure in combination with government policies. As a reader, I am very impressed with the following aspects.

First is an unbalanced industrial structure of Bangladesh. Service sector accounts for a much bigger share than industry in Bangladesh. Although the service sector can effectively alleviate unemployment, economic development without a strong secondary industry can hardly be regarded as ideal and stable. More importantly, service industry can hardly solve the unemployment problem as it is the manufacturing industry (rather than service industry) that can work as the fundamental driving force for economic growth and consumption. Although Bangladesh has established a rudimentary industrial system, its demographic dividend and natural conditions determine that the industrial advantages of Bangladesh are still concentrated around the labor-intensive industries of textile and garment. This has helped to empower women and create many jobs. However, with the increasing employment of artificial fiber and other new fabrics, the added value of advantageous industries in Bangladesh gradually declines. It is difficult to cultivate high value-added industries in the short term. Important products such as steel and metal are still dependent on imports as heavy industry is underdeveloped. This has generated vulnerability of economic development in Bangladesh.

Second is the unbalanced poverty reduction. Thanks to the effort from the Government of Bangladesh, remarkable progress for poverty reduction has been made as the poverty rate has dropped by 52.5 percentage points from independence to 2018. However, the poverty reduction process exposes many problems as well. The data indicates that poverty reduction in rural area is far from satisfactory, as the urban poverty reduction rate is 4.68% while rural poverty reduction rate is just 1.97%. The Gini coefficient, on the other hand, indicates a widening gap between the rich and the poor in Bangladesh. It is learned that the income gap among urban residents has widened as the wealth is concentrating into the hands of a few. The East-North poverty gap remains unchanged while there is big deference of income and regional development. In short, the uneven effect of poverty reduction across regions and the imbalance of poverty reduction have become a prominent challenge that will impede the sustainable and healthy development of Bangladeshi economy.

Third is the insufficient transportation, power and energy supply. In terms of transportation, the comprehensive transportation system of Bangladesh is in urgent need of development. Highways remain the major method for passenger and cargo transport in Bangladesh, with country roads of low transport capacity accessible in an area three times in coverage as compared with national highways. Other transport methods, such as railways, shipping and air travel, are in poor situation. What's more, the development of highways, railways, shipping lines and air routes in Bangladesh has once come to a standstill. The mileage of highways and railways even regressed instead of increasing due to flood and other reasons (the total mileage of Bangladeshi railways was 2,884 km in FY 1981–1982; that reduced to 2,877 km in FY 2015–2016). As an elementary industry in the economic structure, the inefficient transportation facilities impede the economic development in Bangladesh. Meanwhile, in energy sector, Bangladesh has been suffering from a power shortage as it is in shortage of coal, oil and other resources. Natural gas extracted from Bangladesh has been its major source of power generation, but the supply gap will widen as production from most fields would reach a plateau. The outstanding contradiction between energy supply and demand poses a serious challenge to the economic development of Bangladesh and its future prospects.

Fourth is the insufficiency in exportation. Textiles and garments occupy an absolute advantage among the export commodities in Bangladesh. Obviously, this export structure needs optimization as the main export commodities are still at the lower end of the international industrial chain with low value-added. In addition, the target market of Bangladesh is highly concentrated in North America instead of others. Such an unbalanced export distribution brings about great dependence and heavy fluctuations. Considering the need for expansion of market share and economic security, it is extremely urgent for Bangladesh to develop a diversified, multi-level and multi-channel export market pattern.

I would like to advise the Chinese readers to be aware of both the progress and problems for the economic development in Bangladesh and make a road-map for cooperation with Bangladesh to meet its concern. In this process, the Chinese side needs to give full play of its infrastructure development and industrial advantages, while an optimization of bilateral trade structure also needs to be realized. For example, considering the power demand in Bangladesh, Chinese enterprises can actively participate in the construction and operation of power projects there and help develop new energy power generation facilities in Bangladesh. Chinese enterprises are encouraged to take this opportunities in Bangladesh market where private enterprises are encouraged to play a role and offered 15-year duty-free treatment in addition to exemption of value-added tax and customs duties for power generation equipment. This would help the export of both Chinese standards and the capacity for power generation equipment production.

III. Outlook: Suggestions for Further Explorations and Studies

Based on a summarization of the basic situation, industrial structure, monetary policy, financial market and other elements of Bangladeshi economy, the book further analyzes the contradiction between supply and demand of electricity, transportation, and external economic development and other key issues. I would be very interested if further work could be done on the following aspects.

Firstly, to incorporate content relevant to business customs. This book provides a remarkably clear overview of the economic development of Bangladesh. Further incorporation of informations on the customs, society and culture as well as other aspects that shape the business environment of Bangladesh would help provide a very useful reference for the investment cooperation between Chinese and Bangladeshi enterprises and thereby help Chinese enterprises' business enter Bangladesh.

Secondly, to make a comprehensive review of trade exchanges and progress of bilateral cooperation. Since China and Bangladesh established diplomatic ties in 1975, the bilateral economic and trade cooperation has been developed in a consistent way. Bangladeshi imports from China have been growing year by year, while bilateral joint projects have been flourishing in recent years. Despite a focus on the latest situation, the author can consider to make a comprehensive introduction of the economic and trade cooperation, trade agreements, financial investment and other economic exchanges between China and Bangladesh over the past 40 years. A review of the profound tradition, opportunities and challenges of China–Bangladesh cooperation from a historical perspective can provide a powerful intellectual support for the research and decision-making of government agencies and researchers. I would also suggest that the author can make an in-depth evaluation of the achievements and problems of China–Bangladesh cooperation projects under the background of the Belt and Road Initiative, covering social and economic progress in terms of hydropower, energy and traffic.

Finally, to focus on long-term economic development and grasp the future direction of cooperation. As the Belt and Road Initiative has progressed into a new stage, we need to explore the future direction of cooperation based on a forward-looking mindset. Technically, the planning can be made based on a comprehensive collection of data such as GDP growth, domestic financing as a ratio to annual development plan, public expenditure, before it makes an evaluation of investment, trade and financial environment of Bangladesh. A study of the short-term, medium and long-term growth prospects of Bangladesh, with analysis of the risks and challenges to China–Bangladesh cooperation in the new stage, will be a valuable reference for investment decisions for Chinese enterprises, as well as an exploration to the new direction for the bilateral cooperation in the new stage. This will boost the leap-forward development of China–Bangladesh relations. In fact, the author's relevant papers in recent years (such as *"Current Situation and Future Prospects of Economic Development in Bangladesh"* , *"Financial Reform and Effectiveness in Bangladesh"* and *"Current Situation and Future Prospects of China–Bangladesh Economic and Trade Relations"*) have covered many of the above contents. If the latest data can be used for an re-evaluation in this study, it might be able to make a bigger contribution to the development of both China and Bangladesh as well as the bilateral cooperation between them.

As the instability of world situation becomes more evident, it is urgent for all countries to strengthen economic and trade cooperation in order to effectively cope with the challenges and risks brought about by the great change unseen in the past century. Bangladesh is an important node of the 21st Century Maritime Silk Road and a major participant in the Silk Road Economic Belt. China and Bangladesh have jointly built key projects such as the Bangabandhu Sheikh Mujibur Rahman Tunnel (Karnaphuli Tunnel) and the Padma Bridge, bringing about major improvement on the lives of the Bengal people and the industrial capacity of Bangladesh as well as the economic growth of the two countries. In recent years, a series of books on the economies of countries along the belt and road have been published in China. The series incorporate 14 countries inclusive of India, Kazakhstan, Turkey, Pakistan, among others. However, Bangladesh has regretfully not been included. In fact, the economic research on Bangladesh under the background of The Belt and Road Initiative has a big academic significance. In *BRI Partner State Economy: Bangladesh*, the author made full use of his own research expertise and experience in addition to a wide access to papers and monographs of Bangladeshi experts and scholars as well as government documents. His work will be a major intellectual support for the development of China–Bangladesh economic and trade relations. I am confident that a great number of such studies and hard works of researchers will lay a solid foundation for a more vigorous and robust progress of the Belt and Road Initiative (BRI). This will definitely help the earlier realisation of the rejuvenation of China.

An Uneasy Cooperation: A Book Review of *China-India Maritime Security Cooperation Studies*

Xie Feifei, translated by Yang Yulu[①]

Both China and India are maritime powers with similar maritime historical experiences. The unfortunate historical suffering of colonial aggression and the tragic consequences due to lack of maritime defense made both countries aware of the importance of sea for national security. The geopolitical attributes of land-and-ocean countries made both countries realize the difficulties for maintaining a balance between land and sea. In the globalization context, the rapid growth of economic strength and comprehensive national power offers another momentum for the two countries to develop themselves into sea-powers. In the context of the simultaneous rise of China and India, the transformation of maritime strategies and naval modernization of both countries, as well as the maritime interaction between the two countries or among China, the United States and India have been turned into hot topics. In terms of maritime interaction between China and India, discussions on maritime competition and conflicts receive much more attention than discussions on maritime cooperation. Considering the China–India relations have encountered difficulties recently, a rational discussion on maritime security cooperation between China and India is very valuable as it is of unique theoretical and practical significance.

A Study on China–India Maritime Security Cooperation (Zou Zhengxin from Center for South Asia and West China Cooperation and Development

---

① Xie Feifei is a doctoral candidate at the Innovation Center for West Frontier Security and Development at Sichuan University. His research interests mainly cover Indian maritime strategy, maritime security and China–India Relations. Yang Yulu studies International Relations (South Asian Studies) at the Institute of South Asian Studies at Sichuan University. Her main focus is on development and security in northeast India.

Studies of Sichuan University, International Culture Publication, November 2020) makes a tentative discussion of some important issues concerning Sino-Indian maritime security cooperation, including the background, the present situation, characteristics, influencing factors, policy measures for an strengthened cooperation and other important elements. It also incorporates a discussion on Sagar Mala project and the latest development of the Indian navy in its appendix. This book elaborates various factors affecting China–India maritime security cooperation, and puts forward certain innovative suggestions for further enhancement of China–India maritime security cooperation. I would like to take this opportunity to share some of my understanding and further considerations over China–India maritime security cooperation with all the readers.

I. Cooperation and Maritime Security

Cooperation and Maritime Security are key concepts of this book. A brief analysis of such concepts is helpful to understand the maritime security cooperation between China and India from the macro level. Cooperation is an important concept for international relations theories. Robert O. Keohane, a major proponent of neo-liberal institutionalism, used to make a classic interpretation of cooperation. He divided international communication modes into three categories: harmony, cooperation and dispute. Cooperation, he believed, is a mode between harmony with identical interests and dispute with totally conflicting interests. Keohane pointed out that cooperation refers to a state that there is conflict of interests between actors, but after policy coordination the behavior of both parties conforms to mutual interests. Cooperation can only emerge in a complex situation where conflict of interests and convergence of interests coexist. Keohane pointed out that the plight of international cooperation under the anarchy is the information imbalance and deceptive behavior of actors in international communication, and the international system can provide effective information and reduce the possibility of deception so as to coordinate actor's behavior and strengthen the international cooperation.

Maritime security is an extension of the concept of "security" in the marine field. Maritime security in general can be divided into two categories, namely the traditional maritime security (mainly involving political, military, and other areas of the "high politics") and unconventional maritime security (smuggling, terrorism, piracy, marine environment, etc.). Maritime security can be subdivided into marine political and military security, marine economic security, marine social security, marine environment security, etc. These security issues are closely related to the concepts of maritime rights, blue economy, maritime peace and the population vitality of coastal areas, which constitute different aspects of maritime security. Theoretical analysis of these assumptions is not completely applicable to the highly practical maritime security cooperation between China and India; however, it will help to construct a framework to understand maritime security cooperation and specific issues such as "cooperation dilemma" and "mechanism development" in maritime security cooperation between China and India.

II. China–India Maritime Interaction from the Perspective of Maritime Security Strategy of India

China–India maritime security cooperation must be based on shared maritime interests. It must be implemented under the maritime security strategies of the two countries. Based on the situation of maritime security in the Indian Ocean, the author analyzes the similarities and differences of maritime security strategies between China and India and the possibility of maritime security cooperation between them. The author elaborates a tentative discussion on the maritime security strategy of India in a separate chapter on the recent development of Indian navy in the Appendix part, although such discussion is limited in the main text part. In recent years, India has significantly raised its maritime awareness, accelerated the transformation of its maritime strategy, and made consistent modernization effort for its navy. India has achieved remarkable progress in sea (especially in terms of naval modernization), despite challenges in terms of financing, technology and coordination between land and sea power. As the author indicated, the Indian Navy is actively adjusting its strategic intention and striving to develop a balanced and reasonably "ocean-going" blue-water navy. It is trying to make a synergy of indigenization with imitation to accelerate the modernization and localization of naval equipment. Naval diplomacy is being used to expand the strategic space for India. There is nothing wrong with India's efforts to safeguard its maritime interests and accelerate development itself into a maritime power. However, the strong "China factor" has cast a shadow over the maritime security cooperation between the two countries. The Indian strategic community has developed a strong suspicion over the normal exchanges and cooperation between China and other countries such as Myanmar, Pakistan, Thailand and Sri Lanka, believing that China is following a synergy of "Alfred Thayer Mahan" and "Halford John Mackinder" to enter the Indian Ocean from both land and sea. Other Indian experts tended to interpret China's move to enter the Indian Ocean and strengthen ties with countries bordering the Indian Ocean as "China's attempt to implement a 'strategic encirclement' of India from the Indian Ocean." Although the Indian navy's maritime strategy documents in recent years haven't highlighted the so-called China threat to India (as some strategists suggested), they did have a negative interpretation of Chinese navy's presence in Indian Ocean. Against this background, it is conceivable that China–India maritime security cooperation will be very difficult and complicated.

The author in the book made a detailed discussion on China and India's maritime security interaction at all levels in recent years, including the maritime security dialogues and exchanges between officials and research institutions, joint actions in maritime security such as naval vessels visits, joint exercises and anti-piracy escort, as well as maritime security cooperation in science and technology and marine infrastructure development. The discussion on China–India maritime interaction has covered multiple dimensions and all levels of the two governments' high-level officials, foreign ministries, marine departments, navies, think tanks, universities, social organizations, enterprises and individuals. However, China–India maritime security interaction in frequency, scale and content are far from satisfactory. The author also pointed out quite sharply that the current China–India maritime security cooperation presents a contradictory situation. That is to say, the cooperation is weak without much substance despite a high frequency of interaction covering a wide spectrum. Since the maritime cooperation framework is underdeveloped, maritime security cooperation between the two countries is vulnerable to international political environment and fluctuations in bilateral political relations. The high-level political leadership of China and India have few macro-plans on maritime affairs, while documents signed by the two countries and marine science and technology cooperation projects have yet to be implemented. Maritime security cooperation between the two countries is stagnated at "talking-without-doing" stage. Compared with the hesitancy in maritime security cooperation between the two governments and navies, maritime exchanges between think tanks and universities in China and India have increased significantly in recent years. However, considering the tension in border area since 2020 and India's cooling-down attitude toward China as well as the tightening government policies, chillness for Sino-Indian maritime security interaction in this level might not be a surprise.

Ⅲ. China–India Maritime Security Cooperation as Perceived Through Indo-Pacific Perspective?

The author focused its discussion on "Sino-Indian maritime security cooperation" in Indian Ocean region. This help a concentrated discussion over Indian Ocean. The relatively few bilateral maritime security cooperation in other regions is also a reason behind this approach. In light of the current situation, when considering the maritime security cooperation between China and India, it might be workable to expand the geographical scope and take the "Indo-Pacific" as a geographical background for China–India maritime security cooperation.

The concept of "Indo-Pacific" has been well known because of the peddling and promotion by the United States. China does not have to "dance with the US". However, out of its own strategic considerations, China may consider to use the Indo-Pacific as a perspective to enhance the China–India maritime security cooperation. For one thing, the intersection of Sino-Indian maritime interests covers a vast area from the Indian Ocean to the Pacific Ocean. Considering maritime security cooperation between China and India from a Indo-Pacific geographical perspective might be conducive to develop a comprehensive consideration of maritime affairs in the greater region and to ensure the regional balance of China–India maritime security cooperation. This will also help relieve an extreme vigilance of Indian side due to the complete focus on Indian Ocean. In addition, Sino-Indian maritime security cooperation throughout the Indian and Pacific oceans (Pacific ocean in particular) is weak and less influential. However, India is in fact paying an increasing attention to Pacific waters. In recent years, India has upgraded its "Look East Policy" to "Act East Policy" with focus on its own "Indo-Pacific" initiative. In this context, developing a China–India maritime security cooperation in the Pacific through bilateral or multilateral platforms can, to a certain extent, play a positive role in influencing India's Indo-Pacific outlook and deepen the mutual understanding of the two sides on maritime issues.

IV. China–India Maritime Security Cooperation and Its Future

For China and India, there is a necessity for bilateral maritime cooperation as well as for an enhanced maritime security governance. The two countries have a certain complementarity and feasibility of mutual assistance in this regard. However, why the bilateral maritime security cooperation after more than a decade is still lagged in the primary stage? This is a big problem that the author focused on in the book. I would like to pick naval exercise as an example to illustrate the "dilemma of cooperation" in Sino-Indian maritime security field. The author enumerated a few China–India joint naval exercises since the new century. The most recent one was in 2007 when the two fleets made joint manoeuvre in the Yellow Sea for exercise on signal lamp communication, semaphore communication, changing formation, etc. The "Qingdao" missile destroyers from China as well as the INS Rana and INS Ranjit missile destroyers from India participated in the exercise. It is obvious that the exercise is of small scale with relatively elementary items. In the second decade of the 21st century, the two sides rarely conduct bilateral joint exercises except for some under multilateral framework. By contrast, India held frequent, large-scale and complex naval exercises with the United States, Singapore and other countries. For example, in November 2018, The 25th Singapore–India Maritime Bilateral Exercise (SIMBEX-18) was held in Port Blair (capital of the Andaman-Nicobar Islands), Andaman Sea and Visakhapatnam. The exercises included live-fire drills (involving launches of various types of missiles, heavy torpedoes, medium-range artillery and anti-submarine rockets), advanced anti-submarine warfare exercises, submarine rescue drills and joint surface and air defense operations exercises.

For "the dilemma of cooperation", the author used a whole chapter to analyze various factors affecting China–India maritime security cooperation. He pointed out that the security environment in the Indian Ocean region is quite complex. In addition, the two countries, having developed very different maritime strategies, lack mutual trust, while the mechanism and theory of maritime security cooperation are deficient. What's more, external players such as the United States, Japan, and ASEAN have been playing a major role in plaguing China–India maritime security cooperation. At the same time, we need to be aware of some specific issues for this cooperation. For example, some Indian experts believe that the naval exchanges between China and India are still at a very early stage. One of the reasons is that the two navies are very different in terms of future direction, doctrine and ideology of warfare, and there are also some obstacles in communication and equipment interoperability between the two navies. Although this conclusion may not be comprehensive, it can still help us reflect on these specific issues concerning China–India maritime security cooperation.

The author's discussion on the countermeasures and suggestions for enhancement of the Sino-Indian maritime security cooperation is a highlight of the book because of its comprehensiveness and creativity. The author suggested to promote China–India maritime security cooperation through strengthening maritime communication and dialogue, establishing a systematic maritime security cooperation mechanism, improving the integration of maritime cooperation initiatives and policies, developing marine economy, and making full use of multilateral platforms and international organizations. As for the establishment of maritime security cooperation mechanism, the author systematically elaborated the high-level consultation mechanism, early warning mechanism, emergency response mechanism, joint cruise mechanism in the Gulf of Aden and marine information sharing mechanism in the maritime security issues from early warning to practical handling. The author's general idea is to start with fuller use of existing opportunities and multilateral platforms at the very beginning and to proceed with cooperation on as the breakthrough points such as non-traditional security issues, maritime economic issues and infrastructure construction such as ports. In this way, he in fact suggested a "top-down" approach to strengthen the maritime security cooperation between China and India. This approach of course has its own merits. However, it will be difficult to implement this approach considering the frequent setbacks in China–India relations and stalled maritime security cooperation.

In light of the complicated situation, I would like to recommend a "focus on priorities" and "bottom-up" approaches as supplementary to the author's suggested method. Indian strategic community does not have a monolithic understanding on issues such as the development of China's maritime strategy, the presence of Chinese navy in the Indian Ocean region, and China–India maritime security cooperation. While critics and suspicions are playing a leading role, there are anyhow other opinions which believe that "India should give full consideration to China's interests and concerns in the Indian Ocean" and "the participation of the Chinese navy can effectively supplement the collective security forces in the Indian Ocean region". Some scholars even pointed out that "in order to ease China's concerns, India and the US can invite China to participate in Malabar Exercise at some appropriate time". Such voices make it possible for maritime think tanks and research institutions of both countries to carry out joint study for an enhanced bilateral cooperation on specific maritime affairs. At the meantime, China and India can work together to foster Maritime Security Communities involving various actors, considering the diversity of maritime interests and diverse aspirations of all parties. Evolved from the concept of Security Communities initiated by IR integration theorist Karl Deutsch, maritime security communities are used to describe an ideal form of cooperation among various participants in the maritime domain. Stakeholders in maritime security communities, through day-to-day participation to maritime affairs, information sharing and action coordination, can enhance mutual understanding, mutual trust and collective identity consciousness among members. The relationship between members of maritime security communities is different from alliance. Their sense of identity and collective identity is developed in the process of maritime interaction with strong practicality. Maritime security communities, in this sense, can be regarded as an effective form of security governance. In addition, although maritime security communities involve high-level political and diplomatic activities, their major focus remains the lower and middle-level maritime security practitioners, experts and the way in which they interact with each other. Despite being an idealized model, the concept of maritime security communities might help expand the common maritime interests and cultivate a sense of maritime identity. This will consolidate the foundation of the maritime security cooperation between China and India.

《南亚评论》征稿启事

　　《南亚评论》是以南亚现实问题研究为主题的中英双语学术丛书，每年12月1日和6月1日出版。《南亚评论》常设：南亚政治/经济/外交/安全、南亚历史/文化/社会和南亚书评三个栏目，另不定期开设特稿、热点问题笔谈、综述与评述等栏目。《南亚评论》常年面向国内外研究人员征集中英文稿件，特将相关要求说明如下。

一、权利义务声明

　　1.只接受原创作品，保护著作权，来稿文责自负。署名作者应为研究的主要参与者，能够对研究内容及结果负责。

　　2.对于伪作和抄袭作品，《南亚评论》不承担鉴别之责，其作品经《南亚评论》发表后所产生的一切后果，均由作者承担。

　　3.《南亚评论》对稿件有技术性删改权。经编委审定并确定录用的稿件，在不影响文章中心思想和基本内容的前提下，编辑可在必要时对稿件进行删改。作者投稿时如未作特别声明，则视为投稿时即向本丛书授权。

　　4.来稿中英文均可，《南亚评论》负责对确定录用的稿件进行翻译，中英双语稿件将出版于同辑。《南亚评论》提供尽可能准确的译本，但不担保译文的绝对准确性。

　　5.凡在《南亚评论》发表的作品，均视为已获得作者的著作权使用许可，《南亚评论》可代之行使，将所出版的作品加入中国知网等相关网络电子版、数据库、光盘版或另行结集出版。对此作者如有异议请务必在投稿时声明。

　　6.《南亚评论》不收取版面费，暂不提供稿费。

　　7.出版后，《南亚评论》按作者提供的通信方式向作者寄送样书，单一作者寄送样书二册，多作者人手一册。

8. 作者投稿请直接以电子邮件发送电子版至指定邮箱（zengxiangyu@scu.edu.cn），请勿邮寄纸本稿件。

9. 稿件经编委审定录用将及时发出录用通知。若三个月内未接到录用通知，作者可另投。

二、稿件规范

1. 文章内容：作者原创，思想性强，观点正确，资料翔实，结构严谨，体例规范。

2. 研究论文字数一般在中文10000字左右，特稿一事一议。书评一般为中文3500～5500字。

3. 首页信息应完整、明确。请按下列项目提供：题目（中英文对照），中英文摘要（200字左右），中英文关键词（3～5个）；中英文作者署名（多作者署名排序、作者工作单位、邮编号）。另请提供作者简介（姓名、性别、单位、职称、研究领域、电子邮箱等），以脚注形式放于首页。

4. 图表应有明确完整的图题、表题及序号等，采用图（表）随文的方式，在正文中标出图表的位置。图表中的计量单位，一律采用法定计量单位。

三、注释体例

（一）中文文献

1. 专著

马加力：《东南亚国家市场经济》，北京：时事出版社，1995年，第11页。

2. 编著

汤晶阳等主编：《世界主要国家军事战略》，北京：国防工业出版社，2005年，第12页。

3. 译著

［美］吉姆·罗沃：《亚洲的崛起》，张绍宗译，上海：上海人民出版社，2003年，第10页。

4. 报刊

吴艳红："明代流刑考"，《历史研究》，2000年第6期，第34页。

邱永峥："美印日都想拉拢缅甸"，《环球时报》，2009年10月23日。

5. 文集及书信集、档案汇编等

王宏纬："印度与巴基斯坦的关系"，孙士海、江亦丽主编：《二战后南亚国家对外关系研究》，北京：方志出版社，2007年，第122页。

"中共中央最近政治状况报告"，1927年10月，中央档案馆编：《中共中央政治报告选辑（1927—1933）》，北京：中共中央党校出版社，1983年，第20页。

6. 未刊文献

方明东：《罗隆基政治思想研究（1913—1949）》，博士学位论文，北京师范大学历史系，2000年，第67页。

"傅良佐致国务院电"，1917年9月15日，中国第二历史档案馆藏，北洋档案1011—5961。

（二）英文文献

1. 专著

Randolph Starn and Loren Partridge, *The Arts of Power: Three Halls of State in Italy, 1300–1600*, Berkeley: University of California University, 1992, pp. 19–28.

2. 编著

T. H. Aston and C. H. E. Phlipin (eds.), *The Brenner Debate*. Cambridge: Cambridge University Press, 1985, p. 35.

3. 文集

R. S. Schfield, "The Impact of Scarcity and Plenty on Population Change in England," in R. I. Rotberg and T. K. Rabb (eds.), *Hunger and History: The Impact of Changing Food Production and Consumption Pattern on Society*, Cambridge: Cambridge University Press, 1983, p. 79.

4. 报刊

Heath B. Chamberlain, "On the Search for Civil Society in China," *Modern China*, Vol. 19, No. 2, April 1993, pp. 199–215.

（三）互联网

陈雷:《农村女性外出务工与家庭性别关系的变迁》,2005 年 10 月 26 日,http://www.sachina.edu.cn/Htmldata/article/2005/10/457.html,2010 年 4 月 20 日访问。

（四）补充说明

1. 本丛书采用脚注,每页重新编号。

2. 注释序号一律放在标点符号之后。

3. 正文中的引文不必变字体或字号,大段引文则使用楷体表示。

Call for Papers

South Asian Review: A Bilingual Publication is a bilingual academic periodic publication focusing on studies on contemporary issues in South Asia. It will be published on every December and June in both Chinese and English languages, covering irregular columns and three regular columns: South Asian Political / Economic / Diplomatic / Security Studies, South Asian History / Culture / Society Studies and South Asian Book Review. *South Asian Review* solicits contribution of research papers and book reviews in either Chinese or English language focusing on contemporary South Asian studies from both Chinese and international researchers all the year round.

I. Rights and Obligations Statement

1. The submitted work must be an original piece that has not been previously published. The author(s) take(s) the responsibility for his/her views. The author(s) must be the major researcher(s) responsible for the study and its outcome.

2. *South Asia Review* is not responsible for identifying fake or plagiarized works. The author(s) is responsible for the consequences of his/her works.

3. *South Asia Review* reserves the right of technical revision on submitted works. After the manuscript is accepted by the editorial board, the editor may revise the manuscript when necessary on the premise of making no distortion to its core idea and major content. After submission of a work the author(s) will be automatically deemed consent in this regard if the author does not make a special statement of disapproval.

4. *South Asian Review* solicits submissions in either Chinese or English language. The editorial board will try to make a translation (Chinese to English or English to Chinese) of accepted work for publication in the same issue. *South Asian Review* shall try its best to make an accurate translation although it can not guarantee absolute accuracy of the translation.

5. All works published in *South Asian Review* shall be deemed to have obtained the copyright license of the author. Such copyright might be exercised by *South Asian Review* to incorporate the published works into online platforms/databases such as CNKI, or to republish in other platforms. A special statement of disapproval needs to be submitted if the author(s) do(es) not agree in this regard.

6. *South Asian Review* does not collect page charge. It does not provide contribution fee for the moment.

7. Hard copy of *South Asian Review* will be sent to the author(s) in accordance with the address they provide. 2 copies will be sent to a sole author, while 1 copy for each author will be sent in case of multi-authors.

8. Please send your contribution of paper/book review to zengxiangyu@ scu.edu.cn and do not mail hard copy of your manuscript.

9. Confirmation of Acceptance Notice from *South Asian Review* will be sent in a timely manner to the author(s) of an accepted work. The author(s) may submit to other publications or journals if the author(s) do(es) not receive such Confirmation of Acceptance Notice within 3 months of submitting his/her work to *South Asian Review*.

II. General Guideline

1. A research paper shall be the author(s)' original piece that has never published before, well-researched and well-organized, substantiated with in-depth discussion.

2. A research paper shall be 6500–9000 English words in length. A book review shall be 2000–4000 English words in length.

3. Please offer the paper title, the abstract (150 words), key words

(3–5 words), the author(s)' identification (order of authors in case of multi-authors, institution, post-code) in the first page. Please offer as a footnote an introduction of the author(s), inclusive of the name, institution, academic title, research interests and email.

4. All charts and tables should have clear and complete titles and serial numbers. Such marks shall appear in the main text immediately following the charts and tables. Metric units or China statutory measurement units shall be used.

III. Annotation Style

Please use footnote (instead of endnote) and renumber in each page. Note numbers shall be placed after punctuation. Citations in the main text do not have to use a different font and size, while citations in big length shall be in Arial font.

1. Books

Randolph Starn and Loren Partridge, *The Arts of Power: Three Halls of State in Italy, 1300–1600,* Berkeley: University of California University, 1992, pp. 19–28.

2. Edited Works

T. H. Aston and C. H. E. Phlipin (eds.), *The Brenner Debate,* Cambridge: Cambridge University Press, 1985, p. 35.

3. Collected Works

R . S . Schfield, "The Impact of Scarcity and Plenty on Population Change in England," in R. I. Rotberg and T. K. Rabb (eds.), *Hunger and History: The Impact of Changing Food Production and Consumption Pattern on Society,* Cambridge: Cambridge University Press, 1983, p. 79.

4. Newspapers

Heath B. Chamberlain, "On the Search for Civil Society in China," *Modern China,* Vol. 19, No. 2, April 1993, pp. 199–215.

5. Internet information

Jamil Danish, "Afghanistan's Corruption Epidemic is Wasting Billions in

Aid," *The Guardian*, November 3, 2016, https://www.theguardian.com/global-development-professionals-network/2016/nov/03/afghanistans-corruption-epidemic-is-wasting-billions-in-aid, accessed February 13, 2018.